American Media Politics in Transition

Critical Topics in American Government Series

Voice of the People: Elections and Voting in the United States
Alan Abramowitz

Women and American Politics: The Challenges of Political Leadership
Lori Cox Han

Organized Interests and American Government
David Lowery and Holly Brasher

American Media Politics in Transition
Jeremy D. Mayer

Understanding the U.S. Supreme Court: Cases and Controversies
Kevin McGuire

Campaigns in the 21st Century
Richard J. Semiatin

American Media Politics in Transition

Jeremy D. Mayer

George Mason University

Boston   Burr Ridge, IL   Dubuque, IA   Madison, WI   New York
San Francisco   St. Louis   Bangkok   Bogotá   Caracas   Kuala Lumpur
Lisbon   London   Madrid   Mexico City   Milan   Montreal   New Delhi
Santiago   Seoul   Singapore   Sydney   Taipei   Toronto

Higher Education

This book is printed on acid-free paper.

1 2 3 4 5 6 7 8 9 0 DOC/DOC 0 9 8 7

ISBN: 978-0-07-287788-5
MHID: 0-07-287788-X

Editor in Chief: *Emily Barrosse*
Publisher: *Frank Mortimer*
Sponsoring Editor: *Monica Eckman*
Developmental Editor: *Kate Scheinman*
Editorial Coordinator: *Jessica Badiner*
Marketing Manager: *Jennifer Reed*
Project Manager: *Carey Eisner*
Manager, Photo Research: *Brian J. Pecko*
Manuscript Editor: *Kay Mikel*
Senior Designer: *Cassandra Chu*
Cover Designer: *Srdj Savanovic*
Production Supervisor: *Richard DeVitto*
Composition: *10/12 Palatino by International Typesetting & Composition*
Printing: *45# New Era Matte Plus, R. R. Donnelley*
Cover: The McGraw-Hill Companies, Inc./Jill Braaten, Photographer

Library of Congress Cataloging-in-Publication Data

Mayer, Jeremy D.
    American media politics in transition / Jeremy D. Mayer.
      p. cm.—(Critical topics in American government series)
    Includes index.
    ISBN-13: 978-0-07-287788-5 (pbk. : alk. paper)
    ISBN-10: 0-07-287788-X (pbk. : alk. paper)
    1. Mass media—Political aspects—United States. 2. Mass media—Influence.
   3. Journalism—United States—History. 4. United States—Politics and
government—2001- I. Title.
    P95.82.U6M37 2008
    302.23—dc22
                                                 2006046927

The Internet addresses listed in the text were accurate at the time of publication. The inclusion of a Web site does not indicate an endorsement by the authors or McGraw-Hill, and McGraw-Hill does not guarantee the accuracy of the information presented at these sites.

www.mhhe.com

About the Author

JEREMY D. MAYER is an associate professor in the School of Public Policy at George Mason University. He is the author of *Running on Race: Racial Politics in Presidential Campaigns 1960–2000* (Random House, 2002) as well as the brief textbook *9-11: The Giant Awakens* (Wadsworth, 2002, 2nd ed., 2006). He has written articles on diverse topics including constitutional law, presidential image management, Christian right politics, federalism and gay rights, and comparative political socialization, in journals such as *Presidential Studies Quarterly, Social Science Quarterly,* and *The Historian.* Dr. Mayer also trains new American diplomats for the State Department at the Foreign Service Institute. He has offered political commentary to major networks, including the *World News Tonight, Headline News,* BBC, PBS *NewsHour,* CNBC, and local affiliates, as well as many national newspapers. He received his PhD in 1996 from Georgetown University.

This book is dedicated to Ed Beiser and Clyde Wilcox, the former for inspiring me with his legendary lectures to pursue a graduate degree in political science and the latter for mentoring me through that degree and the career that has followed.

Contents

Preface

I decided to write this book because I found the topic of the media creeping more and more into my courses and research on American politics. No course on the presidency, Congress, foreign policy, public opinion, or elections can be considered comprehensive without at least a week focusing on the media. Even my courses on statistics discuss how the media misuse statistics on a regular basis.

My second motive for writing this book was my growing disappointment with how the media cover politics in this country. If you detect in these pages an author who is saddened by media that focus more on attractive missing blond women than on questions of war and peace among nations, you are reading accurately. If those who read this book take any small steps toward reducing the role of sensationalism, sex, scandal, and celebrity in our political journalism, I will be gratified.

At the same time, the third motive for writing this book was my own raw joy at how technological changes have begun to bring media power to the people. In courses at Kalamazoo College and Georgetown University, I encourage my students to craft news broadcasts and political ads. Working with some stellar media folks at both institutions, dozens of college students graduate with exposure not just in media theory but in media practice as well. They learn to shoot and edit video and post it online. There is reason for hope about a generation of young people savvy enough to challenge the large media corporations.

How to Use This Book

I wrote this book to be used in introductory courses on American government and courses on the media and communications. There are many fine books on the media, but most of them do not address all the topics I wanted covered. In particular, most were weak on mixing the historical evolution of American political journalism with theories about its current practice. I also wanted a text that was cutting edge about emerging technological change.

Each chapter of the book is relatively self-contained, and instructors should feel free to assign a selection of chapters. Each chapter also

contains discussion questions, suggestions for further reading, online
resources, and a list of key terms and people. A few chapters also have
suggestions for assignments that instructors might consider, such as a
content analysis project or creating a political ad.

Acknowledgments

I first must thank my editor at McGraw-Hill, Kate Scheinman,
whose support and patience and advice are present on every page;
and Monica Eckman, who first greenlighted the project and brought
Kate to it. Thanks to my copy editor, Kay Mikel, for her relentless
vigilance in improving my prose and grammar.

I should also thank Murky Coffee, in Arlington, VA, where
much of it was written. A bohemian haven for a professor whose
office lacks a window, Murky Coffee is a good place to write about
politics inside the Beltway.

Kingsley Haynes, Jim Finkelstein, Cathy Rudder, and my other
colleagues at George Mason University were all encouraging as the
project grew. I'm also grateful to Frank Sesno of GMU, who team
taught a media course with me that used this textbook in electronic
form. Frank's style of journalism, in which facts trump glitz, shows
what television at its best can do.

McGraw-Hill and I would also like to thank the following people
for reviewing my manuscript at many stages along the way: David
Barker, University of Pittsburgh; Cynthia Boaz, University of San
Francisco; Sharon Bramlett-Solomon, Arizona State University;
Dianne Bystrom, Iowa State University; Tereza Capelos, Leiden
University; Lane Crothers, Illinois State University; Alison D. Dagnes,
Shippensburg University; Tracey Gladstone-Sovell, University of
Wisconsin-River Falls; Lori Cox Han, Chapman University; Anthony
Mughan, Ohio State University; Lewis S. Ringel, California State
University Long Beach; Robert Sahr, Oregon State University; Robert
Spitzer, State University of New York Cortland; Nicholas A.
Valentino, University of Michigan; and David Woodard, Clemson
University.

Finally, I must thank all my students from Kalamazoo College,
Georgetown University, and George Mason University who have
shared insights into the evolving nature of America's political journalism. In particular, thanks to Paul Trampe of George Mason for an
insight that appears in the final chapter.

CHAPTER 1

The Political Medium Shapes the Political Message

A brilliant and famous man is tried before five hundred jurors on charges of atheism and corrupting young people with his dangerous ideas. After a nine-hour trial, the man is sentenced to death. Almost three thousand years later, the meaning of his trial and his death are still debated: Was he killed because he was a threat to the social order or because he was an opponent of democracy?

A leader of a blossoming rebellion in a restless colony pens angry and bold words of defiance. After a passionate statement of universal human rights and the principles of self-government, the author goes on to list all the ways in which the mother country's authorities have violated the rights of colonists. The powerful and stirring document is quickly distributed throughout the region, further fanning the rebellion into a broader war.

A young and relatively inexperienced candidate for public office faces his better known and seasoned opponent in a public debate. Those watching the debate on television believe the younger man is besting his rival; those listening on the radio feel the debate is a tie. Because more people are watching, a victory is declared for the challenger.

A political movement begins in a small room in a dingy apartment. Over the Internet, one person's ideas are broadcast, first to thousands, then to millions. Using e-mail, Web pages, streaming video, interactive chat rooms, podcasts, and instant messaging, the movement quickly becomes more powerful than the established political parties of the country even though the leadership of the organization has never met in one physical location.

What do these four scenarios have in common? All of them are about politics, of course, about the classic "who gets what when how" decisions that every society makes. But more important than what they have in common is what is different. In each case a different method of communication is used to express a political message. Also, in each case the message could not have been sent with equal force, or even equal meaning, using a different method of communication.

This is a book about how the means of communication changes the message of politics. Watching a political convention on television is extraordinarily different from being there in person or reading about it in a newspaper. The difference is not just that reporters and TV cameras will focus on different speeches and issues than you would if you were in attendance. The structure and content of conventions have radically altered over time to respond to print and television media, changing the nature of American presidential politics itself. This is true not only for what the media choose to cover but also for how the coverage affects citizens—and how political elites design conventions in response to television coverage. If you have ever seen a movie made from a book, you understand some of the vast changes that take place as a message is conveyed in different forms. Like great stories, political phenomena cannot simply be translated from one medium to another. Something is lost and something else is gained when a new form of communication rises to dominance.

Today the dominant form of political discourse is television; we live in an era of video politics. Video has been dominant in American politics for just a few decades but already a challenger has emerged: the Internet. If the Internet soon replaces television as the most important form of political communication, it will be the swiftest shift in political communication in world history. American political media are on the precipice of vast changes even though we have barely absorbed the alterations produced by television media. To understand what such a shift might mean, it is important to see how previous political communication eras have operated and to examine the strengths and weaknesses of each.

ORAL POLITICAL CULTURE

You may have recognized some of the scenarios described at the beginning of the chapter. The man on trial for his life in the first scenario is the Greek philosopher Socrates, who lived in Athens in the fifth century BC. Socrates' entire life was emblematic of oral political culture. He spent most of his days in the center of town talking over questions of morality, religion, politics, and science with anyone who would enter into conversation with him. He was famous for taking on the smartest and most self-satisfied members of the community, exposing how little they knew about what they believed, and teaching his followers lessons through these conversations.

Even today we do not know what it was that finally caused the authorities of Athens to put Socrates on trial for his life. The initial charges had to do with teaching atheism and corrupting young people with his ideas.[1] If we are to believe Socrates' disciple Plato, Socrates himself testified that he was on trial because he had been an annoyance to the Athenians, because his questions made the government and the citizens uncomfortable.[2] Others have alleged that Socrates was put on trial because he was an opponent of democracy and an ally of tyrants.[3] The trial was conducted almost entirely via oral debate between Socrates and his three accusers. The five hundred jurors listened carefully as Socrates and his opponents debated the accusations against him.

Unlike a modern trial, almost the only evidence before the jurors was oral testimony and allegations. In such a situation, Socrates claimed to be worried that too much would depend on which side was more eloquent rather than on which side was correct. As he put it:

> How you, O Athenians, have been affected by my accusers, I cannot tell; but I know that they almost made me forget who I was, so persuasively did they speak; and yet they have hardly uttered a word of truth.[4]

Whether because of his accusers' eloquence or not, Socrates was convicted and sentenced to death by the Athenians. Today his thoughts are taught in almost every introductory philosophy course in the United States. Moreover, his oral style of teaching has become so associated with him that we use his name to identify it: the Socratic method. In the Socratic method, an instructor begins asking simple questions about the topic and uses the students' answers to illustrate his or her points, just as Socrates did in his teaching and during his trial. Although most textbooks focus on Socrates' message and meaning, our concern here is with his method of communication. Socrates lived, and very literally died, in the midst of oral political culture.

During most of human history, every government has relied on **oral political culture** to communicate its ideas, its laws, and its decisions. Even though writing emerged centuries before Socrates, the difficulty of reproduction as well as low levels of literacy allowed oral political culture to remain dominant. Writing made the administration of the Roman Empire much easier, but at the apex of power in the Roman senate and among the emperor and his top advisers, debate was still oral. Leaders still spoke to each other, and rebellious or conformist ideas were still conveyed by word of mouth.

Every form of communication that is used to send political messages has specific strengths and weaknesses. Let's examine the advantages and disadvantages of oral political culture.

Advantages of Oral Political Culture

Interactivity Inherent in the Socratic method is one of the great advantages of oral political culture: interactivity. When political leaders speak directly to the masses, the masses have a chance to individually address the leaders with questions. Even nonverbal communication such as cheers and boos or claps and whistles conveys a message from the masses to the leaders. Political leaders also have a chance to confront each other, depending on the nature of the political system. The Lincoln-Douglas debates, which took place in Illinois in 1858, pitted two candidates for the U.S. Senate against each other in debates that often went on for more than six hours. The speakers, Abraham Lincoln and Stephen Douglas, had to respond not only to each other but also to the shifting moods of their audience. They could see immediately how well their points were faring with their fellow citizens.

Low Barriers to Participation Oral political culture is relatively open. To understand it, all you need is the language. To participate, all you need is a voice. This was particularly important in those ancient republics in which some limited form of democracy was practiced. Even today there are "free speech zones" in some democratic countries where any citizen can speak or listen. Part of Hyde Park in London, England, is taken over every Sunday by speakers of all varieties: evangelists, atheists, socialists, and anarchists. Speakers stand on a soapbox and harangue, cajole, plead, and caterwaul to passing tourists and British citizens. Almost any type of speech is permitted, including obscenity, blasphemy, racial slurs, and sedition.

Truth Ascertaining   Oral political culture involves face-to-face confrontation between the governor and the governed. Many people believe that this type of politics allows citizens to judge whether their leaders are honest. Would you have a better idea if someone were lying to you by reading a letter she wrote to you or by talking to her for ten minutes? Of course, an honest politician may still make bad decisions and advocate poor policies out of misguided thinking, but at least she will not be purposefully deceptive. Beyond merely assessing truthfulness, many people believe that in directly speaking to someone they get a much better sense of the person's general character. It is likely that the writers of the Constitution of the United States believed this. They allowed for direct election of members of Congress because they thought the people would have sufficient knowledge of the character of local politicians. At the same time, they feared people would lack enough direct knowledge of national candidates for the presidency, and might choose unwisely. This was one reason they gave the power of presidential selection to an elite, the members of the Electoral College. If character matters in political leadership, oral political culture may provide the best means for the people to judge the character of candidates for office.

Disadvantages of Oral Political Culture

Impermanent   One problem with politics conducted through oral means is that what is spoken may not be remembered accurately. As time and distance from the moment the words were originally spoken expand, the chance that context, meaning, and details will be omitted, changed, or added increases. Although we have several accounts of what Socrates said during his years of lecturing in Athens, the accounts do not seem to agree. The most extensive account, that of Socrates' pupil Plato, probably includes much of Plato's own thought. Because Socrates spent his days engaging in lengthy conversations in Athens rather than in writing his ideas down, we cannot be sure what he actually said.

   The impermanence of oral culture has posed continuing challenges for major world religions. Much of what is written about Buddha,

Mohammed, Moses, and Jesus has its earliest origin in oral accounts, told by witnesses and passed around by followers. Some scholars of Christianity regularly debate whether Jesus said precisely what is attributed to him in the Bible. Specific debates can have important political ramifications, but more broadly they illustrate how ephemeral thoughts and even facts can be if they are communicated orally.

Low Complexity   Oral political culture limits the complexity of what can be said. Imagine a college class conducted without any writing by either pupil or professor. The class would consist only of the professor talking and the students occasionally asking questions. No books would be read, and no notes would be taken. Such a college class could not cover even a fraction of the material dealt with in a class that uses books to create a common basis of understanding among the students. Oral culture also affects the meaning of intelligence itself. In an oral culture, the "smartest" person is the one with the strongest memory, someone who can retain thousands of stories and parables. Even in the modern era, some small African, Asian, and South American societies still rely on leaders with good memories to hold the legacy of the people in their heads. Does this attention to simple memorization prevent more attention to synthesis and cognition?

The Danger of Demagoguery   When oral political culture involves some degree of participation, a new danger arises: demagoguery. A **demagogue** is a cunning speaker who manipulates the fears and prejudices of his or her audience to whip them into a dangerous emotional frenzy. A crowd can turn into a mob under the influence of a demagogue. More broadly, oral political culture may contain several biases that produce negative outcomes. When a debate between two positions is held before a public assembly, it is very likely that the best course of action, if espoused by a weaker speaker, will lose out to a less logical argument put forth by a better speaker. Socrates spoke disparagingly of those who used **rhetoric,** or skill with words, to make false ideas look true. Psychological studies show that better looking people are perceived to be smarter and more moral than they actually are. Thus oral political culture may have a bias for charisma and speaking talent.

Limited Scope   Oral political culture limits the size of any participatory political system. While vast empires ruled the earth for centuries before the printing press, the earliest forms of democratic government, such as the Greek cities or the Italian city-states of the Middle Ages, were uniformly small, not only in size but also in population. When the human voice is the only means of expressing political ideas, the conversation is limited to at most the number who can fit in a small stadium.

Aspects of the American Political System That Reflect Oral Political Culture

Even today, in this video politics era, elements of our system reflect oral political culture. We look at three of these elements next.

The Judicial System   More than any other aspect of U.S. politics, the judicial system reflects a faith in oral communication. The Constitution guarantees to every American the right to a trial by a jury and the right to confront witnesses. Whenever feasible, testimony is required to be in person. Our system of justice is founded on the idea that it is much more difficult to get away with lying in person than on paper. Requiring oral testimony also provides the advantage of interactivity. The opposing lawyer may confront a witness and question each claim of the prosecution. At the apex of the judicial system, the Supreme Court requires that petitioners present their claims in oral as well as written form. Lawyers face a withering crossfire of questions from the nine justices, and although some experts question the worth of these exchanges, it is unlikely that oral arguments will disappear any time soon.

Local Governments and Caucus Voting   Within electoral politics, the more local the level of government, the more the business of government is conducted orally. A town council often debates issues for hours and hears directly from citizens. Even the path to highest office in the land, the presidency, is not without an oral element. The first chance for average voters to participate in the presidential nomination contest is the Iowa caucuses. In a caucus election, voters gather in a large hall, and speakers for each candidate attempt to woo supporters to their cause. After hearing from all the speakers, the voters vote by converging in different areas of the hall. This is as close to the Athenian style of politics as the American presidential race gets.

"Word of Mouth" Politics   When political scientists study public opinion about politics today, they don't ignore oral political culture entirely. Although television and newspapers are the main sources of information for most Americans, oral communication among peers and family remains vitally important according to some scholars. In your own life, imagine which would have more impact on you: a newspaper column about abortion or an impassioned discussion with your parents on the same topic. Or suppose your best friend believed that one of the candidates for president was simply a dishonest and immoral person. Of course, your best friend probably got this opinion from the mass media or from talking to someone who did. This is called the **two-step flow process** of political communication, in which the mass media send out messages that are received by opinion leaders.[5] These opinion leaders, who can be just ordinary citizens who pay a lot of attention to politics, then talk about what they have learned with others. Opinion leaders can have a great deal of impact because they individually decide which tiny piece of the day's news will be discussed.

WRITTEN POLITICAL CULTURE

Thomas Jefferson was the rebellious writer in the second scenario at the beginning of this chapter. As the author of the Declaration of Independence, Jefferson was widely known as the most gifted of the Founding Fathers, and his fame is second only to George Washington's. Yet Jefferson could not have been a political leader in any other era of politics. Jefferson was shy and hated speaking in public. His voice was faint, and to some listeners it sounded almost feminine. When Jefferson became the third president of the United States, he ended the tradition of giving the State of the Union in person, preferring to deliver his views in writing.[6] Indeed, for the entire eight years of his presidency, it is possible that he gave only two speeches. Historian Joseph Ellis aptly called Jefferson's tenure at the White House the "Textual Presidency."

When Jefferson arrived in Philadelphia in 1776, he was known to the other colonial leaders because of an incendiary pamphlet he had authored the previous year. Even after he penned the Declaration, few understood how important the document would become. For years Jefferson was much less famous than several other Virginians, including the fiery Patrick Henry, who was a brilliant orator.[7] Indeed, July 4, 1776, is arguably the moment when the printed word became the dominant mode of political communication. In the American Revolution words were at least as powerful as bullets, not just Jefferson's Declaration but Tom Paine's anti-British pamphlets such as *Common Sense* as well. Without the printing press, there could have been no American Revolution, no Declaration, and, a decade later, no Constitution. Written political culture made the United States of America possible. Americans are, in the words of media scholar Neil Postman, children of a typographic revolution. Let's examine some of the advantages and disadvantages that characterize **written political culture.**

Advantages of Written Political Culture

Permanence   Each day thousands of tourists in Washington pass by a climate-controlled display case containing the Declaration of Independence. The words that Jefferson wrote remain unaltered; ideas expressed in print last unchanged so long as a single copy survives. Of course, the interpretation of Jefferson's words may change with the times, but at least there is no debate about what the Declaration of Independence actually says.

Broad Scope   Unlike oral culture, written communication can speak to diverse audiences separated by vast distances. Without printing, the far-flung thirteen colonies could not have coordinated their rebellion against Great Britain. The ability to make exact copies of pamphlets and documents and to distribute them widely made the Revolution possible.

Complexity and Rationality   Written political culture is able to handle extraordinarily complex ideas and concepts. Writing itself is an abstraction and trains the mind to think in complex ways. Memorization becomes a less important trait of intelligence; if you don't remember a precise fact, you can always look it up in a book. What matters most is the ability to synthesize complex ideas from diverse sources and analyze their significance. Also, the process of reading allows a citizen to acquire objectivity and distance so that the claims of the writer may be assessed more rationally and unemotionally. At a public speech, the mood and opinions of others, as well as the emotional appeals of the speaker, may pull the listener in an irrational or unwise direction. French public opinion expert Elizabeth Noelle Neumann has shown convincingly that many citizens adapt their views to what they perceive to be the majority's beliefs. These psychological forces are surely stronger on the spectator in a crowd of people than on a person reading a newspaper alone at home.

Blind to Appearance   If oral political culture is biased toward better looking politicians who are glib speakers, written political culture makes looks largely immaterial. Could Abraham Lincoln have been elected in an era of televised politics? Lincoln was called a "baboon" by his political opponents, and he was an unusually homely man. Would William Howard Taft, the fattest man to ever serve as president, have had a chance in a televised election? When words on paper are dominant, looks become much less important.

Disadvantages of Written Political Culture

Access and Cost   When writing is the dominant form of political expression, inequality naturally appears. First, the illiterate are left out of politics to a large extent. Many of the Founding Fathers were opposed to those without property participating in politics because they feared that the uneducated and landless lacked the proper perspective to engage in politics. In part, what worried them was that many of the landless could not read. How could they cast an intelligent ballot if they could not read the newspaper? For decades certain states prevented illiterate citizens from voting (although in most cases this was a way for racist whites to keep blacks out of politics). Even without these barriers, politics conducted in an era of printing is not fully accessible to the illiterate. At best an illiterate person could keep informed by talking to others about the news of the day, but it would be very difficult for that person to get his or her own views heard.

Beyond the barrier posed by literacy, a written political culture also introduces economic inequality. When Jefferson became president, he had the support of the majority of the people, but many of the young nation's largest newspapers were held by his well-off political opponents in the Federalist Party. Owning a newspaper has always been a costly endeavor. The wealthy can communicate political ideas much more easily than the poor because printing is expensive. Not only has the cost of printing a newspaper risen substantially in the last two hundred years, but larger and fewer media conglomerates own most of the newspapers in the country. Domination by the elite may be more possible in a written politics era.

Danger of Propaganda   Just as oral culture poses the danger of the demagogue, written culture contains the danger of **propaganda.** The use of the media to deceive the public in a coordinated fashion, by a corporation, a political party, or, most commonly, a government, is called propaganda. Nazi newspapers and pamphlets brilliantly exploited the fears and grievances of the German people from 1928 to 1933 in preparing Germany for Hitler's rise to power.[8] Joseph Goebbels and other masters of propaganda helped the Nazis capture the affection and support of the German people.

Propaganda is the extreme case of biased writing pulling politics in one direction, but even when there is no intention to deceive or inflame the reader, written discourse has a bias—for good writing. Writing is a skill, like piano playing or public speaking. Consider two newspaper editorials with competing viewpoints. One is written by a brilliant and clever craftsman of English who convincingly argues a weak case. The other is authored by a terrible writer who mangles grammar, uses trite clichés, and has poor organization. Even if the second writer actually has the better position, which editorial is likely to sway more voters?

Aspects of the American Political System That Reflect Written Political Culture

Perhaps because the written era of political culture begins with the birth of the United States, the American political system has been built around the printing press. It should not be surprising that many aspects of our system retain a reverence for the written word.

Print Journalism   Although more Americans now get their news from televised sources, print journalism remains a vibrant part of political discourse. Many television reporters take their cues from such vital newspapers as the *New York Times* and the *Washington Post*. The political elite must remain responsive to the concerns of these newspapers, even if their daily circulation is just a fraction of the viewership of a nightly news broadcast.

Laws and Rulings   The U.S. legal system remains centered around the written word, even though it retains elements of oral political culture. The written Constitution is upheld by a judiciary that releases lengthy documents defending its interpretation of the laws and the Constitution. The U.S. Supreme Court operates behind closed doors and resists any effort to televise its proceedings. Lawyers at all levels of the judiciary file briefs arguing over the meaning of written laws. Although the system does usually require attorneys to defend their written arguments orally, most believe that a good brief is far more important than a good presentation.

Party Platforms   Every four years the two major political parties release documents during their national conventions. These party platforms contain the party's agenda and its views on a variety of public issues. In the past, party platforms were often quite important and were studied carefully by journalists and even voters. Although their importance has diminished, platforms still convey important messages about a party's principles. If the Republican Party ever removes its anti-abortion plank, a part of every Republican platform since 1980, pro-life groups will take this as a highly offensive act. Similarly, if the Democratic platform did not endorse the pro-choice position on abortion, the electoral costs would be high. Not only do platforms matter at the ballot box, some research suggests that a high percentage of platform promises are carried out after the election.

Petitions   Before running for office in most areas, a candidate must acquire a list of signatures of citizens who support his or her candidacy. In many states, signing another document, called a referendum, allows citizens to demonstrate their support for placing an issue before the voters. These petitions are relics of the era that produced the Declaration of Independence and the Constitution, which were both signed by their authors and supporters.

VIDEO POLITICAL CULTURE

The third scenario at the beginning of the chapter describes the first televised presidential debate. It occurred in September of 1960 between Vice President Richard M. Nixon and Senator John F. Kennedy. The debate was a contrast of looks and speaking styles as well as issue positions. Indeed, there was no large ideological gulf between Nixon and Kennedy, but the stylistic differences were great. Nixon spoke in the formal style of a traditional debate, rebutting his opponent's points before making his own. Recovering from a serious illness, Nixon also appeared pale and uncomfortable before the harsh television lights. Kennedy was much more at ease with the camera, and much healthier looking. Although both men refused to wear makeup, this didn't affect Kennedy's image nearly as much because he was bronzed from several days' rest on the beach. Kennedy also

WHAT ARE THE MEDIA?

What exactly is meant by the term *media*? The *Oxford English Dictionary* defines it as "the main means of mass communication, esp. newspapers, radio, and television, regarded collectively; the reporters, journalists, etc., working for organizations engaged in such communication." A broader definition could include talk shows like *Oprah,* popular films and novels, cartoons, and even cell phones, fax machines, and advertising. For the purpose of this book, however, media refers to outlets such as newspapers, television networks, radio stations, and Internet Web sites that cover politics.

Many refer to "the media" as if it were a singular entity; others consider media as a plural entity, with the singular being "medium." This book uses media in the plural form because it captures the tremendous diversity in the media. Conservative critics, in particular, often use the singular form, as if to imply that there is a liberal uniformity to media outlets. They also use the term *mainstream media,* or MSM, often in the pejorative, to distinguish it from some conservative outlets.

was, objectively speaking, one of the most handsome men to ever run for president.[9] He didn't debate in the formal style of Nixon; Kennedy talked to the viewers at home, making short concise points that tended to ignore Nixon's arguments.[10]

Those listening on the radio were said to have felt that the debate was a tie, whereas those watching on television felt Kennedy had bested Nixon. Recent research by political scientist James Druckman confirms that Kennedy had the advantage on television and that Nixon fared better when only their voices were heard.[11] Perhaps because this is one of the best examples of how the medium of television affected politics, many scholars have identified the Nixon-Kennedy debate as a turning point in American politics. From that day onward, television has been the most important medium in politics. Elections would be won and lost on television, just as many believed Nixon lost the election in that debate.

What strengths and weaknesses have been observed in **video political culture** since September 1960?

Advantages of Video Political Culture

Immediacy   In oral political culture, news arrived only as fast as humans could travel. News from abroad sometimes came months later. Much the same was true in written political culture until the invention of the telegraph. Printing itself was hardly immediate, requiring many hours of manual labor well into the twentieth century when printing was finally mechanized and eventually computerized. Even with today's rapid printing, newspapers are delayed by the process of writing, printing, and distribution. Television networks using satellites and phone lines can take their viewers to distant crises around the globe instantaneously, and it is this speed that sets the pace of modern journalism, not the newspaper's schedule. Cable news has a constant twenty-four hours a day, seven days a week news cycle. This affects politics directly because decision makers have access to news from afar as it is being made. Politics moves faster in a video era.

This advantage is not without its downside. The time available to make decisions has been shrunk by video technology. Today's politicians have access to more information about recent and distant events than yesterday's leaders ever did, but they also face the challenge of having to make many more decisions much more quickly. Perhaps the quality of the choices they make has been hurt by the speed with which they must react.

Vividness and Scope   Is a picture worth a thousand words? Consider the depiction of war. Writers from Thucydides to Ernest Hemingway have tried to paint a portrait of war in words to bring home the tragedy, heroism, and brutality of conflict to those who will never see it firsthand. Yet some have argued that it was the television pictures of American boys dying in Vietnam that brought that bitter conflict to an end.[12] For the first time, the moving images of death and dismemberment were in the living rooms across America. Perhaps the vivid and gripping character of television limits the ability of political leaders to choose war, or at least wars with high casualties in which the national interest is unclear. Is it any accident that since Vietnam all of America's conflicts until the Iraq War have been depicted with prettier pictures and low casualties? Often, when the pictures become ugly or indefensible, such as with the deaths of 19 soldiers in Somalia in 1994 or the deaths of 242 Marines in Beirut in 1982, the troops are quickly withdrawn.

Video politics may also expose brutal injustice better than the written word. It is arguable that television was a crucial ally in the civil rights movement that removed the worst stain on America's record as a just nation. When Martin Luther King Jr. launched his "children's crusade" to free Birmingham from segregation and white supremacy, he sent boys and girls out to face police dogs and powerful water cannons. The images of children being viciously oppressed by white police rocked the whole nation. No more could northern and western whites remain indifferent to racial violence against blacks in places like Alabama. Any educated American in the 1950s had been aware that black Americans had few rights in the South, but television brought the plight of the black American into the nation's living rooms and gave the civil rights movement an urgency it had never had before.

Accessibility   Video politics, like oral politics, is accessible to everyone who speaks and can watch, so long as they own a television. Currently, an estimated 99 percent of American homes have at least one television. Cable television, although not as widely accessible, is in a solid majority of American homes. Whether broadcast over the airwaves or through a cable, television distributes its messages with great ease compared to print media. Given that some studies suggest that a significant minority of Americans are "functionally illiterate," and given that the percentage of Americans who read newspapers is also dropping, the accessibility of politics on television is of vital importance.

Sense of Character   Television gives many viewers the sense that they know their leaders in an intimate fashion. Viewers of a presidential debate are now asked by pollsters about how comfortable they felt with the candidates. Indeed, during the 2000 presidential campaign, voters were asked whether they would rather have a beer with George Bush or Al Gore as if this were a relevant question. And, in a sense, every four years Americans choose not only a president but a television "show." The president is in their living rooms more than any other political leader, and if they find him pompous, supercilious, boring, and arrogant, as many apparently did find Al Gore, it may be a long four years. Many Americans also believe they can gain some idea of the character and honesty of a candidate after watching him or her on television. This claim has been made since the earliest days of television's dominance. In 1962 the head of the Democratic Party was asked how television had changed politics:

> Men on television or women on television being interviewed if they are not telling the truth and if they are not sincere in their answers,

it's obvious to those who are watching them . . . the viewers of the program know whether the truth is being told and for that reason I think great strides have been made in television. . . . I don't think demagogues can do as well on television as they could on radio.[13]

Many Americans even today still believe that watching a debate or an interview with a politician gives them the ability to judge a leader's character firsthand, an element lost in our politics since the rise of printed communication. Would you feel closer to a presidential candidate after seeing him on television in a debate or after reading an essay he wrote?

Permanence   Like printed media, video preserves political messages in a protected, unchanging format. Given adequate attention to storage, a video of a presidential debate could last for millennia.

Disadvantages of Video Political Culture

Cost and Elite Domination   Video media are very accessible to most Americans, but video politics is primarily a one-way street. It is very easy for a citizen to receive messages, but it is extraordinarily difficult for the citizen to send them. When politics is mostly discussed through video, only those messages supported by millions of dollars can easily be heard.

One change in American life that has been much discussed by sociologists is the **death of public space:** there simply aren't many places left where Americans can congregate together that are not controlled by corporations. It is very difficult to send a message about politics at a privately owned sports stadium or mall because the owners may object to any controversial political information that might distract customers from shopping or entertainment. Suppose you wanted to send a message to your fellow citizens but could not get mainstream media coverage for your cause. What could you do? Most malls and stadiums ban soliciting. Going door to door is extremely time consuming, and many Americans resent or resist solicitation on their front stoop. More and more Americans also live in gated communities or high-rise buildings where soliciting is banned. The only "place" where Americans congregate on a regular basis is in front of the national television networks. Yet without vast sums of money, that venue is out of reach. This leaves a great deal of power in the hands of corporations and the wealthy. Video has become the most centralized form of political discourse in world history.

Manipulation   Is video "truth"? Every slice of life shown on video is a truncation of reality. For many citizens, seeing a videotape is believing. The Rodney King incident in Los Angeles that sparked the bloody riots of 1992 began when King's brutal beating by L.A. cops was captured on video. Defenders of the cops argued that the few seconds of video that many news organizations showed did not include King's allegedly dangerous lunge at officers. However convincing, no video is "real"; it is a representation of reality, a partial and incomplete picture of the way the world actually is. The gap between reality and video may allow for manipulation because for most Americans video equals truth more so than print or oral communication.

If oral political culture is vulnerable to demagoguery and written culture to propaganda, video politics is susceptible to manipulation. The creator of a video image may use editing, sound effects, and even digitalization to create a powerful message that may differ sharply from reality. "Morphing" has become a common tactic in political campaign ads. An unpopular political figure, such as Bill Clinton in much of the American South in 1994, is linked to a local Democrat by digitally morphing their faces together. The local Democrat's face slowly becomes that of Bill Clinton, sending a blunt message to every viewer.

As with propaganda under the Nazis, manipulation is most powerful when all video outlets are controlled by the government. When dictator Slobodan Milosevic controlled Serbia in the 1990s, his rule was bolstered by manipulative news on the national networks. During the brief air war with Serbia, the United States felt it necessary to target Serbia's television broadcast facilities because these powerful images were boosting Serb morale.

These examples of video manipulation are relatively minor, but the video form is only in its infancy. It may be waiting for its Goebbels to show the evil possibilities of the form. Consider that digitization technology is only a few years away from being able to create a fake video of John F. Kennedy giving a speech endorsing radical antiterror tactics with a degree of realism that would fool his surviving family. The movie *Forrest Gump* inserted actor Tom Hanks into interactive scenes with several U.S. presidents. Soon such scenes will be so well crafted that they will be indistinguishable from "real" video without extensive technical analysis.

Bias to Simplicity   As critics have warned for decades, video culture dumbs down politics, reducing its complexity. Both campaigns and political journalism revolve around brief simplistic sound bites, with substantive issues seldom debated. In watching political news shows, have you ever seen someone say "that's a good point, I've never considered that before. I guess you are correct." Chances are that you haven't because such an exchange would require television commentators to listen to each other with open minds. Almost all political talk shows are set piece dramas with positions decided before the cameras are turned on, and no one budges from established ideologies. When comedian and political commentator Jon Stewart appeared on the CNN show *Crossfire*, he attacked the hosts for "doing theater, when you should be doing debate!" As Stewart put it, most political talk shows were as far from true debates as televised wrestling is from a true sport.

It may be the video form itself that prevents complex arguments from appearing on television. Anything that takes longer than thirty seconds to explain cannot typically be stated on television. An average story on the evening news runs less than one minute, including introduction and video. The average sound bite from a presidential speech is now around seven seconds. Imagine if Thomas Jefferson had lived in an era of televised politics. Could he convey the famous statement of principles in the Declaration of Independence in a seven-second sound bite on the evening news?

> We hold these truths to be self-evident, that all men are created equal, that they are endowed by their Creator with certain unalienable Rights, that among these are Life, Liberty, and the pursuit of Happiness. That to secure these rights, Governments are instituted among Men, deriving their just powers from the consent of the governed.

The entire Declaration ran to more than 1,300 words, not counting signatures. How would the whole document ever be conveyed in the abbreviated form of video? Television's problem with simplification may be the gravest of all.

Bias to Looks and Telegenic Cool   Television is an unforgiving medium. If the dawn of the television age was the presidential debates of 1960, the moment of its total mastery may well have been the 1992 vice presidential debates. Those debates pitted Democratic Senator Al Gore against Republican Vice President Dan Quayle and independent candidate Admiral James Stockdale. Anticipation of the event was perhaps greater than for any previous vice presidential debate, because very little was known about Stockdale, Ross Perot's running mate. Stockdale opened his remarks with a braying and odd "Who am I? Why am I here?" a rhetorical tactic that fell flat on television. Intended to make him look homespun and honest, it instead conveyed that he was befuddled and out of his league. From a bad start, Stockdale's performance got worse. When it was over, Stockdale was fodder for every late night comic, most cruelly the brilliant mockery on *Saturday Night Live*, which depicted him as a brainless, senile, and unbalanced stooge of Perot's.

The truth was starkly different. Stockdale was a decorated war hero, whose mental toughness had gotten him through six years in a brutal North Vietnamese POW camp, where torture and isolation were regular occurrences. After his release, he had become a PhD scholar of political philosophy, an acknowledged expert in the Greek philosophy of Stoicism. But this brilliant man had committed the unpardonable sin in modern America—he had been bad on television.

Television rewards good-looking people who are "telegenic," a vague concept that simply means that the viewers at home feel comfortable and secure watching them. A politician who is telegenic has an immense advantage over his or her opponents. Ronald Reagan ably advocated his conservative positions on television because he understood the conventions of video discourse. When Reagan made his political debut in 1964 with a riveting nationally televised speech that instantly made him a hero to conservatives everywhere, he had been on movie and television sets for decades. Unlike almost every other political figure of the day, he was as comfortable in front of the camera as he was talking to a friend.

Image may be even more important in the video era than in the oral era because the images a politician puts out over the airwaves are carefully staged and planned today. In the oral era, a political figure such as Socrates, who was allegedly quite physically unattractive, could still compensate for this by verbal displays of brilliance. Today the looks of a candidate for higher office are essential to success. Since the dawn of television as the dominant form of political discourse, no bald candidates have won the White House. Politics may be becoming the sport of the telegenic, eliminating from national leadership the modern Lincolns and Jeffersons simply because they lack the looks and the screen presence necessary today. In a television era, we judge our leaders harshly on the basis of looks. In discussing the Nixon-Kennedy debates of 1960 in which Nixon, in addition to his many other image problems, was also much sweatier than Kennedy, political scientist Kathleen Hall Jamieson observed, "The argument can be made that whether or not a candidate perspires under the hot studio lights should have no bearing on his possible performance as president."[14] Television draws our attention to the irrelevant aspects of appearance and attractiveness and away from issues and facts or even deeper questions of character and judgment.

Surveillance   Video politics may have one final disadvantage: surveillance. Government's ability to regulate every aspect of human behavior has grown immensely as a result of the availability of cheap video cameras. From red light cameras to hidden surveillance cameras on the National Mall, the eye of "Big Brother" is on Americans as never before. How many times a day are you videotaped without your consent or most likely even your knowledge? Many apartment building lobbies, gas stations, elevators, banks, convenience stores, and even parks are now under constant video surveillance. In 2002 it was estimated that the average resident of the Washington D.C. area appeared on security cameras more than eight times a day. The all-seeing camera eye may change the definition of what "alone" means. Overseas, few places in downtown London or Amsterdam are without video surveillance as a deterrent against street crime. These measures have reduced crime, and it is not surprising that many American cities are considering similar measures.

Aspects of the American Political System That Reflect Video Political Culture

Although video has been part of American politics for only a few decades, it has taken over several areas almost entirely.

Television Ads and Television Campaigns   Today television ads are the most important part of most presidential and congressional campaigns. More money is spent on creating and broadcasting political ads than on any other single campaign endeavor. Along with television news, ads are the most popular source of campaign information. Campaigns still spend money on more traditional activities, but many of them, such as political rallies, are no longer directed at the actual participants. A modern political rally is all about playing to the cameras, and the audience members are extras in a short political film. The politician is not really talking to the comparatively few people at even the largest rally; he's talking to the viewers at home.

Television News   Even though the nightly network news broadcasts have been losing audience share to cable channels and to the Internet, broadcast news remains the largest single source of news for American citizens. Compared to newspapers, television news simplifies politics to an extraordinary degree.

Congressional Debates   During the early years of the video era, television cameras were rarely allowed to cover congressional debates or committee meetings except at moments of high drama, such as the Watergate hearings. The House of Representatives has broadcast its floor debates since 1979. The Senate long resisted the idea, fearing that the introduction of cameras would change the way the Senate operated, but both houses now broadcast floor debates and many committee meetings over C-SPAN, reaching an estimated eighty-nine million American homes every day. Members of Congress are almost always in front of cameras when questioning a witness, crafting compromise legislation with colleagues, or casting a vote. According to some congressional scholars, many things that legislators now say on the floor or in committee are not directed at their fellow members but at the cameras. The values of video culture work to prevent compromise and cooperation because members become fixed into positions through posturing for the cameras. They may be forced to choose increasingly simplistic and harsh rhetoric in order to get coverage by the broadcast networks.[15]

Video culture brought many aspects of legislative life to the attention of Americans for the first time in our history, which might have boosted Congress's approval. Unfortunately, Congress has been brought into American homes just as television's appetite for simplified and rigid discussions may have made congressional debate a farce.

Trials   Increasingly cameras have become a part of the U.S. legal system. Sometimes this is unquestionably a good thing. The growing practice of videotaping the questioning of suspects aids both the prosecution and the defense. It is harder for a suspect to disavow a confession if the police possess a complete record of that confession to show the jury. At the same time, many defense lawyers believe it may be harder for police to brutalize or coerce suspects in pursuit of confessions if the entire interrogation process is videotaped.

Cameras have also intruded into the courtroom itself, and that worries many legal scholars. The rise of Court TV, a cable station that focuses on televised trials, illustrates some of these fears. Will judges in high-profile trials rule differently in pursuit of television popularity? Given that several of the figures in the O. J. Simpson trial of 1995 later went on to reap millions of dollars from books and television appearances, it seems probable that others will seek similar gains. Will juries worry about freeing an unpopular, but innocent, defendant now that some trials have become daytime dramas rivaling the networks' soap operas?

Cyber Political Culture?

The fourth scenario from the opening of this chapter has not yet happened. No Internet-based political movement has yet brought down the established order in the United States or any other country. There is as yet no Socrates, Jefferson, or JFK who symbolizes the dominance of cyberpolitics, but it is conceivable that this day is coming. Important aspects of American politics are already deeply affected by the Internet. The first outlet to cover the 1998 Monica Lewinsky story was the DrudgeReport, an online political gossip site. Many months later the Starr Report appeared online, detailing the president's sexual relationship with the young intern. In 2000 and 2004, every presidential candidate had a Web site, and some were extraordinarily sophisticated, attracting millions of visitors. Most mainstream media outlets now have a presence on the Web, and more Americans go online every day. In the 2004 presidential campaign, dark horse Democratic candidate Howard Dean used the Internet to rally his supporters and raise money, briefly shocking the Democratic establishment. In the general election, independent political groups (groups not directly affiliated with the presidential campaigns) such as Moveon.org and the Swift Boat Veterans for Truth acquired money and notoriety through the Internet.

Chapter 11 deals directly with the emerging problems and benefits of cyberpolitics.

BENJAMIN'S HOPE, POSTMAN'S NIGHTMARE

Now that we have seen that every method of political communication comes with drawbacks and benefits, how should we feel about the current era in which video is the dominant form for conducting politics?

Most analysts bemoan the current state of political campaigns and journalism in the television era. Many accuse television of dumbing down U.S. elections and news coverage and making campaigns more relentlessly negative. No one has better stated the broad case against television than media theorist **Neil Postman** in his book, *Amusing Ourselves to Death*.[16] Postman argues that entertainment has become the subtext of American politics because of the role television plays in our politics. Newscasters and politicians feel it necessary to entertain citizens, to offer up "infotainment" to the viewers. Postman believes that in shifting from written politics to video politics we have lost much that was vital in American democracy and culture.[17] It is easy to find elements in the writings of political scientists that echo Postman's pessimism about what television has done to American politics, and what it will do in the future.

There is surely a great deal of truth to Postman's critique. Many of the disadvantages of video politics discussed here should worry Americans. Yet is Postman's portrait of America under video politics accurate? Are we really a nation of political couch potatoes, knowing almost nothing about current events because the news provides only shallow or sexy stories that emphasize celebrity and trivia rather than real issues? Do we sit back and apathetically accept whatever the television tells us, allowing for elite manipulation? If this is so, why has the American political system improved by many measures during the era of video dominance? Although racial discrimination is still present in American life and politics, surely television has helped to end legal discrimination against blacks. When Americans sit down to watch the evening news, they see black leaders who possess enormous political power and influence, including Cabinet secretaries and members of Congress. The argument for women's equality in politics began well before the nineteenth century, but it is only since the 1970s—during the video politics era—that women began to be important political figures in Congress.

If American campaigns today are considered to be the worst examples of television's perverting and pervasive effect on politics, then it would follow that the presidents elected during the television era would be much worse than those elected in the print era. Some of the least successful presidents in history have been elected during the television era (Richard Nixon, Jimmy Carter), but several mediocre and incompetent presidents (including dimwit Warren Harding) managed to get elected long before television ads appeared. Although Postman and others bemoan that the presidential campaign today is a battle of thirty-second ads featuring personal attacks and unsubstantiated allegations, campaigns in the nineteenth century could be just as lurid. It is not clear that U.S. political culture has gravely declined during the television era.

Postman's critique of video politics is important, but others have put forward a more positive view of what video politics might mean. One person who thought deeply about what video would do to culture was critical theorist **Walter Benjamin.** Benjamin, who committed suicide to escape capture by the Nazis in the 1940s, never experienced television, only film. But in his visionary essay on what film would do to art and culture, he anticipated some of the positive effects of video on politics.[18] Although Benjamin wrote mostly about art, his ideas translate well into a discussion of politics. He believed that film would be a democratic force. First, cameras would take viewers places they would never otherwise go. This would change politics forever, in his opinion, because it would reveal previously hidden aspects of life. If Benjamin is right, the civil rights movement succeeded in the video era because television showed a hidden aspect of American life to northern and western Americans in a vivid and direct fashion.

But Benjamin's positive vision of video politics did not end there. He also believed video would give the people more power to make their own decisions. Benjamin compared a painting to a film. When a painting was shown, because there was only one copy of it, the masses could see it only in small groups, and they were already told what to think about it by the wealthy elites. But in a darkened theater the masses may immediately respond with laughter or applause without filtering by elites. As these words are being written, the number one movie in the United States has been widely labeled a pathetic and shallow piece of sophomoric trash by newspaper and television reviewers. The immediacy of video transmission limits the influence of cultural gatekeepers.

Does this sort of thing happen in politics? It did in 1992. Ross Perot was widely dismissed by the media and the political experts as an inexperienced rube. He had no political record, his policy proposals seemed flimsy and shallow, and no third-party candidate had been a significant player in electoral politics for decades. When Perot rejected traditional campaign tactics and decided to speak directly to the public in one-hour national broadcasts, the political experts expected that few would watch long lectures on topics like the deficit. These expectations were wrong; Perot's shows were highly rated, and his standing in the polls went up.[19] Like an audience in a movie theater, the citizens made decisions independent of elite cues.

Benjamin's positive vision of what film and video can do for politics is certainly open to debate. Perot had billions of dollars and was able to afford national television time; only the ultra-wealthy can readily speak over the heads of the established authorities in a video era. And Benjamin saw grave dangers in video politics as well. He worried that a powerful government could use film to make war terribly attractive by emphasizing its drama and even the glittering beauty of gleaming war machines in action.

The point to remember is that every change in the means of communication may offer as many new opportunities for positive change in politics as for decline in the quality of political life. As you read, consider whether the effects of new forms of political communication should be seen as negative, positive, or both.

KEY TERMS AND PEOPLE

Walter Benjamin   propaganda
death of public space   rhetoric
demagogue   two-step flow process
oral political culture   video political culture
Neil Postman   written political culture

DISCUSSION QUESTIONS

1. Do you agree that oral political culture gives citizens a better sense of the character of their leaders? If you had a chance to hear the president give a speech and answer questions in person, would your assessment of the president's character be more accurate?
2. Do you think video political culture makes wars more difficult to wage by showing the viewers at home ugly pictures of conflict?
3. Has video technology made American politics worse? How and in what ways?
4. How do you typically learn about politics, through oral, written, video, or Internet means? Is your most frequent source of political news also your most influential, or have you been most shaped by some other force, such as conversations with a relative or friend?
5. Of all the disadvantages of each era of political culture, which do you believe are the worst?

ADDITIONAL RESOURCES

Neil Postman's *Amusing Ourselves to Death* is the best critique of
what television has done to politics, religion, and culture in the
United States.

ONLINE RESOURCES

Socrates' speech during his trial (according to Plato) is available
here: www.law.umkc.edu/faculty/projects/ftrials/socrates/
socrates.htm
The full text of Benjamin's essay "The Work of Art in the Age of
Mechanical Reproduction" is available here: http://bid.berkeley
.edu/bidclass/readings/benjamin.html
A transcript of the Jon Stewart appearance on *Crossfire* is available here:
http://politicalhumor.about.com/library/bljonstewartcrossfire.htm

NOTES

1. Thomas C. Brickhouse and Nicholas D. Smith, *Plato's Socrates*
   (New York: Oxford University Press, 1994), 173–75.
2. Plato, *The Trial and Death of Socrates: Four Dialogues,* trans. Jowett
   (New York: Dover, 1992).
3. I. F. Stone, *The Trial of Socrates* (New York: Little, Brown, 1988).
4. Ibid.
5. Paul F. Lazarsfeld and Elihu Katz, *Personal Influence: The Part
   Played by People in the Flow of Mass Communications* (New York:
   Free Press, 1955).
6. Joseph J. Ellis, *American Sphinx* (New York: Knopf, 1996).
7. Garry Wills, *Inventing America* (New York: Doubleday, 1978).
8. William L. Shirer, *The Rise and Fall of the Third Reich* (New York:
   Simon & Schuster, 1990).
9. Christopher Matthews, *Kennedy & Nixon: The Rivalry That
   Shaped Postwar America* (New York: Simon & Schuster, 1996),
   148–49.
10. Theodore White, *1960: The Making of the President* (New York:
    Atheneum, 1961), 346–47; Kathleen Hall Jamieson, *Packaging the
    Presidency* (New York: Oxford University Press, 1984), 158–59.

11. James N. Druckman, "The Power of Image: The First Nixon-Kennedy Debate Revisited." A paper presented at the annual meeting of the American Political Science Association, San Francisco, CA, 2001.

12. This view has not been universally accepted. See David L. Paletz, *The Media in American Politics* (New York: Longman, 2002), 305.

13. *Meet the Press*, John Chancellor interview with James A. Farley, November 11, 1962.

14. Jamieson, 1984, 159.

15. Timothy E. Cook, "Media Power and Congressional Power." In *American Government: Readings and Cases*, 14th ed., Peter Woll, ed. (New York: Longman, 2002), 376.

16. Many of the themes about the evolution of cognition and the advantages and disadvantages of various types of political communication had their genesis in Postman's work.

17. Neil Postman, *Amusing Ourselves to Death* (New York: Penguin, 1985).

18. Walter Benjamin, *Selected Writings, Volume 3* (Cambridge, MA: Belknap Press, 2001). The essay is also widely available online in full text searchable format.

19. Jeremy D. Mayer and Clyde Wilcox, "Understanding Perot's Plummet." In *Ross for Boss: Mass and Elite Perspectives*, Ted Jelen, ed. (Albany: State University of New York Press, 2000).

CHAPTER 2

Theories of Media Influence

As we have seen, the mode of a political message affects its content. But what about the effects of the content itself? Do media send messages that influence how citizens think about politics? Beyond merely giving information, can the media shape the opinions we have about these facts? Can they change our minds? Do they intend to?

FUNCTIONS OF THE MEDIA

First, it is important to understand what is meant by the term *media*. Political scientists consider the "media" as a whole to be a mediating institution. It is neither the citizens nor the government but a collection of organizations that speak to both citizens and government about matters of political importance. The smallest monthly independent newspaper and the vast multimedia empire of Time Warner are both included in this simple term *media*. Indeed, some definitions of media also include films and television programs. The following discussion focuses primarily on political journalism. The news media fulfill five key functions in a democratic society: to inform, filter, analyze, investigate, and act as the voice of the people.

The media **inform** citizens about politics. Through the media, citizens learn about important government actions and changes in policy. Although it is possible for government to speak around the media directly to the citizens, it is far more common for media outlets to be the conduits of the information. Sometimes the media simply transmit what politicians say, without editing and almost without commentary. When television stations broadcast a presidential speech or a newspaper prints the full transcript, there is very little room for bias in the presentation.

However, there is too much political information to be covered in full. The media must **filter** the crucial news from the merely important, and both types of news from the marginal and insignificant. To take but one example, consider a session of Congress. Thousands of bills are proposed, hundreds become law. Thousands of committee and subcommittee meetings are held, and thousands of speeches and press conferences are given. The media act as gatekeepers, determining which of these millions of pieces of information belong on the front page of your newspaper or as the lead story of a newscast, which merit smaller notice, and which deserve no coverage at all.

The media also **analyze** the political world on behalf of citizens. The media do not rely solely on the interpretations of facts that politicians and other political actors provide. Newspaper editorials and columns provide commentary on matters of public concern. On television it is more common for opinions to appear on political talk shows such as the *McLaughlin Group* or the *O'Reilly Factor.*

The media also **investigate** matters of public concern and serve as watchdogs on government behavior. When public officials have hidden information about policies and practices from the public, it is the media's job to report the facts to the citizens. The media cannot simply accept what politicians say about an issue. Sometimes they have to dig into a story and find out what is not being said. Many historians feel that the media did a poor job of reporting the early days of the Vietnam War: reporters were too accepting of the statements of government spokespersons about the likelihood of victory and the costs of defeat. By the middle years of America's longest war, the media were scrutinizing the speeches of the president and other officials with greater care and trying to check the facts they were given against what they saw in Vietnam directly. Similarly, it was two journalists at the *Washington Post,* Bob Woodward and Carl Bernstein, who discovered that the Nixon administration had been bugging political opponents and using secret slush funds of money to engage in illegal acts.

The media's final function is to serve as the **voice of the people.** The media inform our leaders about what we are thinking. In the past, members of Congress paid careful attention to the number of letters a newspaper printed for or against a certain issue. Although entirely unscientific, before the onset of polling this was one good way for a politician to find out how many voters felt a certain way. Today, of course, the media rely on polling to a great extent. When

CNN reports the result of its latest survey on Social Security reform, that result can change the outcome of the policy debate on Capitol Hill. Although polls are the dominant way journalists gauge public opinion today, letters to the editor, online chats hosted by media outlets, and call-in shows on television and radio still provide an outlet for the people to be heard as individuals. This function also provides a way for citizens to talk to each other and learn what people beyond their circle of friends and family think. We look to media to tell us about the political views of our fellow citizens.

WHAT IS BIAS?

If the media have five key functions—to inform, filter, analyze, investigate, and speak for the people—then accusing the media of bias suggests that they are not conducting one or all of those functions in an objective fashion. At its core, the media's job is to take political reality in all its messy complexity and vast substance and transmit the most important elements in a way that will be comprehensible and useful to the citizenry. No matter how much the media strive for objectivity, of course, the picture will be incomplete; reality cannot be accurately summarized by even the most conscientious journalist. Something is inevitably lost "in translation." But most of the complaints about bias in the media allege that the media intentionally twist reality to fit some political agenda.

Examples of bias can be found in all five functions. If a certain media outlet does not inform the public of a particular political event, it may be doing so out of bias. Are presidential press conferences and national speeches always newsworthy, and should they always be broadcast without immediate commentary? If an outlet makes different choices depending on its views about a particular president, the possibility of bias appears.

Deciding when and what to filter always opens the media to accusations of bias. The *CBS Evening News* gave much less attention to the scandal involving former Democratic Congressman Gary Condit in 2001 than did other national networks. Several conservatives suggested this was because Condit was a Democrat and Dan Rather and CBS did not want to hurt the more liberal party. Biased filtering can also occur when journalists are deciding which political figures to quote or to invite to appear on their programs.

Analysis is another source of bias. Even though columnists and television pundits do not usually hide their biases, and indeed are often hired for their provocative and strong opinions, the editors and producers who decide which voices get heard can be biased. Is the editorial page roughly balanced between conservative and liberal voices? Does a particular talk show book an equal number of liberals and conservatives, and does it pick pundits of equal stature, charisma, and eloquence for each side? One subtle method of biasing the news is to pick fringe representatives to speak for the side you dislike. A liberal producer for a political television show could bias the program by picking a radical or extremist figure to represent conservatism. This gives the appearance of balance and objectivity, but the viewers will be much more likely to side with the more moderate voice.

Investigations can be conducted in a biased fashion as well. If a media outlet aggressively searches for any whiff of scandal with an administration it dislikes, and then relaxes its standards for one it favors, the average viewer will have no idea that biased reporting is occurring. This may be the toughest type of bias to detect. Both the Reagan and Clinton administrations experienced a high number of official investigations of Cabinet members and other top government officials. The two largest scandals, Iran-Contra (Reagan) and Whitewater-Lewinsky (Clinton), were followed by thousands of journalists, each trying to track down new and hidden information. Yet the press coverage of Reagan overall was more positive than that given to Clinton by a number of accounts. Reagan was known as the "Teflon" president; nothing stuck to his public image, at least not until the Iran-Contra investigation. Clinton, by contrast, had a contentious relationship with the press almost from his inauguration.[1]

Assume for the moment that it is true that Clinton was treated "worse" by the press than Reagan (although many conservatives would disagree). Was this because the Reagan presidency was more ethical and the media covered the two presidents in a relatively objective fashion? Or did the Clinton scandals attract more media attention due to market forces because they often involved, at least peripherally, illicit sex? Perhaps the media covered the Clinton scandals more intensely because they knew the ratings would be better. Did Reagan simply do a better job of wooing the press, whereas Clinton's press office seemed to go out of its way to alienate them? Perhaps the Reagan administration was less ethical than the Clinton administration overall, but the media and the public didn't notice because of the contrast between the two men in charge. Reagan's personal probity gave his administration a veneer of ethics, whereas Clinton's reputation for womanizing and shading the truth tainted the rest of his administration.

Even if we assume that the Clinton and Reagan scandals were given equal treatment by the media, one can question whether this was "fair." Despite the intense coverage of the Clinton administration's scandals, such as Travelgate, Filegate, and Lewinskygate, no Clinton appointees were convicted of criminal violations for acts committed in office, whereas more than thirty Reagan administration officials were convicted (although some convictions were overturned on technicalities or removed by presidential pardons). In looking at bias in the media over time, it is always tough to compare the treatment of one event or political figure to that of another because the situations are rarely exactly the same.

Finally, the media can be terribly biased in fulfilling their obligation to speak for the people, both to the nation and to the government. Suppose a liberal with very strong views is in charge of polling for a major media outlet. When a Republican is in the White House, perhaps the monthly poll features items on homelessness, unemployment, and aid to the elderly. When Americans tell the pollsters that these are important issues that are being neglected, this becomes headline news. By not asking similar questions when a Democrat is in office, it might appear that these problems have been solved or lessened, but in fact what has changed is the poll. Bias in polling is seldom this obvious. Often it has to do with the question wording and with journalists' interpretations of the poll.

Studies show that many Americans don't read much more than the headlines on newspapers. Imagine a poll showing that President Bush's support has dropped from 62 percent to 53 percent in a one-month period. A conservative might think a fair headline would be, "President Bush's Support Still at High Levels; Majority Supports White House in Difficult Economic Times." A liberal might want the same poll reported as, "Bush Approval Drops Sharply; Lowest Since 9/11." Both headlines can be defended as true, and both fulfill the function of being a "voice of the people." Yet the impression given to the citizens about the poll is starkly different.

The selection of which letters to the editor are published, or which callers to a talk show get on the air, can also be a source of bias. Some outlets strive for balance in such forums, but is balance unbiased? If *Time* magazine receives four hundred letters complaining that the magazine's coverage of the 2004 presidential election was too liberal, and five letters complaining that it was too conservative, is it balanced to publish one of each? Defining and measuring bias and fairness are quite challenging.

ARE THE MEDIA REALLY LIBERAL?

Most Americans have heard arguments that the media are too liberal. For at least forty years, Republicans, particularly conservative Republicans, have argued that the media have a liberal bias. Conservatives have created organizations such as Accuracy in Media (AIM) to act as conservative watchdogs on the media. AIM argues that 80 to 90 percent of the mainstream media vote for Democrats:

> They (the media) admit they're anti-business, pro-big government, anti-family and anti-religion. A couple of years ago, CBS commentator Bernard Goldberg caused quite a stir by saying in a Wall Street Journal op-ed piece that he couldn't believe people were actually still arguing about whether or not the media were liberal, because it was so obviously true . . . the journalism profession has become a powerful manipulator of public opinion.[2]

In the view of AIM and many other conservatives, the media are not only powerful but heavily tilted toward the left. Studies do show that many national reporters voted Democratic in particular years, but few scholars feel the percentage is as high as AIM claims. Some polls suggest that substantial numbers of Americans are convinced that there is a liberal bias in the media. A bestseller by conservative pundit Ann Coulter, entitled *Slander,* outlined a number of different ways in which Coulter claims the mainstream media expresses its hatred for conservatives. Coulter believes liberals in the media unfairly use vicious and personal attacks against conservatives instead of rational arguments against conservative positions. However, given that Coulter called newscaster Katie Couric an "affable Eva Braun" (Hitler's wife), and that she expressed regret that terrorists did not blow up the "liberal" *New York Times,* it appears that at least some conservative voices in the media are able to defend themselves with equal if not greater ferocity.

Indeed, many liberals claim that the media now in fact have a conservative bias. Even if it is sometimes true that surveys of national reporters show them trending toward liberalism, other surveys suggest that most publishers and owners of media companies are quite conservative. Liberals ask which job has more influence, owning the company or writing the stories that can then be changed by editors and publishers? Publishers also can exert tremendous control over the most obviously opinionated section of a newspaper, the editorial page. In 2004 one of the largest media moguls in the world, Rupert Murdoch, was quoted as fulsomely endorsing President Bush and his Republican policies. Imagine the outcry if a national anchor had said something similar about a Democratic president. Of course, owners of media outlets are not uniformly conservative. The founder and former owner of the Cable News Network (CNN) is Ted Turner, who espouses many liberal policy positions.

Still, some liberals believe the media are heavily biased against them. The campaigns by AIM and other groups have cowed the media according to some observers. As *Time* magazine columnist Jack White observed in an interview:

> I'm constantly amazed when people complain about the so-called liberal bias in the press. . . . I keep wondering "When are you gonna declare victory fellas?". . . Sooner or later I think we're all going to have to acknowledge that the myth of liberal bias in the press is just that, it's a myth. May have been true at one time, but it's been beaten out of 'em.[3]

When the Democratic Party suffered substantial losses in the 2002 midterm elections, its most prominent member, former President Bill Clinton, blamed part of the setback on "an increasingly right wing and bellicose conservative press." His former vice president, Al Gore, agreed, complaining that prominent elements within the media have become extremely conservative "day after day injecting daily Republican talking points into the definition of what's objective."

Many liberals point at the Fox News Network (FNN) as an example of conservative bias in the media, but Fox defends itself as providing balance rather than bias and accuses the rest of the media, particularly CNN and the three broadcast network news divisions, of having a liberal bias. Fox's slogan is "Fair and Balanced," and it aggressively asserts its objectivity. It seems obvious, however, that Fox leans conservative, to say the least. The leader of the news division is Roger Ailes, a prominent conservative Republican operative, who crafted cunning media strategies for Republican presidents Nixon and Bush, among others. Many of the most prominent on-air personalities are well-known conservatives, such as Sean Hannity and Bill O'Reilly. And in 2005 Fox's London bureau chief told the *Wall Street Journal:*

> Even we at Fox News manage to get some lefties on the air occa-
> sionally, and often let them finish their sentences before we club
> them to death and feed the scraps to Karl Rove and Bill O'Reilly. . . .
> News is, after all, a private channel and our presenters are
> open about where they stand on particular stories. That's our
> people watch us because they know what they are getting.[4]

Whatever the truth about bias in the mainstream media, the topic is occupying the political elite's attention as never before. In addition to the conservative groups and authors, liberals have banded together, forming groups such as Fairness and Accuracy In Reporting (FAIR) and Media Matters to counter some of the conservative media watchdog groups. A defender of the mainstream media might observe that if both liberals and conservatives feel the media are biased, perhaps the media are doing their job.

SCHOLARLY MODELS OF MEDIA INFLUENCE

The debate about partisan or ideological bias in the media will certainly go on, but within scholarly circles a different set of issues are debated. Media scholars want to know whether the media can influence us at all, and if so, when and how. A number of thinkers have examined these questions. What follows are brief summaries of the major academic theories of media influence.

Classical Model of Media Influence: The Free Marketplace of Ideas

In the **classical model,** citizens absorb the variety of messages about politics that the media put out. Each citizen evaluates the veracity of the claims and opinions that the media make and independently arrives at his or her own views. The media may attempt to sway opinion, and are not assumed to be unbiased in their presentation of the facts, but in the classical model an informed individual will have the ability and the motivation to sift through the biases.

Although there is no single spokesperson for this view, several strands of thought can be linked to form the classical model. British political philosopher John Stuart Mill (1806–1873) argued that the "free marketplace of ideas" would result inevitably in true claims defeating false ones. So long as all ideas and viewpoints were permitted to be distributed, citizens would eventually figure out which ones were accurate. A similar faith in citizens to arrive at truth is contained in Thomas Jefferson's famous comment that if forced to choose between a government without newspapers and newspapers without government, he would take newspapers without government. The "pen" of the press was not only mightier than the "sword" of government, it was to be preferred.

Today the idea that individuals will eventually find their way to truth through discussion may seem naïve, but it was a powerful and new idea at the time. Prior to the Enlightenment, individual citizens were typically not perceived as capable of arriving at independent judgments of political truth. However, the classical model was never universally accepted. Many remained skeptical that the public as a whole could remain uninfluenced by widespread bias. Walter Lippmann, a famous journalist and scholar of public opinion in the early and mid-twentieth century, felt that citizens were largely dependent on the **pseudorealities** created by the media; these impressions of the real world often varied greatly from the truth, and citizens could not be expected to perceive this. When the first large scientific surveys of public opinion were conducted beginning in the 1930s and 1940s, scholars were shocked at the low levels of information that most citizens had about politics. If the public knew very little about politics, could they be making the kind of careful judgments that the free marketplace of ideas would require? New models had to be devised to explain how the media might be affecting citizens who had less interest in politics and less information about the political world.

Propaganda Model: Media Messages as Hypodermic Needles of Opinion

Perhaps the greatest challenge to the free marketplace of ideas model was the rise of Nazism in Germany in the 1920s and 1930s. At that time, the German people were among the most educated and cultured in Europe. Gradually, the Nazis became more and more popular, creating their own newspapers and radio programs. Pioneering director Leni Riefenstahl's movie *Triumph of the Will* conveyed heroic and mythic images of Hitler to Germans everywhere. The German public was sold a series of lies and half-truths about domestic and international politics. Hatred of the Jews and pseudoscientific ideas of racial purity became widely accepted. Although much of the German public were already anti-Semitic, they clearly became more so. The brilliant and devious propaganda machine of the Nazis was key to their triumph over other political parties. Hitler's top media adviser, Josef Goebbels, has become synonymous with propaganda, and the coordinated messages that he devised preserved the obedience of the German people even as the war became desperate and hopeless.

In part in response to the success of the Nazis, a newer model of media influence was created. In the **propaganda model,** the media could wield vast influence in shaping the opinion of citizens. This was particularly true if the media were unified in their biases, as they were under the Nazis. This was also called the "hypodermic" model of media influences: once the message from the media gets under a citizen's skin, it changes his or her views about politics almost irrevocably—like a powerful drug.[5]

If one accepts the propaganda model, then controlling the media becomes paramount. Under this model, the leaders of the media have the ability to influence the outcome of political debates and even to decide on war or peace. The citizens are seen as highly vulnerable to messages encoded in the media. The propaganda model is not limited to fascist states such as Nazi Germany; the word first came into wide usage to describe how America and its allies in World War I maintained the morale of the populace as more and more young men perished in the war. Under the hypodermic model, the citizens are captives of the media's powerful messages, unable to exercise much independent judgment.

This same picture of the media as all-powerful was brutally depicted in George Orwell's dark vision of the future, *1984.* To those, like Orwell and Walter Benjamin, who fought against fascist dictators who used newspapers and films to mislead entire nations, the media would always be a fundamental concern. They would always believe that the media were central to politics. Those who came after them came to a different conclusion.

Minimal Effects Model: The Media Barely Matters

The first scientific surveys of public opinion in the United States, conducted in the 1930s and 1940s, found that Americans had very little information about politics. However, they also found that Americans seemed somewhat immune to the influence of media messages about political campaigns and issues. Public opinion on politics seemed much more influenced by religion, party, occupation, class, or union membership than by which newspaper a citizen read or what the newspaper said. As scholar Paul Lazarsfeld observed in the mid-twentieth century, "the mind erects high tariff barriers to alien notions." Once a citizen, however poorly informed, made up his or her mind about a political matter, it was very difficult for the media to change that opinion. A new school of thought about the media emerged that has come to be labeled the **minimal effects model:** This model suggests that the media only affect political opinion at the margins, even when they make the attempt to influence citizens.

Why might the media be so weak in influencing opinions? Both psychologists and political scientists have studied this question. One explanation is the concept of **selective exposure.** If a media outlet has a strongly conservative message, is it likely that liberal citizens will expose themselves to it on a regular basis? Conservative radio talk-show host Rush Limbaugh does have a few liberal listeners who seem to enjoy his provocative and entertaining style of bombast and satire, but it is safe to say that the vast majority of his audience is made up of conservatives. Indeed, they even label themselves "Dittoheads" to humorously signal their total agreement with everything Rush says. It is rare to find an American home that subscribes to both the *Nation* (a liberal and even occasionally radical journal) and the *National Review* (a leading magazine of conservatism). People who are interested in politics tend to follow sources that already agree with their basic worldview, thus limiting the media's ability to change minds. At best, the media reinforce existing views, an important function, but this is far weaker than the hypodermic effects of altering opinions.

Another reason the media may have minimal effects is **selective perception.** Suppose a liberal feminist who normally would avoid conservative publications nonetheless receives a media message about former President Clinton committing sexual harassment as part of a thirty-minute evening news broadcast. Suppose further that this liberal feminist believes Clinton has been the greatest defender of women's right to control their reproductive health, and she is consequently a big supporter of both women's rights and President Clinton. She may change her definition of sexual harassment so that it no longer includes Clinton's specific conduct, or she may simply ignore the report and not process it. Studies consistently show that viewers pay more attention to information that agrees with their existing opinions. They even may willfully misperceive or ignore confounding information.

This is because of the influence of what psychologists label **cognitive dissonance.** When two competing and mutually exclusive ideas have been absorbed, this creates dissonance (so long as the thinker is smart enough to realize that the ideas are in conflict). Dissonance is inherently unpleasant; the mind rejects it if it can possibly do so. Cognitive dissonance is present in all areas of human interaction, not just politics. It explains our pain when someone we love does something that hurts us or that we reject on moral grounds. This dissonance can be resolved by altering one of the views that produced the dissonance, but it is often resolved by the mind misperceiving or ignoring the event that produced the dissonance.

A related phenomenon is **selective retention.** Each week a reasonably attentive citizen receives a barrage of data about politics from the media. If, despite selective exposure and selective perception, the citizen receives information that challenges one of his core beliefs, it is likely that that fact will be forgotten far sooner than data that agrees with his core beliefs. This is the principle of selective retention; our minds forget facts that produce cognitive dissonance because in so doing we resolve the "pain" that dissonance produces. Selective retention is not a new idea; the German political philosopher Nietzsche put it this way in the nineteenth century:

> "I have done that," says my memory. "I cannot have done that"—says my pride, and remains adamant. At last—memory yields.[6]

Another limiting factor on the media's ability to influence our opinions is the competitive media market. At least in the last hundred years, media outlets have been judged by consumers on their ability to be objective and unbiased. If a media outlet is perceived to be so biased that it twists the facts to suit its views, many consumers will simply choose not to watch or read. Journalists are trained to present "both" sides of political issues, and that limits the ability of any one media outlet to send a distinctive and unified message on politics. The most popular newspapers (the *New York Times,* the *Wall Street Journal, USA Today*) and the most popular news programs (the nightly news broadcasts on NBC, CBS, and ABC) all strive to be perceived as objective, at least in their news coverage. Even Fox News, a network owned and run by committed conservatives, with many prominent conservative figures, denies in its promotional

WHO STUDIES THE MEDIA?

The Academic Perspective

This book approaches the media from a political science perspective, but many of the most important scholars who examine the media are not political scientists. Neither Walter Benjamin nor Neil Postman was a political scientist, nor are some of the major theorists discussed in this chapter. The political media are studied in many academic disciplines, including communication studies, political science, law, sociology, linguistics, cultural studies, journalism, public relations, advertising, public policy, semiotics, philosophy, psychology, and even economics. The topic of the media remains resiliently interdisciplinary, with tendrils extending throughout the social sciences and humanities, and even into neuroscience.

You can find media topics in a host of journals. Three of the most important journals that publish academic research exclusively on media and communication are the following:

Journal of Communication
    http://joc.oxfordjournals.org
Political Communication
    www.tandf.co.uk/journals/tf/10584609.html
Media, Culture and Society
    www.sagepub.com/journal.aspx?pid=208

If you find the media particularly interesting and are considering a graduate education in the topic, the good news is that so many disciplines are examining the media that you will have many choices for your master's or doctoral degree.

materials that it is anything but "fair and balanced." Although both liberals and conservatives often accuse various reporters of bias, top journalists at least attempt to be objective in their coverage of politics. In so doing, they are trying to give consumers what they say they want: objective news on important political issues.

Thus, for many years in political science, it was widely believed that the media did not greatly affect public opinion. The minimal effects model was even called the "law of minimal effects."

The Uses and Gratification Model

Within the field of communication studies, the propaganda model was replaced not by the minimal effects model but by the **uses and gratification (U&G) model** of media usage, originated by sociologist Elihu Katz in 1959. U&G theorists argued that prior models had seen the individual as too passive in his or her relationship to media. Instead of asking how the media influence consumers, U&G asks what drives consumers of media to watch or read. Instead of asking what function the media fill in the American political system, the U&G model asks what function the media fill for each individual. These researchers looked at media consumption as any other human activity and found that certain types of media consumption were favored because they fulfilled certain basic human needs. The human need to have topics to discuss with friends and family is fulfilled by cable news outlets. Political news also provides diversion from the routine problems of everyday life and "value reinforcement." You feel better about your existing beliefs because a certain column or news story confirms their correctness. Finally, political news may also provide "surveillance," or information that is necessary to a particular individual.[7] Sometimes the media tell us things that we need to know. Many investors carefully watch financial news to monitor their stock portfolios. Some commuters religiously follow traffic and weather reports to help them select their daily routes.

Although few political scientists have utilized the U&G framework to guide their studies, it is an important way of thinking about the media because it frames the entire question of media effects in a different fashion. It asks why anyone watches political media at all or, indeed, chooses any kind of media over another at a given point. By emphasizing what the individual may get out of a particular act of media consumption, it helps us understand such phenomena as the declining audience of political conventions and presidential debates. Prior to the onset of cable television, more Americans watched conventions and debates. The decline in viewership can be seen as evidence of alienation from politics; perhaps viewers are being turned off by the negativity of modern campaigns. This is a content-based explanation with very important political implications. However, from the U&G perspective, in which individuals choose from an array of media and nonmedia pursuits to fill every moment of leisure, it is simply that other shows provide greater pleasure and fill more pressing needs. In the past, the debates were the only option for watching television, but with cable television other shows are always available.

THE SOCIAL CONSERVATIVE VIEW

Many conservative Christians in the United States perceive that the media are not just liberal but have adopted a worldview, secular humanism, that is opposed to their core beliefs. According to social conservatives, secular humanism is an anti-God ideology that advocates the perfectability of humans and emphasizes moral relativism. Moreover, social conservatives believe that the mainstream media are suffused, often unconsciously, with the doctrine of secular humanism. Even when mainstream journalists attempt to be objective, they fail because they don't understand how their ideology shapes their news decisions.

Consider the case of Matthew Shepard, a young gay man who was brutally murdered by allegedly homophobic killers in Wyoming in 1998. His death became a rallying point for gay rights activists across the country. Major media outlets covered his murder quite extensively, as well as covering the ensuing marches and television ads by his supporters. Many Christian conservatives questioned why the media made Shepard's death such huge news. Amidst the thousands of Americans who were murdered that year, why focus on this one death? Although not supporting Shepard's killing in any way, they asked whether Shepard became news because most national journalists believe that gay rights is a just cause and that opposition to it is religiously motivated prejudice.

Some social conservatives made an even more direct attack on the mainstream media's alleged objectivity by raising the case of Jesse Dirkhising, a thirteen-year-old boy who was kidnapped, tortured, repeatedly raped, and killed by two homosexuals in 1999. His death, which occurred about the same time as Shepard's, merited almost no national coverage. Social conservatives asked why, when two heterosexuals killed a homosexual, it was national news from Maine to California, but when two homosexuals killed a heterosexual, it was barely a footnote.

Mainstream media outlets such as the *Washington Post* defended their journalistic judgment. Shepard's death ignited a national debate about hate crimes legislation, and there were marches and candlelight vigils in his honor. No such events occurred in Dirkhising's case. But social conservatives might respond with a simple question: Without the coverage of Shepard's killing in the first place, would the marches have occurred? Another defense offered by mainstream journalists was that the Shepard case directly addressed a current political debate, gay rights. No such debate surrounds the rape of children; it is universally viewed as evil by all political factions. However, many social conservatives believe that homosexuals tend to prey on children, although most research fails to support this, and for them this is a current political debate ignored by the mainstream media.

Even a gay conservative pundit, writer Andrew Sullivan, criticized the media for its disparate treatment of the two cases:

> In the month after Shepard's murder, Nexis recorded 3,007 stories about his death. In the month after Dirkhising's murder, Nexis recorded 46 stories about his. In all of last year, only one article about Dirkhising appeared in a major mainstream newspaper. The Boston Globe, the New York Times and the Los Angeles Times ignored the incident completely. In the same period, the New York Times published 45 stories about Shepard, and The Washington Post published 28. The discrepancy isn't just real. It's staggering.[8]

Sullivan even raised an additional issue: prevalence. According to Sullivan, very few gay Americans are killed due to homophobia in any given year; the rape and murder of children, by straight and gay men, is much more common. Why the disparity? According to Sullivan, "Some deaths—if they affect a politically protected class—are worth more than others. Other deaths, those that do not fit a politically correct profile, are left to oblivion." Sullivan, a gay man, can hardly be labeled a social conservative, but his arguments were echoed by many conservative Christian leaders who believed that the Shepard/Dirkhising comparison proved the media was biased. Social conservatives in this case are accusing the mainstream media of filtering the news in a biased way so that a liberal cause, gay rights, is protected and advanced.

Many social conservatives are also upset about government subsidies given to what they perceive to be secular humanist media outlets, such as the Corporation for Public Broadcasting (CPB) and National Public Radio (NPR). The CPB, which helps support almost 350 public television stations and more than 700 public radio stations, receives nearly a third of its budget from federal, state, and local taxes. Until recently the government did not exert any direct editorial control over the content of the broadcasts, but some ask whether a dependence on government funds will naturally lead to the station's favoring the Democratic Party, which tends to advocate maintaining or increasing government funding of public broadcasting. During the Bush administration, an ally of social conservatives was appointed to head the CPB to try to provide "balance."

For many social conservatives a core problem with public television remains: their tax dollars go to promulgate views they abhor. Many public television and radio programs address homosexuality and abortion with frankness and even at times full-throated support. The emphatically pro-gay show *In the Life* has been broadcast on public television since 1992 and is now seen on 130 stations nationwide. Although the show itself is made without tax dollars, the stations that air it are government supported. There is no equivalent voice for socially conservative viewpoints about sexuality on public television.

Social conservatives also object broadly to the cultural elements of the mainstream media. Right-wing film critic Michael Medved, in his book *Hollywood vs. America*, argues that America's television and movie studios put forth an almost relentless stream of secular humanist programs. According to Medved, these shows tend to be pro–gay rights, pro-abortion, pro-adultery, and politically liberal, anti-Christian, anticapitalist, antifamily, and antimilitary.

In response to what they perceive to be widespread bias in the mainstream news and cultural media, social conservatives have advocated creation of an independent media for conservative Christians. Hundreds of Christian radio stations, television stations, magazines, and Web sites seek to help their followers combat or at least avoid the secular humanism in the mainstream media.

THE RADICAL VIEW: A UNIFIED CAPITALIST DOMINATION OF MEDIA

In many ways the polar opposite to the social conservative view of the media's influence is the neo-Marxist, or radical, school of looking at the media. While having deep roots in elite theory, such as the work of sociologist C. Wright Mills, the neo-Marxist view is best represented today by linguist Noam Chomsky. In his book *Manufacturing Consent* (cowritten with Edward Herman), Chomsky paints a portrait of a news media deeply committed to reinforcing the existing power structure. The media gave much more coverage to the death of a Polish priest killed by his communist government than to the rape, maiming, and murder of four American nuns by right-wing death squads linked to the government of El Salvador. One might have expected that the deaths of four U.S. citizens would have received at least equal coverage to the death of a foreign priest, but Chomsky believes that because the nuns were working to help the poor and were killed by forces allied to a friendly government, their deaths were largely ignored. Chomsky documents how even tens of thousands of deaths committed by allies of the United States in the 1970s and 1980s were widely ignored because they didn't fit the unified media elite's ideal of legitimate victims. More recently Chomsky has argued that the media accept the definition of terrorism put forth by the American government without questioning actions taken by our government and its allies that would fit anyone's definition of terrorism. When America plants naval mines that threaten the civilians of a country we are not at war with (Nicaragua), the media do not call this terrorism. However, if al Qaeda put mines in New York Harbor, the media would not hesitate to label this terrorism. When the U.S. government protects Cubans who set off bombs that killed innocent Italian tourists and shot down civilian airplanes, the media do not call that harboring terrorists. The media tend to accept the government's definition of who is and is not a terrorist rather than establishing some objective standard unaffected by the biases and preferences of our leaders.

Many radicals see the surface differences of the media outlets as a sham. Although there are several different national networks and many different newspapers, all of them are owned by corporations wanting to avoid raising fundamental questions about the nature of the U.S. economy. Even public television stations are increasingly reliant on corporate donations for survival. The media also constrict political debate as they try to be fair and balanced. Recall that journalists try to get "both sides" of a political debate to appear fair to the viewers. From a radical perspective, hearing from both Republicans and Democrats on the question of tax cuts is inherently unfair because it leaves out all but a narrow range of ideologies. By talking only to those who already are in power, such as top officials in the two parties, the media leave out those who would ask broader questions about the nature of the U.S. economy and society. From a radical perspective, both parties are biased in favor of corporate America, so hearing from both sides is merely an illusion of diversity.

"Balancing" between Republicans and Democrats, or liberals and conservatives, is hardly "fair" from a radical perspective.

Radicals pay particular attention to incidents in which the media seem to be directly obeying the corporations that own the major outlets. In 1995, when ABC squelched coverage of a sex scandal at Walt Disney World, many pointed out that Disney owned ABC and had a vested interest in spiking the story.[9] Fewer and fewer media outlets are independent of mammoth international conglomerates, and the number of companies in the media business has been declining rapidly over the last four decades as companies merge.

Chomsky and others point out how extraordinarily difficult it is for authentic working-class voices to be heard in the modern media in America. There are no longer any working-class or blue-collar newspapers, and network television, which is run through advertising, does not seek out working-class viewers. Working-class Americans are the least desirable viewers to most advertisers because they don't have the purchasing power of the middle class.

Another radical critic of the media, former reporter William Greider, in his book *Who Will Tell the People,* argued that journalism as a profession abandoned the working class when it began to employ wealthier and better educated journalists instead of rough-edged non-elites in gritty reporting jobs:

> In the end, the educated city room betrayed its promise. When the quick but unschooled working-class reporters were displaced and the well-educated took over the work, that social dislocation might have been justifiable if the news media were going to serve democracy more effectively, if the educated reporters were using their professional skills to enhance citizens' ability to cope with power in a more complicated world. The educated reporters instead secured a comfortable place for themselves among the other governing elites. The transformation looks more like a nasty episode of social usurpation, a power shift freighted with class privilege.[10]

Instead of being a relatively low-paid profession with few entrance requirements (most reporters throughout American history lacked even a college degree let alone a graduate degree in journalism), national journalism has become a profession of the well-paid elite at its top levels. Reporters on television are media superstars with fan clubs and highly paid speaking tours.

Ironically, much of Greider's critique of modern reporters mirrors that of some social conservatives. Radicals on both the right and the left perceive that modern reporters have different values than they once did, and that these conscious and subconscious perspectives shape the news and separate the news profession from "the people." Just as social conservatives believe that the media paid more attention to Matthew Shepard's death than to Jesse Dirkhising's because of reporters' liberal bias, radicals wonder why so much more attention is paid to deaths in white suburbs than in black inner cities. Is it fair that a murder in a "safer" area becomes bigger news, either because most reporters are white or because most viewers are or simply because it is more rare? Doesn't this convey the message that black lives are less valuable?

Much as social conservatives have done, some radicals have attempted to set up their own independent media. However, left-wing radicals lack the deep pockets of many social conservatives, so the number of hard-left media outlets with any national presence is extremely small.

THE CURRENT PARADIGM

All of these various schools have their proponents within the field of American political science, but scholars are coalescing around a new paradigm to replace the minimal effects model of media politics. There is an emerging sensibility that media are far more influential at shaping public opinion and political behavior than the minimal effects proponents believed. Scholars Kathleen Hall Jamieson, Lance Bennett, Robert Entman, Doris Graber, Shanto Iyengar, and others have shown through surveys and experiments that the media play an important role in American politics. Modern scholars may differ over how the media affect public opinion, but these new approaches are linked by the consensus that the media matter. Chapter 3 describes some of the ways the media directly shape our political attitudes, knowledge, and actions.

KEY TERMS

classical model

cognitive dissonance

five key functions of the
   media (inform, filter,
   analyze, investigate,
   voice of the people)

minimal effects model

propaganda (hypodermic) model

pseudorealities

radical perspective

selective exposure

selective perception

selective retention   uses and gratification
social conservative perspective   (U&G) model

DISCUSSION QUESTIONS

1. Do you believe the media are consistently biased against liberals or conservatives? What evidence shows this?
2. Do you think you are affected by any biases in the media? How?
3. If you were the news director of a large metropolitan television station and had to decide how much coverage to give the murder of a poor young black man in the inner city in a drive-by shooting, versus the murder of a wealthy suburban white kid in a school shooting like Columbine, how would you make the decision? Assume that in your area drive-by shootings are relatively frequent and school shootings rare.
4. If there is some truth to the propaganda model, but the media are only that powerful when almost all outlets are sending similar messages, should we be concerned about the increasing dominance of American news by fewer and fewer companies?
5. Do you think Hollywood or the news media are hostile to conservative Christian values?

ADDITIONAL RESOURCES

Hollywood vs. America: Popular Culture and the War against Traditional Values, by Michael Medved, argues that the entertainment industry sends out liberal messages in movies and television shows.

Manufacturing Consent: The Political Economy of the Mass Media, by Edward S. Herman and Noam Chomsky, argues that the mainstream media are inherently and overwhelmingly conservative. A film of the same name as the book is widely available.

Liberty and the News, by Walter Lippmann. This short book from 1920 can serve as an introduction to Lippmann's thought. He calls for a more professional media with rigorous standards. Lippmann talks about the media in *The Phantom Public* as well as in his most famous book, *Public Opinion.*

1984, by George Orwell, is a futuristic look at a world in which the government runs every media outlet and teaches citizens to support every war, blindly.

Triumph of Will, a film by Leni Riefenstahl, was a seminal moment in the development of political video and propaganda. Through the use of powerful images of mass obedience and physical activity, Riefenstahl portrayed Hitler as the savior of Germany.

ONLINE RESOURCES

For a conservative perspective showing that the media are biased in favor of liberals, see Accuracy in the Media (AIM) at www.aim.org or The Media Research Center at www.mediaresearch.org. The more social conservative perspective on the media can be found at the Parents TV Council, at www.parentstv.org.

For a liberal perspective showing that the media are biased in favor of conservatives, see Fairness and Accuracy in Reporting (FAIR) www.fair.org or Media Matters at www.mediamatters. org.

NOTES

1. W. Lance Bennett, *News: The Politics of Illusion* (New York: Longman, 2003), 28.
2. Accuracy in Media Web site, www.aim.org
3. Interview with Jack White, C-SPAN's Washington Journal, November 18, 2002.
4. Timothy Noah, "Fox News Admits Bias!" *Slate.* May 31, 2005.
5. Daniel L. Paletz, *The Media in American Politics* (New York: Longman, 2002).
6. Friedrich Nietzche, *Beyond Good and Evil: Prelude to a Philosophy of the Future,* trans. R. J. Hollingdale (New York: Penguin 1987), Aphorism 68, p. 72. (Orig. pub. 1886.)
7. D. McQuail, J. Blumer, and R. Brown, "The Television Audience: 'A Revised Perspective.'" In *Sociology of Mass Communication,* D. McQuail, ed. (New York: Penguin, 1972).
8. Andrew Sullivan, "Us and Them." *The New Republic.* April 2, 2001.
9. Nikki Finke, "The Untold Story: How Corporate Takeovers Make the Media Less Curious." *LA Weekly,* November 22, 2002.
10. William Grieder, *Who Will Tell The People?* (New York: Simon & Schuster, 1993).

CHAPTER 3

Media Matters: Measuring the Effects

There are many theories about how the media influence American politics, but most mainstream researchers today have rejected the extremes of the propaganda model as well as the law of minimal effects. The media are seen as neither weak nor all-powerful but somewhere in between. This "media matters" school is methodologically and politically diverse but shares some core assumptions and approaches: Most media consumers are inattentive, most citizens are low in political knowledge, and media effects are subtle and difficult to measure. Social scientists have increasingly studied the effects media consumption has on Americans. Indeed, the field of media studies as a separate discipline has emerged fairly recently. Perhaps this growth in the study of the media is only natural. When the minimal effects model was dominant, the study of the media was hardly a promising field. Why study something that has only a marginal impact? Today, however, some of the most exciting work in a number of disciplines relates directly or indirectly to media effects.

ANALYZING THE EFFECTS OF MEDIA ON CONSUMERS

Social scientists examine the effects of media on consumers in three main ways: content analysis, experiments, and survey research. The best media studies often combine two or three of these methods.

Content Analysis

Content analysis is the systematic study of the messages and meanings encoded in the media. Although it began as the study of texts, content analysis today can include all aspects of media, including radio, video, and the Internet. Content analysis is the primary method for establishing whether a media outlet is biased. For example, researchers may examine how a newspaper covers the same political event over a one-week period. If twice as many liberal sources are quoted as conservative ones, could the researchers conclude that the paper has a liberal bias? What if conservatives had little to say about this issue because it was a debate among liberals? What if few conservatives were in power at that time, so the newspaper focused on actual decision makers? To truly establish bias, even in this simple example, content analysis has to be comparative. If several other papers covering the same event in the same week have roughly equal quotes from conservatives and liberals, then the first paper may well have a liberal bias.

Content analysis performed by professional researchers today is usually much more sophisticated. Rather than simply counting sources, a study might use multiple readers (called coders) to assess the stories for deeper evidence of bias. Some content analysis projects ask coders to evaluate the whole story as biased or tilted toward one side or the other based on the feel they get after reading the story. A story on the occupation of Iraq with a final sentence comparing the situation to Vietnam might leave the reader with a very different feel than one that ends with a quote from Secretary of Defense Rumsfeld about how well the occupation is going. The final sentence in an article or broadcast is called the *tag*, and it may be influential because it is the last word on the subject that the reader or listener gets, and appears to be a conclusion. On the other hand, the headline or the first line of the story, called the *lede*, may be the most influential because studies show that a number of readers read only the headline or first paragraph. Some content analysis studies assess the tag, headline, and lede separately.

Researchers who use coders always have to answer this question: Are these coders unbiased and neutral? A story about Al Gore read by a determined liberal may seem very biased against Gore if it is about Gore's involvement in campaign finance improprieties in 1996. However, a conservative coder might see the story as a fair discussion of a relevant part of Gore's past. Although almost all researchers instruct coders to put their personal views aside as they rate stories for bias, this is a very difficult thing to do, even if we assume that the coders wish to comply. Coders can even lose their neutrality by overcompensating in an effort to achieve objectivity. A conservative striving too hard to be objective may code conservative media as biased and liberal media as neutral. Researchers address this difficult problem by using multiple coders. A project might require two readers to separately code each story, and if their assessments of bias differ significantly, a third coder is brought in to resolve the dispute. In addition, when two or more coders evaluate the same material, statistical techniques can measure "intercoder reliability" to ensure that the subjectivity of the assessment of bias is addressed. Multiple coders, however, add greatly to the cost and length of content analysis studies.

Perhaps because of these costs, many media researchers now use computers in their content analysis work. Computers are certainly objective if given the proper instructions, and they eliminate the possibility that the coder will introduce bias. Used creatively, computers can answer questions in seconds that would take human coders thousands of hours to answer. A computer can be programmed to identify every instance in which the word *Hispanic* appears in hundreds of stories about the 2000 election to see which media outlets focused attention on that voting group. However, a poorly written computer program can be worse than biased coders. The old adage about "garbage in, garbage out" applies to computerized content analysis. Computers are faster than humans but currently lack crucial judgment. A computer-based content analysis would count a story headlined "Hispanic vote is a myth" as attention to Hispanic concerns. Also, many print resources are not yet in computerized databases, which limits the scope of computerized content analysis.

Another limitation of computers is that they are not yet able to scan video media with the flexibility and nuance humans employ. A computer will do a poor job of assessing whether the video footage used by one network is biased. Suppose one network tended to show harsh video footage of poverty every time Bush's economic plans were discussed. This network is showing a bias against Republicans, but only human coders who compare the video footage for each story would pick this out. Most content analyses of television news focus on the words the broadcasters use because it is much easier to examine and quantify words from a transcript than images on a screen. More sophisticated analyses also look at the most powerful aspect of television—the images on the screen. Political scientist Robert Entman studied how local television news portrayed black and white crime and found that black criminals are more likely to be displayed in a physically threatening way than are white criminals. Content analysis of video media, as well as of Web sites, is an exciting field of study and can even be conducted in a limited way by ambitious undergraduates. You can try your hand at this by completing the exercise in the box titled Content Analysis.

Experimental Studies of Media Effects

Content analysis focuses on the nature of the message encoded in the media, but it typically does not assess the effects of the message on viewers. It is assumed that a message framed in a certain way or biased in a particular fashion will have an effect on some consumers of the media. However, a central assumption of the minimal effects theory of media influence is that consumers of the media are often unaffected by bias due to cognitive barriers such as selective perception. Perhaps content analysis can discover that some media outlets are heavily biased against conservatives, but it cannot reveal if anyone is watching or whether any viewers are persuaded by this biased content. For this reason, content analysis cannot claim to show any real-world effects.

Experimental studies offer researchers a method to address these issues. In a media experiment, the amount and nature of media can be precisely controlled, and subjects can be carefully divided into test and control groups. (As with any social science study, it is vital that the group be representative of the population you are studying. A sample of undergraduates at a private college is not a good substitute for the nation as a whole.) Suppose a researcher wants to know if extensive coverage of crime makes viewers more likely to vote for law and order candidates. One group of subjects could be shown news footage that included lurid coverage of violent crime while the control group viewed a more typical news broadcast. Afterward, both groups would be asked to respond to a political ad by a candidate who is "tough on crime." If the first group (or "test" group) has a significantly more positive response to the ad than the control group, we can tentatively conclude that the media's coverage of crime does affect voters' opinions.

This method of research differs in important ways from content analysis. It tests for media effects on specific individuals and, by using a control group, isolates the effect of the specific stimulus that is of interest to the researcher. However, there is an obvious limitation to this method as well: artificiality. The researcher has much more control in the laboratory environment, but is it really similar to the environment in which most Americans consume media? Is watching TV or reading a newspaper in a laboratory on a college

CONTENT ANALYSIS

An Exercise

Of all the methods of studying media effects, the one that is most easily replicated by undergraduates is content analysis. If you have a term paper requirement in your course, consider doing some original research using content analysis in a quantitative fashion.

First, you will need a testable hypothesis about some aspect of the media that could be examined using content analysis. Here are some examples of such questions:

> Is the *Washington Post* more liberal than the *Wall Street Journal*?
>
> Are female candidates treated differently from male candidates by the media?
>
> Do television stations cover black crime differently from white crime?

In every content analysis, you must first choose your sample or the materials you will examine in your study. Be realistic about what you can do. If you try to analyze too much material, you will not be able to give enough attention to each assessment. In answering the question about the *Washington Post* versus the *Wall Street Journal,* set reasonable limits. Although you may want to read and code every story in the two papers for a month, this is probably not a realistic goal for an undergraduate paper. So set limits, such as only reading stories in the two papers about one specific political event in a two-week time period. For the broader question about female and male candidates, you will have to pick your outlets based on availability and feasibility. If you choose televised media accounts of crime, you will need access to a VCR or Tivo because you will not be able to code a program in one sitting.

Each content analysis must have a coding protocol. This is true even if you are the only coder. If you are analyzing the question about female candidates, you might want to track how early in an article about a candidate the reporter mentions the family of the candidate. Or how frequently does an article mention the candidate's clothing, hairstyle, and overall appearance? As part of the coding protocol, you'll need to develop a data collection sheet, which will be used to record whatever data you need from each unit of analysis. A unit in a content analysis study could be an article from a newspaper or a news segment from a television program.

If you do have more than one coder, you will have to provide a small amount of training. Each coder should at least attempt to apply similar standards in filling out the data collection sheets. You may also want to adopt a method for accounting for situations when your coders disagree about the evaluation of a unit. You might use two coders for each unit, and if they disagree greatly, bring in a third coder who has not seen their sheets to resolve the dispute. If you wish to be even more sophisticated, you can administer a short survey on political attitudes to prospective coders to make sure you have a diverse group of coders. If all of your coders are liberals or conservatives, that might affect your results. Knowing that one of your coders is a political radical or an extreme social conservative might explain some outliers in your coding!

Finally, before you analyze your coding data, you should have an idea about what results will allow you to conclude that the effect you were examining is actually present. A good researcher will not hesitate to say that no effect was found. Indeed, this can be the foundation of an excellent paper, and most professors will appreciate that you did not twist your data to get the result you predicted. Also look out for partial effects. Suppose that a study of the coverage of black and white crime on local television news reveals that the words used by newscasters are not significantly different in stories about black criminals or white criminals. However, if you found that in 60 percent of the stories about black criminals a photo of the victim was shown on the screen, whereas this was true in only 30 percent of the stories about white criminals, you may have an important finding. Showing the victim of the crime is likely to induce viewers to consider the crime to be far more serious than they otherwise would. Viewers may experience greater anger at the perpetrator and have greater sympathy for the victim. Thus your expectation is partially confirmed, and you have a powerful paper about the visual aspects of media bias.

Be creative in your selection of topics as long as it is okay with your professor. Remember that a broad definition of the "media" can include movies and television shows. Bob Lichter, a media researcher who has studied popular culture extensively, did a groundbreaking study on the role of religion on popular dramas and sitcoms. In a careful study of more than four hundred television characters, he found that only a handful showed any evidence of religious faith at all. (His study was conducted before the runaway success of such religious-themed shows as *Touched by an Angel*.) Many conservatives have used Lichter's study to argue that the "Hollywood elite" are biased against religion. You might want to do a study of the politics of popular culture on a much smaller scale.

You can also be creative about the ways in which bias manifests itself. One of my students did a study of the physical attractiveness of guests on Fox News versus CNN. She hypothesized that a Fox show could have a conservative bias if it invited less attractive liberals as guests and paired them with more physically attractive conservatives. Although the show might give the appearance of being "fair and balanced," it would not be because people are more likely to believe what they hear from attractive spokespersons. To make sure that the imbalance was not simply a result of conservatives being more attractive in general, she also studied CNN. She taped ten hours of each cable news network, identified guests as conservative, liberal, or neutral, and asked ten of her fellow students to rate the guests on physical attractiveness. She found that Fox News did, in fact, book liberals who were significantly less attractive than their conservative guests, but no such imbalance appeared on CNN. (It should be noted that her results, while intriguing and certainly sufficiently sophisticated for an undergraduate paper, did not meet the standards for a professional political science publication.)

If you decide to conduct your own content analysis study, be sure to consult a book on the methodology of content analysis and conduct a substantive review of the literature related to your topic. There are several good books on content analysis, including *Basic Content Analysis*, by Robert Weber, and *The Content Analysis Guidebook*, by Kimberly Neuendorf. You will not be able to fully emulate the methodology of a professional political scientist or media scholar, but in reading what has gone before, you will get many good ideas and avoid potential pitfalls. You may be able to partially "replicate" or redo a study by a professional researcher to see if his or her finding is still true. And, of course, do clear your idea with your professor!

campus comparable to doing the same activities in your home? Isn't it possible that viewers will be more attentive in the laboratory, because none of the distractions of home, such as family, pets, telemarketers, food, and friends, will be present? Or will viewers be less attentive because they are less comfortable? Behavior in laboratory settings can be very different from normal behavior.

Tali Mendleberg, a leading scholar of racial politics, tried to get around this limitation in an innovative study of media effects. She selected a random group of residents in a Michigan county and contacted them to see if they would participate in a university study. Those who agreed were visited by an undergraduate student who brought a videotape containing fake news coverage of fictional candidates for governor. Mendleberg wanted to know if the media's news coverage could activate hidden racial prejudice among whites. In *The Race Card*, she reports that when pictures of blacks were used to represent the typical welfare recipient, it increased racial resentment among whites toward blacks, which has important political implications. When pictures of white welfare recipients were used with the same voice-over, prejudice was not activated.

Yet even an innovative study like Mendleberg's cannot conclusively show that the effects found in an experiment last after it is over. Perhaps the racial resentment she found, or other media effects discovered in laboratory experiments, dissipates rapidly. It is difficult to prove that media effects matter weeks or months after a citizen consumes a particular media outlet. It is immensely challenging to replicate the complexity of media effects in the real world, no matter how sophisticated your laboratory or research design. Even so, a well-done experiment on media effects can be a powerful technique to explore the influence of media.

Survey Research on Media Effects

As we have seen, the greatest limitation of experimental studies is that they may not accurately replicate what happens in the real world. Similarly, content analysis looks at the media and merely assumes that significant effects discovered in the media must have real-world consequences. Researchers who are particularly bothered by these problems often do research on media effects using surveys of citizens. A typical survey on media effects includes an exposure component and an attitudes component. In the exposure component, respondents are asked which types of media they consume, how often, and which outlets. In the attitudes section, respondents answer an array of questions about political figures and issues. Then the researcher looks for some correlation or relationship between the two areas.

Survey research is often used to study the effects of using different types of media. If watchers of TV news are more likely to think crime is a serious social problem than those who get their news from newspapers, we might tentatively conclude that television causes an increased fear of crime. Of course, it is always possible that those who think crime is a more serious problem simply watch more television. To make conclusions about causes and effects rather than about simple relationships, researchers must use more sophisticated research designs and statistical techniques.

One famous study of the effects of consuming different types of media appeared in Robert Putnam's book, *Bowling Alone,* on civic life in the United States. Putnam argued that Americans in the last thirty years have become increasingly disconnected from their communities and from important community groups, such as Parent Teacher Associations (PTA), Kiwanis, and even bowling leagues, that make up civic life. One of the many causes of this change, Putnam argued, was watching television. By analyzing surveys, Putnam found that for every hour spent watching television each week, a person was significantly less likely to join a community group. Yet for every hour spent reading a newspaper, a person became more involved in community groups. It is possible that Putnam was confusing cause and effect. Perhaps those who are already involved in civic groups read the local newspaper because they know the issues and the players and derive less pleasure from television, which is seldom about local matters. But even finding a relationship between types of media and level of community involvement is quite valuable.

Survey research can also make claims about the level of bias in specific media outlets and the effects this bias may have. To study the effect of Fox News on attitudes toward Hillary Clinton, for example, one could use a panel study of television viewers. A panel study is a specific type of survey in which the same respondents are asked questions at least twice. If we found that all types of voters (liberals, moderates, and conservatives) who watched Fox News felt worse about Clinton after watching Fox for six months than did similar voters who regularly watched CNN, we might conclude that watching Fox contributed to having a low opinion of Hillary Clinton. This would not necessarily prove that Fox is biased against Clinton. A conservative might feel that Fox News presents the unvarnished truth about Clinton whereas other media treat her with unwarranted deference because of their liberal bias. Proving that a media outlet presents a biased picture of the world is quite difficult without some objective measure of reality.

Those who study the effect of political ads often rely heavily on survey research. Voters are asked if they saw a specific ad and are compared to voters who did not. Respondents can also be asked directly if they felt the ad affected how they voted. And here we encounter perhaps the greatest limitation of surveys: How can we trust the answers that are given? Many people are reluctant to admit that watching a thirty-second ad affected their vote. As with other advertising, most of us like to think we are immune to the effects of ads—even while believing that advertising affects those around us. Also, people are often reluctant to admit that they never read newspapers or magazines about politics. This is called the "social desirability effect." Respondents in surveys want to give the answers that will make them look better in the eyes of the person asking the questions. Sometimes they even want to look better in their own eyes. When respondents don't want to tell the researcher the truth, the answers they give are questionable.

But the reliability of the answers in surveys is a broader problem than just the case of respondents not wanting to answer honestly. Even if we assume that everyone wishes to answer honestly, we run into the problem of memory. Ask yourself how many hours of television news you watched this year. How many hours this month or this week? Isn't it possible for voters to see a negative news story about a politician, have it affect their judgment of that politician, but then a month later not remember where they learned about the story? If we cannot accurately recall our exposure to the media, then much of the validity of survey research on media effects is faulty.

In addition to questions about the reliability of answers about exposure, surveys have other problems. They can be quite expensive to do at the national level, requiring a carefully selected random sample of between 600 and 1,000 respondents. Less expensive methods, such as online surveys, are nonscientific, and their results should not be trusted without careful investigation. Also, all survey results are very sensitive to biases in question wording.

WHAT MEDIA STUDIES TELL US

Content analysis, surveys, and laboratory experiments are the three main ways that media effects are examined in academia. Of course, there are others, such as focus groups, interviews with elites, analysis of accelerating media conglomeration, and firsthand observation of the media. But these three form the core of most quantitative studies of the media. What types of effects have researchers discovered using these methods?

Assessing Bias: Measuring the Media's Spin

The first and most basic question asked about the media is whether the picture of the political world presented to media consumers is systematically biased in some way. As we explored in Chapter 2, there are many views about the nature of bias in the media. Media analysts have attempted to answer this perennial question using a number of techniques, including those just discussed.

When political scientists and academic media analysts talk about bias in the media, they are looking at specific instances and want to test whether the media attempt to or actually do influence the opinions of the public. This is a question that has not been asked as often as you might think due to the lingering influence of the minimal effects school. Scholars have spent far more time examining how the media has framed issues or set the nation's agenda, and far less time examining the persuasive power of the media in directly changing political opinions.

One study of the power of media shows how difficult it is to show persuasive effects in a rigorous manner. Dalton, Beck, and Huckfeldt wanted to see if reading negative or positive stories and editorials about a particular presidential candidate made a reader more likely to support that candidate.[1] They used a massive data set of editorials and stories from newspapers in more than forty counties randomly selected across the United States. After coding all their data, they analyzed whether readers of newspapers that were identifiably biased affected readers' views about the presidential election. In other words, if you read a newspaper that was opposed to Bill Clinton, did it make you more likely to oppose him yourself? They found, in fact, that readers' attitudes toward the candidates could be changed by reading a newspaper that editorially endorsed one of the candidates. But the effect was small and was dwarfed by the impact of the readers' own partisanship. Moreover, they found that most readers got both positive and negative information about all the candidates, even in newspapers that were strongly supportive of one party or the other.

Interestingly enough, this same study found that many readers felt that their newspaper was biased: in most cases Republicans thought the paper was biased against Republicans, and Democrats thought the paper was biased against Democrats. This perception has been found by other researchers and has been called the "hostile media effect." Vallone, Ross and Leper defined the hostile media effect as the tendency of partisans to perceive news coverage as biased against them, almost without regard for the content. They showed pro-Arab and pro-Israeli undergraduates the same videotape about a 1982 massacre of Palestinian civilians by Israeli allies. Both pro-Arabs and pro-Israeli students felt that the coverage was biased against their position, that it would convince a neutral viewer to take the opposite side, and that the people who made the video were opposed to their worldview.[2] Partisans of either side use different standards of assessment, seeing facts and arguments supportive of their side as more valid, and thus equal treatment between falsehood and truth cannot be fair.

Another key question that has been examined is "exactly who gets persuaded by the media?" A communications model, building on earlier research by Converse and McGuire, has been put forth by political scientist John Zaller. The power of a media message can be assessed by multiplying the likelihood of its reception by the probability of its acceptance. This deceptively simple model is actually quite complex conceptually. The likelihood of a citizen receiving the media's message and understanding it is proportional to the person's general political awareness, according to Zaller. In simpler terms, the most likely recipient of political news is a person who has already received a lot of political information. Zaller calls this the "reception axiom." What about accepting the message? Zaller labels this the "acceptance axiom": The greater a person's political awareness, the less likely the person is to uncritically accept the media message if it differs from his or her existing political views. This could be called Zaller's paradox: Media messages will have their greatest impact on those who are least political aware, but those individuals are the least likely to receive such messages.[3]

Discovering direct persuasive effects of media remains challenging, in part because of the hostile media effect and because of the limitations on the media's influence that inspired the minimal effects school. Yet the evidence that the media matters, and indeed contains important biases, remains strong, as we shall see.

Transmission of Information: The First Function of the Fourth Estate

Journalists have been called the Fourth Estate for centuries, ever since the French Revolution.* The name implies that journalists play a fundamental role in government in any democracy or republic even though they are not formally part of the government. The most obvious political role the media play is to inform the public about issues and controversies and provide relevant facts that will enable the public to be informed citizens. What do the media teach the public about politics?

One prominent study argues that Americans are ill informed by the media, in part because they are so reliant on television news. Using a questionnaire in seven different countries (the United States, Spain, Germany, Canada, Great Britain, France, and Italy), Dimock and Popkin found that Americans were near the bottom in terms of political knowledge, just ahead of Spain. This was true even though the United States has a far more "educated" populace in terms of number of years in school. Why do Americans know so little? It is not because Americans spend less time consuming news media; in fact, adding together time spent reading newspapers and watching television news, Americans consumed more news than any other nation's citizens in the study. The reason may be that no other nation was as reliant on television news. As the authors concluded, "If American TV news viewers are abysmally ignorant, some of the fault lies with American television news."[4] Television, with its biases for simplicity and entertainment, is again the villain, as Postman would predict.

---

*The First Estate was the religious leadership, the Second Estate the aristocracy, and the Third Estate the mass of the populace. Originally, each estate was given a certain number of representatives in French government. The media was first called the Fourth Estate by British statesman and political philosopher Edmund Burke after the French Revolution had ended. In the midst of parliamentary debate, he gestured toward the press gallery and declaimed, "Yonder sits the Fourth Estate, and they are more important than them all!"

However, it should be noted that this was a five-question survey in which two questions were about Europe (Bosnia and Russia), the third was about the Middle East peace process, the fourth about North Korea, and the fifth about the United Nations secretary general. We might expect Europeans to be better informed about Europe, as well as the Middle East, which is far closer to their region. In addition, the UN is far more popular and salient in Europe and Canada than it is in the United States. If a question involving North America had been included, perhaps Americans would have fared better.

Recent work has again raised the question of how well the media educate the public about politics and whether television news has failed the public compared to other media outlets. In a study of support for the Iraq War, Kull, Ramsay, and Lewis found that those who got their news primarily from corporate television were far more likely to have key facts wrong.[5] The researchers asked respondents three questions: (1) Had clear evidence of a close working relationship between Saddam Hussein and al Qaeda been found? (2) Have weapons of mass destruction been found in Iraq? and (3) Did world public opinion favor the U.S. invasion of Iraq? Prior to the invasion, all three of these ideas were sold heavily by the Bush administration, and many people believed them to be true. After the invasion, however, when the surveys were conducted, it had become clear that the factual answer to each of these questions is "No." As shown in Table 3.1, the likelihood of respondents believing in at least one major untruth about the war in Iraq was directly related to the source of their news.

The majority of those who watched network or cable television news were in error about at least one simple fact about the Iraq War. Only those who read newspapers, watched PBS, or listened to NPR were likely to know the truth. It is, of course, possible that the television media are not directly responsible for the differences. Recall the

TABLE 3.1 Misperceptions about the Iraq War and Source of News

	Fox News	CBS	ABC	CNN	NBC	Print Media	NPR/PBS
Fact-based beliefs	20%	30%	39%	45%	45%	53%	77%
One or more misperceptions	80%	71%	61%	55%	55%	47%	23%

Source: Data from Kull, Ramsay, and Lewis, 2003.

discussion of selective perception and selective exposure in Chapter 2. Perhaps those who still believed that weapons of mass destruction were in Iraq watched media outlets such as Fox News that fed that belief by omission or merely downplayed the significance of it. Rather than misinforming the public, these outlets may have simply allowed many of their viewers to continue to misperceive the facts.

It remains troubling that basic factual knowledge about one of the most important issues in American politics is deeply dependent on what type of media a citizen consumes. It cannot help but reinforce a negative view of television as a source of news, supporting Postman's dark vision of television's dangers.

Agenda Setting: Telling Us What to Think About

The media may be at their most powerful when they engage in **agenda setting.** The media have the power to decide what issues are important, what solutions are legitimate, and which political figures are worthy of our attention.

Not even the most arrogant news director or editor claims that agenda setting is entirely under the media's control. Setting the agenda is at least a three-player game, with politicians, the public, and the media all playing their parts. The president has extraordinary powers to set the public agenda. The media has to cover the president to a great extent, and they cannot entirely ignore an issue that the president believes to be important. The public can also put an issue on the agenda through mass action or by responding to surveys and polls. The interactivity inherent in the process makes any claim of sole responsibility patently false. Suppose Americans are becoming increasingly upset about illegal immigration. This opinion or mood then appears in a few surveys conducted by the media, and the media begin to cover the issue more intensively. Politicians respond, sensing an opportunity to win votes. Although it appears that the public is in charge of agenda setting, it is rare for the public to move in one direction without some elite guidance. Surely some local politicians and public opinion leaders agitated about the issue in ways that led the public to care more. And the public probably found out about those agitations through the media, thus leading to the initial change in poll numbers.

Despite the complexities of studying this phenomenon, many media analysts have attempted to determine how much media influence exists in setting the nation's agenda in specific instances.

Political scientist John Mueller, in his book *Policy and Opinion in the Gulf War*, examined whether the media set the agenda during the lead-in to the first Gulf War. He concluded that the media were not in fact the prime movers in setting the agenda; rather, they responded to the acts of then President Bush and Saddam Hussein.

There is a clear distinction between the power to set the agenda and the power to persuade citizens about the importance or meaning of a political event. When news of a sexual relationship between President Clinton and Monica Lewinsky first broke in January of 1998, many media analysts discussed the situation as if it had the gravity of the Watergate scandal that brought President Nixon down. One pundit opined on the air that if the allegations were true Clinton's presidency might end in days. Week after relentless week the media covered the Lewinsky matter to the point that it seemed the media had become "all Lewinsky, all the time." Remarkably, even as the story turned out to be quite accurate, the public's approval of Clinton's work as president stabilized, and even rose. While the public watched and read stories about the scandal with great interest, polls also showed that many Americans thought the media were spending too much time on it. It was almost schizophrenic the way the public would bemoan the obsessive coverage and then tune in to watch every new development. Who, then, was really controlling the agenda? Is the media, with their need for ratings and sales, in charge, or is the public, which made the Barbara Walters interview with Lewinsky a massive hit, in change?

Media analysts use a number of techniques to measure the agenda-setting power of the media. Several studies using content analysis have tracked how public policy outcomes do or do not mirror the editorials in newspapers. There is no question that specific media outlets have the power to put an issue on the nation's agenda, at least briefly. If the *New York Times* runs a story on its front page, that is part of the nation's agenda. Political elites can choose to respond with new proposals, and the public can decide whether to make the issue part of their responses to surveys and a factor in their voting. But the influence of the *New York Times* is such that some political scientists have used its front page as a measure of what the nation's agenda actually is.

One key problem in measuring agenda setting is providing an objective standard against which to measure a specific media outlet's coverage of a political event. It is very difficult to come up with an objective measure of what is "newsworthy." One way of getting around

TABLE 3.2   Media Coverage of Demonstrations
in Washington, D.C.

Number of Demonstrators	Percent of Demonstrations Covered, 1982	Percent of Demonstrations Covered, 1991
Less than 26	2.9	3.3
26–100	12.3	7.7
101–1,000	34.7	11.9
1,001–10,000	47.1	29.8
10,001–100,000	77.8	37.5
More than 100,000	100	— (none occurred)
Total number and percentage of demonstrations covered	13% (158 of 1,209 demonstrations covered)	7.1% (133 of 1,856 demonstrations covered)

Source: Adapted from McCarthy, McPhail, and Smith, 1996.

this dilemma is for the researcher to create a data set based on non-media sources. A study by McCarthy, McPhail, and Smith in 1996 examined what factors led the media to cover demonstrations in Washington, D.C.[6] Most prior studies of demonstrations relied on the media to report demonstrations and their size. This one, however, looked at permits granted by federal agencies and official estimates of the size of the demonstration and compared these data to the media's coverage of demonstrations. The researchers discovered that the media tended to cover larger demonstrations, as shown in Table 3.2.

The media covered fewer demonstrations in 1991 than they did in 1982, even though there were many more demonstrations in 1991. A fairly large demonstration—10,000 to 100,000 people—in 1982 was twice as likely to be covered as a similar demonstration in 1991. The authors conclude that the media's agenda-setting power is greater in 1991 because the media have greater power to choose to cover or not cover political events. The meaning of a political protest is "mediated" through the filters of the press. If 25,000 people gather in front of the Lincoln Memorial to demonstrate on behalf of a political cause but the media don't report it, the demonstration almost doesn't matter except to those who participated and the few who happened to be walking by.

Agenda setting is perhaps the only media effect that most journalists will admit to causing. The media don't tell us what to think through agenda setting, but they may tell us what to think about.

FRAMING

Framing is a complex process through which the media shape our perception of the political world, often subconsciously. Nelson, Clawson, and Oxley define framing as "the process by which a communication source . . . defines and constructs a political issue or public controversy."[7] Framing can be very subtle. Consider a march through the downtown of your city or town by the racist group, the Ku Klux Klan. If your local television news station covers it, they have helped put it on the political agenda. Framing looks at how the media cover an event once they decide it is news. Framing can be harder to spot than direct political bias or agenda setting. It is how a story is packaged—What set of issues is it cataloged with? A number of frames could potentially be used for the Klan march. A reporter could adopt the "free speech" frame and talk about the march as an illustration of how the Constitution forces Americans to tolerate even hate speech in public places. Or a reporter could adopt a "disruption of public order" frame. Many Klan marches attract counterdemonstrators, and sometimes the clashes turn violent. A reporter could adopt a "civil rights" frame and discuss how the Klan march will remind many black residents of a hateful past, or how it reflects persistent racism among some whites. A reporter could even adopt a "dollars and sense" frame, in which case the cost to the city of the extra police security and the financial losses of downtown businesses shut down by the march would be the theme of the story.

Nelson, Clawson, and Oxley used an experiment to test just how framing of a Klan march would affect viewers. When a Klan march was framed as a civil liberties issue rather than a public order one, the researchers found increased tolerance among viewers. Even when news stories contain exactly the same facts and images, the way the story is presented by the media has a profound impact on how viewers feel about it.

One of the most common and broadest types of framing is the contrast between **episodic** and **thematic framing** of political issues, a distinction made most clearly by Shanto Iyengar in his book, *Is Anyone Responsible? How Television Frames Issues*. Episodic coverage emphasizes the specific people involved in a news story and focuses on their personal struggles. Episodic coverage fails to link the event to any historical or broader forces. A thematic frame, in contrast, puts the specific event into the context of related issues and of history. Iyengar believes television news in particular is prone to episodic coverage of political events because thematic coverage is far less visual and gripping. Thematic coverage also requires more airtime and more explanation, both of which are in short supply on television news. It is also one of Postman's key criticisms of television: the medium tends to present a barrage of unrelated facts, leaving viewers with little sense of how issues might be linked.

How would you frame this issue if you were the news director at a television station in rural America? A small town in your area pulls together to raise money for a popular and well-known waitress at a chain restaurant who has contracted a rare form of deadly cancer. She had worked at the restaurant in the center of town for more than thirty years, and everyone knew her name. More than $200,000 was raised by local community groups, and the waitress was able to travel out of state for very expensive treatments.

There are many ways to frame this story. One frame would emphasize how this woman struggled and how the community rallied to her aid. Touching video footage of bingo games and bake sales would be prominent, as well as images of the woman getting on the plane to get her medical care. This is episodic coverage. What might thematic coverage look like? Questions might be asked such as how, in the richest country on earth, a woman could work thirty years for a multinational corporation and have no health insurance. Coverage might link her difficulties to others in the community, less popular and with a lower profile, who have had medical needs but no insurance, or look at the rate of cancer in this small town compared to neighboring towns. For any of these more thematic frames, reporters would be required to do much more work, and the story would change from a simple, heart-warming human interest story to a far more challenging and controversial story that would take up lots of airtime and lots of the news division's budget.

Do frames matter? Consider the "gotcha" game media often play in presidential campaigns. In gotcha journalism, reporters look for minor misstatements, discrepancies, or past personal imbroglios to pester candidates about. Framing a campaign as being about which candidate has fewer gotcha problems, and which handles them better, is easier for reporters than trying to assess the workability and feasibility of different plans for the economy, the environment, defense, or agriculture. It also avoids accusations of bias. If a reporter says that Gore's plan for the surplus will not result in greater deficit spending but Bush's plan will, someone might accuse the reporter of bias against Bush. The reporter's statement could be seen as an opinion, not a fact. But if a reporter covers Gore's factual misstatement about who accompanied him on a trip to Texas, by definition that's a simple declarative fact, with no obvious bias. The gotcha frame may convey the impression that issues don't matter, or at least that minor miscues and a candidate's personality matter much more.

The way media frame an event can radically change how the public think about politics. In 1976 Republican Gerald Ford was trying desperately to catch up to Democratic candidate Jimmy Carter. In one of the best run campaigns in history, Ford gradually pulled close to Carter after being more than 25 points behind. It was clear that the presidential debates could decide the election. In the second debate, Ford made a misstatement about Soviet control of Eastern Europe. He had been trying to say that the Soviet Union had no right to dominate the captive nations behind the Iron Curtain, but what came out was the statement that there was "no Soviet dominance of Eastern Europe." Viewers paid little attention to the minor misstatement and judged Ford the winner of the debate (44 to 33 percent) in polls taken immediately after the debate. The media, stuck on their gotcha frame, focused almost all their attention on Ford's mistake. Nothing else that Ford or Carter said seemed to matter to the media, and the gaffe was front-page news the next morning. The polling swung so much that soon only 17 percent of the voters thought Ford had won the debate, compared to 63 percent for Carter.

Politicians are not merely victims of frames; sometimes politicians try very hard to get the media to accept a particular frame for an issue. During the months prior to the second war in Iraq, the Bush administration struggled to convince the media and the public that standing up to Saddam Hussein was part of the war on terror. If the media framed the looming conflict with Iraq as part of the larger war against terrorism, this could be seen as evidence that the media had accepted the Bush administration's frame. If, instead, the media framed the war as a fight over natural resources or a conflict between Islam and Christianity or as a replay of the first Gulf War, this would be a sign of an unsuccessful media strategy by the White House. By the time the second Gulf War began, some surveys indicated that a majority of Americans erroneously believed that some of the 9/11 terrorists had been Iraqis and that Saddam Hussein aided in the planning of the 9/11 attacks. Clearly, framing the second war in Iraq as part of a war on terrorism was successfully sold to the public.

Generally, though, a frame is not about giving the public different facts. Rather, it is giving structure to the facts in the news, placing the news in a broader context. Any news event may be put into an infinite number of frames. Perhaps the best thing for the media to do is to offer at least two frames for every story and let the viewers decide. Unfortunately, multiple frames on every news item could more than triple the length of the typical newscast or double the size of your daily paper.

PRIMING

Priming refers to specific changes media coverage produces in the way viewers think and feel about politics. Perhaps watching television news coverage of murders in your community doesn't change how you feel about crime nor persuade you that the death penalty is good or bad. However, if it causes you to weigh a candidate's position on the death penalty much more heavily than you did previously, you have been "primed." In some ways, priming can be thought of as measuring whether the media's agenda setting has any impact on specific voters. As media expert Shanto Iyengar observed, "the more prominent an issue in the news stream, the greater the impact of that issue on political attitudes."[8]

Priming can also be seen as the activation of existing attitudes through exposure to media content. Every citizen has an array of opinions, prejudices, and beliefs that are potentially relevant to politics. The media can prime particular attitudes through their political coverage. In her work on racial prejudice in political campaigns, Mendleberg found that coded racial messages in the media activate some white voters' racial prejudices and make them politically relevant. She didn't argue that the coverage gave viewers new attitudes about racial questions. The media aren't turning random white voters into racists in a propaganda fashion. Rather, the media bring to the forefront existing attitudes about race and crime, thus altering campaigns and elections.

Why does this matter? Consider all the issues and considerations that might be influential in a citizen's decision to vote in an election or to vote for a particular candidate. The number of facts or opinions that might matter is almost infinite. Few voters sit down and list all the pros and cons of the candidates and weigh the choice in a systematic fashion. If the media make a particular issue salient, it will almost inevitably become one of the criteria that some voters use to make their voting decision.

Priming is present in almost every commercial you have ever seen. Think about the ads for pickups and SUVs that boast about how some trucks can pull boats weighing many tons. If one car company succeeds in convincing consumers that a vital criterion for selecting a pickup truck is towing capacity, the other companies will have a very difficult time changing the primed attitude. Instead, they will have to develop ads showing their pickup truck pulling a grain silo or a house. This is so even if the vast majority of truck buyers seldom, if ever, require such large capacity engines.

Priming works on politicians as well as pickup trucks. It can alter the way the public thinks about a particular office. The media can introduce new criteria for judging the worthiness of candidates. At least since the 1960s, the media have increasingly focused on the personal aspects of the presidency. Presidents are now expected to have happy families and to be good spouses. Subsequent presidents have not always met this standard, but it is a new criterion that has been primed by the media and that seems to influence the public's thinking about politics. An innovative study by political scientist Scott Keeter found that television has made the public much more concerned about the personal qualities of candidates for president over the last thirty years.[9] The media primed Americans to care about how a candidate's personality made them feel rather than about whether they agreed with his platform or supported his party. One interpretation is that the media have reduced the role of cognition, of thinking, in American elections and replaced it with facile emotional judgments about who we "like" more. This may be the most negative example of priming by the media. When the media talk about how attractive or unattractive a candidate is, they prime voters to think that looks matter in politics. A viewer exposed to this discourse will be much more likely to apply looks criteria to their voting decisions.

It is important to understand the differences between framing and priming. Framing is the broader context into which a particular news story is placed by the media. Priming is how particular words or images activate existing political attitudes in citizens. If there is an outbreak of a rare disease among an immigrant group in a small community, the media could frame the story as being about the need for greater health care spending, the need to fight poverty among immigrants, or the need for stricter immigration controls. The framing decision is distinct from (although not unrelated to) the priming effects that the coverage might have on an upcoming governor's race. Voters may now consider emergency responsiveness as a new and important factor in selecting a governor. Constant coverage of the outbreak will prime viewers to think about the disease crisis in choosing candidates. If voters have an existing prejudice against immigrants as being dangerous or unhygienic, these views may now become central to their political outlook.

YES, MEDIA MATTERS

The evidence has mounted steadily over the last forty years—the media matters. The media often fail in their attempt to depict politics neutrally and can affect the issue they are attempting to observe. In the hard sciences, this is called an "observer effect." The act of studying an event changes the event that you study. In journalism, the act of reporting on a political event changes that event, both in how politicians prepare for it and in how it affects the public. Compelling research shows that the media can teach correct or incorrect facts, help set the nation's agenda, frame issues in ways that change the attitudes of Americans, and prime citizens to alter their priorities and the ranking of their values and beliefs. There is even some evidence that the media can persuade voters to adopt certain views, in limited circumstances.

Yet the message about the media is mixed. Few in academia argue that the media are attempting uniformly to affect American politics according to some ideological agenda. Moreover, most researchers have found important limits to the power of the media. Many of the components of the minimal effects model, such as selective retention and selective perception, remain real barriers to media influence. And, as we shall see later in the book, political leaders have become increasingly sophisticated in responding to the power of the media.

KEY TERMS

agenda setting	experimental studies
content analysis	framing
episodic versus thematic framing	priming
	survey research

DISCUSSION QUESTIONS

1. Do you feel surveys on media consumption can accurately measure media effects?
2. Do you think the media have too much power in setting the nation's agenda? What could be done about this?
3. Do you think you have ever been primed by the media?
4. Think of the most important political issue to you, personally. Can you think of three different ways to frame it? Which one do you like best? Which one do the media use most?
5. If you have a political view that you consider to be in the minority among your fellow citizens, do you perceive the media as being hostile to that opinion, objective, or in agreement with you?

ADDITIONAL RESOURCES

News: The Politics of Illusion, by Lance Bennett, presents a different take on media bias, including that the media has informational biases in the way it structures the news.

Is Anyone Responsible? How Television Frames Political Issues, by Shanto Iyengar, is an excellent book on framing by one of the best media scholars in the country.

The Nature and Origins of Mass Opinion, by John Zaller, is a difficult but very important text on how mass public opinion works. It has important implications for media studies.

NOTES

1. Russell J. Dalton, Paul A. Beck, and Robert Huckfeldt, "Partisan Cues and the Media: Information Flows in the 1992 Presidential Election," *American Political Science Review* 92(1998): 111–26.
2. The work is discussed in Roger Giner-Sorolla and Shelley Chaiken, "The Causes of Hostile Media Judgments," *Journal of Experimental Social Psychology* 30(1994): 165–80.
3. John Zaller, *The Nature and Origins of Mass Opinion* (New York: Cambridge University Press, 1992). See also John Zaller, "Strategic Politicians, Public Opinion, and the Gulf Crisis." In *Taken by Storm: The Media, Public Opinion, and U.S. Foreign Policy*

in the Gulf War, Lance Bennett and David Paletz, eds. (Chicago: University of Chicago, 1994).

4. Michael A. Dimock and Samuel L. Popkin, "Political Knowledge in Comparative Perspective." In *Do the Media Govern?* Shanto Iyengar and Richard Reeves, eds. (Thousand Oaks, CA: Sage, 1997).

5. Steven Kull, Clay Ramsay, and Evan Lewis, "Misperceptions, the Media, and the Iraq War," *Political Science Quarterly* 118, no. 4(Winter 2003).

6. John D. McCarthy, Clark McPhail, and Jackie Smith, "Images of Protest: Dimensions of Selection Bias in Media Coverage of Washington Demonstrations, 1982 and 1991," *American Sociological Review* 61(1996): 478–99.

7. Thomas E. Nelson, Rosalee A. Clawson, and Zoe M. Oxley, "Media Framing of a Civil Liberties Conflict and Its Effect on Tolerance," *American Political Science Review* 91, no. 3(1997): 567–83.

8. Shanto Iyengar, "'Media Effects' Paradigms for the Analysis of Local Television News." A paper presented to the Annie E. Casey Foundation Planning Meeting, September 17–18, 1998.

9. Scott Keeter, "The Illusion of Intimacy: Television and the Role of Candidate Personal Qualities in Voter Choice," *Public Opinion Quarterly* 51(1987): 344–58.

CHAPTER 4

The History of American Journalism before Electronic Media

*T*he book began by asking the question "Does the method of transmission of a political message matter?" To fully understand how political messages are transmitted today in the United States, we must first understand how news about politics was conveyed in the past.

American journalism in its modern form is very young. Technology changes in the means of communication have radically altered journalism in a thousand ways. For most of American history, journalism referred only to print journalism. Even today print journalism often sets the agenda and the electronic media follow. The social and political roles played by print journalists, and the ethics and ethos of journalism, have changed radically. Before radio and television altered the norms and rules of journalism, print journalism arrived at its own standards, which remain influential. The evolution of journalism has been a fitful and dynamic process in which rapid change has coexisted with persistent echoes of previous eras.

In this chapter, the relationship between the political world and the media is examined for each of the major eras of journalism, but journalism is not just the story of technological and institutional change. It is a story full of vivid personalities, powerful and brilliant men and women who fought to establish their vision of what journalism should be in America. For each era, a prominent journalist who exemplifies aspects of the particular period is profiled.

THE COLONIAL ERA: 1690–1770

Newspapers are almost as old as the American experiment. The first "newspaper" to be regularly printed appeared in London in 1622, only two years after the Pilgrims landed in Massachusetts. The American colonists had no newspapers of their own for decades, instead reading the rare newspapers from Europe, delivered weeks, months, or sometimes years after their date of publication. Even though the first printing press arrived from Great Britain in the 1630s, as late as 1660 there were only two such machines in America, with printing tightly controlled by the New England authorities.[1]

American journalism really began in 1690 when Benjamin Harris of Boston published "Public Occurances" on September 25. Yet long after Harris began his tiny newspaper, there were no journalists in America, at least not as we understand the term. Most publishers of newspapers throughout the colonial period were men with other occupations: booksellers, postmasters, or simply printers for whom newspapers were a small source of revenue amid more profitable printing ventures.[2] Newspapers didn't have a staff of reporters, regular sections, or editorials. The income of the colonial papers could not have supported even the small staff at a modern rural paper. A significant colonial circulation was two or three thousand papers, but newspapers were so valuable that some modern historians estimate that each copy of a paper had more than ten readers. News coverage was a very informal affair, with much of the text of newspapers taken up with letters. A newspaper from Boston might print a letter from a New Yorker about some current trial or debate. The letter writer could be a friend of the printer, a person of some influence in New York, or merely a witty person with a lot of free time. Newspapers also freely stole material from other papers if they felt it would be of interest to their readers. The modern ideas of plagiarism and copyright were largely unknown.[3]

Colonial media were not limited to newspapers. Four other types of printed communication were popular as well: broadsides, magazines, pamphlets, and books. Broadsides were posters covered in writing that were often read aloud for the benefit of the illiterate. The Declaration of Independence in 1776 was a broadside posted around the colonies. Magazines were rarer than newspapers, and far less influential, but some, such as the annual *Poor Richard's Almanac* by Benjamin Franklin, were widely distributed throughout the colonies. Pamphlets were loosely bound short essays on a single topic by a single author, usually designed to advance a particular position on a burning political or religious issue. A pamphlet often was answered by another writer's pamphlet, and printers made money off such controversies. Finally, books were also printed in America during the colonial era, but due to their cost and the time necessary to publish a lengthy hardback book, they were not ideal for conveying current news.

Early printing machines were difficult to operate, and each page took hours of painstaking preparation. Printing was a profession that required not only a long apprenticeship but a commitment to challenging and dirty physical labor. Men of wealth and privilege seldom became printers; it was seen as a profession far beneath banking or plantation farming in social standing. Many printers were quite literate and well read, but they were not the best educated men in the colonies. As a consequence, much of the content in the newspapers of the day was written by others. In many cases, prominent men who wished to be read but did not wish to be known as authors took on pseudonyms. It was not just authorship that was hidden from public view; some newspapers were quietly subsidized by men who wished to make a political statement but worried about taking responsibility for their inflammatory words.

New England was truly the cradle of journalism in America, and most of the colonies were without presses for decades. An early governor of Virginia, a state that was particularly antipress, observed in 1671: "Thank God, we have no free schools nor printing; God keep us from both."[4] New England may have had printing, but it was by no means free of government control. For much of the period, printers could work only if they were licensed by the Puritan authorities.[5] Throughout the colonies, the early American press faced substantial limits to its freedom. That the press should be free to criticize government was a foreign concept to most colonists. This is not surprising because most American ideas at this time were derived from England, and the British press was far from free. Although certain British thinkers such as John Milton, Daniel Defoe, and John Locke had begun to advocate for a free press, the practice in England was often to harshly punish those who criticized political or religious authorities. In particular, printers could be held accountable for publishing "seditious" material or material that could be seen as encouraging public unrest or disrespect for the authorities. In fact, by some measures, the American press may have been more free, although much smaller, than the English press (see Box).

ARCHETYPE OF THE COLONIAL ERA

John Peter Zenger

Colonial governments, like those in England and throughout Europe, did not believe that the press had any right to harshly criticize government, particularly in ways that were likely to incite the people's anger. Satire, ridicule, and even mild admonishment of government officials could lead to lengthy imprisonment, confiscation of presses, and in some cases death. The first major challenge to the idea that the press could be punished for publishing factual material of a critical nature or for publishing bitter satire of the ruling authorities was the case of the printer **John Peter Zenger.**

Zenger was born in Germany and arrived in New York via England at the age of thirteen with his widowed mother; his father passed away on the journey.[6] Zenger became an indentured servant to the most prominent printer in New York City, and then set out to make his living as a printer. In 1733 Zenger began publishing the *New-York Weekly Journal,* a paper funded and written by men who strongly opposed the current colonial governor, William Cosby. Zenger's paper relentlessly mocked Cosby and exposed alleged corruption under his rule. Zenger was arrested by the governor's authorities in 1734 and placed in prison. In his first letter to his readers from prison, Zenger explains what has become of him:

> As you last week were disappointed (with the disappearance) of my Journal, I think it is incumbent on me to publish my apology, which is this. On the Lord's Day . . . I was arrested, taken and imprisoned in the common jail of this City by virtue of a warrant from the Governor . . . whereupon I was put under such restraint that I had not the liberty of pen, ink, or paper, or to see or speak with people, until my complaint to the honorable Chief Justice. . . . I have had since that time the liberty of speaking thro' the hole of the door to my wife and servants.[7]

When Zenger's trial began, it seemed to be a foregone conclusion that he would be found guilty, even though public opinion had rallied to him during his eight months in prison. The common law at the time of Zenger's trial was crystal clear: publications that caused citizens to question their government could be banned and their printers harshly punished. As one contemporary legal ruling put it:

> If people should not be called to account for possessing the people with an ill opinion of the government, no government can subsist. For it is necessary for all governments that the people should have a good opinion of it.[8]

There was no exception made for expressing opinions, or even for printing factual material that put the government in a bad light. The only question the governor felt necessary to put before the court was whether Zenger had published the material.

Zenger's attorney was perhaps the most famous lawyer in the colonies, Andrew Hamilton of Philadelphia. Hamilton boldly admitted that Zenger was the publisher of the libelous words about the governor, which seemed to eliminate any role for the jury. However, Hamilton called on the jury to intervene to uphold a higher principle than the common law, the principle that governments can and should be subject to printed criticism. Moved by Hamilton's eloquence, the jury acquitted Zenger on all counts. The judges in the case, both strong supporters of Governor Cosby, were left without the ability to bring down punishment on Zenger, who was immediately freed from jail.

Zenger's victory did not free the presses throughout the colonies from government control. Indeed, publishers still faced trouble, and charges of libel or sedition, if the words they printed angered government authorities. What the Zenger case did was promulgate the idea that the press should be free. Zenger's case was followed in England and other European countries, further spreading the concept of a free press.[9] Zenger's ultimate victory came with passage of the First Amendment, with its endorsement of free speech and a free press. Zenger remains a hero to many modern journalists, and figures as diverse as Internet blogger Matt Drudge and pornographer Larry Flynt have tried to claim Zenger's mantle.

Several books deal with the Zenger trial as part of the history of American journalism, including *The Early American Press,* by William Sloan and Julie Hedgepeth Williams (1994, Greenwood Press). A recent book focusing entirely on Zenger is *John Peter Zenger and the Fundamental Freedom,* by William L. Putnam (1997, McFarland).

Perhaps the most famous American journalist of this era was Benjamin Franklin of Philadelphia. Franklin first became a newspaper editor at the age of sixteen when his brother was banned from publishing in Boston and named Benjamin to take the heat.[10] Eventually Franklin founded his own paper in Philadelphia and went on to become the first true businessman in the journalism arena. Franklin helped found papers in South Carolina and Rhode Island, indirectly aiding the idea of America as more than just a set of disparate colonies. Franklin, unlike most colonial printers, actually made money at it and eventually retired from the business to pursue his interests in politics and science.

The development of an independent American press, with widely read newspapers, was certainly crucial in developing a sense of a separate American identity. Although no newspapers advocated separation from England at this time, the articulation of distinctly American views unquestionably prepared the colonies for the coming conflict. It should also be noted that a number of newspapers were also published in German, which indirectly reminded all the colonists that they were not exclusively a product of Mother England.[11] In the colonial era, the loyalty of most newspapers and printers to the colonial governments and to the Crown of England was largely unquestioned. But that was all about to change.

REVOLUTIONARY ERA PRESS: 1760–1789

In 1760 America was thirteen relatively small colonies dependent on England for security and most of their trade. Twenty-three years later, America was the victor over the much more powerful English nation in a bloody battle for independence. But the Revolutionary War was not just a battle of men and muskets; it was a battle of ideas and national identity. What was an "American"? What loyalty did an American owe to the English nation or the royal rulers of England? How should the colonies be governed, and who should do it? The answers to these questions changed rapidly during those years. Traditionally, historians argued that the press played a central role in spreading the ideals of independence and democracy. Later, another group of scholars, under the influence of the minimal effects school, held that the press was not crucial to the revolution. They also demanded to see the evidence of such an impact, which is admittedly lacking by the standards of modern social science.[12] But it cannot be argued that the press played no role. It seems, rather, that printers were essential to the establishment of the United States as an independent nation.

The controversies of the day coincided with a phenomenal growth in the American media. From 1760 to 1776, newspaper circulation grew twice as fast as the population did.[13] As in England, newspapers and pamphlets were distributed much more widely than their circulation numbers would suggest. Coffee houses and taverns would keep newspapers available for their customers to read, and passages were read aloud for the illiterate. By the time the revolution came, there were thirty-four newspapers in the colonies, published mostly in the cities and some of the smaller towns.[14]

Printers were indirectly attacked by an early attempt by Britain to raise money from the colonies. The Stamp Act required that every document, including newspapers, be stamped to show that taxes had been paid on it. By increasing the price of newspapers and pamphlets, the Stamp Act greatly angered printers. It almost ensured that many printers would oppose the British government's efforts, and newspapers were crucial in rallying opposition to it.

Newspapers were essential to the cause of revolution because the colonies tended to be thinly populated. The few population centers were separated by vast territories, which made any other form of political communication difficult. There were great orators of the revolution such as Patrick Henry, but their words achieved power only as they were transmitted in print. When Henry proclaimed, "If this be treason, make the most of it!" or "Give me liberty, or give me death!" his boldness and his commitment to the cause of freedom inspired imitators far from his native Virginia. By comparison, a decade later, when revolutionary tensions emerged in France, newspapers were less important because so much of the population and the intellectual elite of France were concentrated in a single city, Paris. Americans, lacking one great capital city that dominated politics, economics, religion, and the arts, had to move toward revolution on the printed page.

Newspapers sometimes became the focal point of tensions between colonists who wished for greater independence from Britain and those who supported the Crown (called Loyalists or Tories). The Boston Tea Party, a famous act of civil disobedience against a much hated tax, was planned in the offices of the *Boston Gazette,* run by influential revolutionary Samuel Adams.* The *Gazette*'s headquarters

---

*Yes, the same Samuel Adams on the label of the beer company.

were frequently the meeting place of those who sought independence from Britain. Adams, after Franklin the most influential printer
of the day, never achieved the prominence of Franklin in part because so many of his essays and comments were printed anonymously, as was the tradition of the day.[15] Indeed, as the tensions with
England became sharper and actual blood was shed, such as at the
Boston Massacre, the tradition of anonymity became even more important. Harsh criticism of the British was often written under a
pseudonym in case the royal authorities sought to enforce the common law against libelous or seditious speech.

Those loyal to England also had reasons to remain anonymous
as the independence movement gained in strength. Neither side in
the revolution accepted the principle of free speech. If the British
took a city from the revolutionaries, printers who had been too
strong in their advocacy of independence often fled. If the forces of
George Washington conquered a town held by the British, historian
Jeffrey Pasley observes,

> the Loyalist press was mobbed, prosecuted, or confiscated out of ex-
> istence when the British army was not around to protect it. Loyalist
> publishers fled for their lives when they were not banned outright.[16]

There was no pretense of journalistic objectivity during the revolutionary era. Although some publishers attempted to portray
themselves as fair and balanced, most were forced by conviction,
fear, or market forces to choose either England or independence.
Those who chose wrongly could lose everything, depending on the
outcome of specific battles during the seven-year struggle for
American independence. While it is difficult to accurately count
how many printers were on each side, in part because some switched
sides, it appears that the Loyalists were outnumbered by revolutionaries by at least two to one.[17]

The ending of hostilities with Britain did not end the upheaval
of the revolution. For six years Americans struggled under a confusing and inefficient confederate government, which led to widespread chaos. The new government system was widely perceived to
be failing. The greatest outbreak of civil unrest was Shays' Rebellion,
in which poor farmers took up arms against the government and
banks of Massachusetts. The rebellion was put down, but it showed
how deeply distressed the population was. Thomas Jefferson, author of the Declaration of Independence, felt that the solution to
the ongoing strife was not greater control of the press but a wider

readership. Jefferson argued that the best way to prevent similar rebellions would be to give the people full information through "the channel of the public papers, and to contrive that those papers should penetrate the whole mass of the people."[18]

However, Shays' Rebellion, as well as ongoing economic and political upheaval, convinced many that a new system of government should be instituted. Much of the debate over how to fix the national government was conducted in the newspapers. When a gathering of representatives from the various states was finally held in 1787, the delegates were deeply aware of proposals that had been aired in the press; indeed, some of them had anonymously authored them. The document that emerged from the Constitutional Convention was a far more sweeping and radical revision of the existing government than most Americans had anticipated.

The press quickly took sides in the debate, and papers, like politicians, were labeled as "Federalists" and "Anti-Federalists." The debate was a battle waged nationally as well as state by state. Each state had to separately ratify the new Constitution. Most of the men engaged in this debate chose to do so under pseudonyms although the identity of a prominent author was sometimes hardly a secret. One of the most famous Anti-Federalists went by the name Brutus, taking his name from the man who killed the dictator Julius Caesar in ancient Rome. Brutus dissected the new Constitution in essay after essay, raging at what he perceived as a far-too-powerful central government that would threaten the liberties so newly won in the revolution.

To answer the many opponents of the new Constitution, three men, Alexander Hamilton, James Madison, and John Jay, agreed to write a series of essays to be published in the newspapers of New York. Hamilton, who later went on to fame as Washington's secretary of the treasury (and who appears on the ten-dollar bill in your wallet), was the organizer and author of the largest number of the essays. Madison, who had been perhaps the greatest influence on the Constitutional Convention, wrote some of the most important Federalist Papers in its defense. The three men agreed to publish their works under the same pseudonym, Publius, another reference to ancient Rome.

The essays by Publius may have directly influenced the outcome of the very narrow ratification fight in New York. In that sense, they may be the most significant editorials in the history of American journalism. Without New York as a willing member, the new union

ARCHETYPE OF THE REVOLUTIONARY ERA
Tom Paine

Without the pen of Paine, the sword of Washington would have been wielded in vain.

—John Adams

Tom Paine's words were fiery, inflammatory, and inspiring. He wrote not for the educated elite but for the rising tide of educated commoners, those who wanted to understand and improve their society. Unlike many of the aristocratic men who led the American Revolution, such as Jefferson and Washington, Paine was born in relative poverty in England. He was a relentless advocate for liberty and free thought, which would eventually lead many more established political figures to reject him as dangerous and radical.

Tom Paine's career as a journalist was indeed an odd one by modern standards. Born in 1737 in Thetford, England, he failed at numerous professions.[19] Emigrating to America in 1774, Paine quickly achieved local notoriety in Philadelphia with the publication of an essay attacking slavery as unjust and against God. One of the earliest abolitionist essays, Paine's words quickly led to the establishment of the first antislavery society in America. Five months later, Paine attacked another injustice in his "Occasional Letter on the Female Sex," in which he advocated greater rights for women at a time when women were considered property and were denied the right of speech or political participation.

Paine achieved his greatest fame, however, with his next major publication, a pamphlet called *Common Sense*, which advocated independence from Britain and was released in January of 1776. After less than two years as a resident of America, Paine was convinced that the colonies should not be governed from afar by Britain. His argument was grounded not only in the fact that Britain was taxing America while denying it representation in Parliament but in his belief that a just government must be popularly elected in regular contests. Paine's words were not written in the style of many political writers of the day, with their frequent references to Greek and Roman authorities. Paine's readers were addressed in a common style that made

forceful points in favor of independence, representative government, and liberty. *Common Sense* sold hundreds of thousands of
copies in just a few months, a staggering figure considering that
the total population of the colonies was just a few million. Even
before Jefferson did so in the Declaration of Independence, Paine
saw the struggle for freedom in America as part of a global struggle against monarchy and injustice, writing that "The Cause of
America is in a great Measure the Cause of all Mankind."
According to Neil Postman, a greater proportion of Americans
read *Common Sense* in 1776 than watch a Super Bowl today.

   During the Revolutionary War, Paine put his beliefs into action, volunteering to fight against the British in the Continental
Army. Paine, however, quickly realized two things: he was not
much of a soldier, and the revolutionaries were losing the war
against the British. After Washington's bloody retreat from New
Jersey, Paine left to write the first of his *American Crisis* papers,
which rallied the embryonic American nation to support the
troops. The first words of Paine's new work have become justly
famous:

> These are the times that try men's souls. The summer soldier
> and the sunshine patriot will, in this crisis, shrink from the
> service of their country; but he that stands it now deserves the
> love and thanks of man and woman. Tyranny, like hell, is not
> easily conquered.

The army made *The American Crisis* required reading for its soldiers, and many felt it spurred new enlistments.[20]

   After the war Paine did not find success in the new America
he helped create. Eventually, in 1787, he left for England, where
he pursued several dubious business deals. Very shortly afterward, the French Revolution began, and Paine, ever eager for
new battles in the cause of liberty, quickly became involved in the
struggle. Paine published *The Rights of Man*, defending the French
Revolution against its conservative critics in Britain and America.
The book was far more radical than an attack on the French
monarchy; Paine's targets now included poverty, arbitrary governments, illiteracy, unemployment, and war. The book was
banned in Britain, and Paine escaped arrest by fleeing to France.
By 1793 Paine's iconoclasm had landed him in jail in France

because, even though he hated monarchy, he had refused to support the execution of the former king of France. While in prison, he wrote what many consider his masterwork, *The Age of Reason*. In it Paine completed his radical alienation from most other American founders by advocating what many saw as atheism.

Upon his release from prison, Paine remained in France until invited to return to America by Thomas Jefferson, now president. Paine's new views, on religion in particular, made it difficult for him to return to prominence in America, and he became a bitter alcoholic in his last years. When he died alone in poverty and near obscurity in 1809 in New York City, his crucial role in the American Revolution was almost forgotten by the newspapers of the day, which wrote more about his atheism and other radical views. The poverty in which he died was another example of his commitment to the nation that later rejected him. Although he was quite possibly the best-selling author and journalist of the revolutionary era, he never received a dime for either *Common Sense* or *The American Crisis*, donating the proceeds to the cause of revolution.

Books on Thomas Paine

Tom Paine: Apostle of Freedom, by Jack Fruchtman (New York: Four Walls Press, 1996)

Thomas Paine: Firebrand of the Revolution, by Harvey J. Kaye (New York: Oxford University Press, 2000)

Tom Paine: A Political Life, by John Keane (New York: Grove Press, 2003)

would have been doomed to failure even if all twelve of the other states had ratified it. But the influence of the Federalist essays extends much further. Today, they are gathered together in book form and studied by students of American politics as well as by designers of new governments in emerging democracies around the world. Federal judges have also looked to the Federalist Papers to help them figure out what the intentions of the Framers of the Constitution actually were with regard to specific clauses. What is truly stunning to the modern reader of the Federalist Papers is the length and complexity of these journalistic writings. Nothing that appears in today's newspapers matches the sustained argument and erudite references of the Federalist Papers.* Perhaps this reflects a decline in the quality of American readers or journalism. On the other hand, it may better reflect the fact that Hamilton, Madison, and Jay were writing for the literate elite of New York, who had the most influence in the ratification fight. These were not essays aimed at the mass public of 1787.

In the end, the Constitution was ratified, and the American republic finally firmly established. A revolution that in some ways began with words in print, gained momentum through printed broadsides such as the Declaration of Independence, and sustained itself through a long costly conflict in part through essays such as Tom Paine's (see Box), was brought to a decisive conclusion through an erudite debate conducted in large part in the newspapers of the day.

However, it was probably not a fair fight, and it was certainly not a fight conducted by objective journalists and publishers. It is impossible today to ascertain what the majority of Americans felt about the new Constitution; there was no mass media to conduct polls. What we do know is that the Federalists tended to be far wealthier than their opponents, and they controlled more newspapers. In some states there was no published debate at all because every paper was owned and operated by a Federalist printer.[21] Some owners, whether for or against the new Constitution, forbade the publication of material from the other side. Today many Americans worry that the media have monopolistic control over the nation's agenda. That may or may not be true, but it is important to realize that the American system did not emerge from an open debate conducted according to the modern standards of a free and objective press. The press during the war against the British was highly partisan, and both sides not only slanted coverage but freely punished opposing printers if the opportunity presented itself. Similarly, the press's treatment of the Constitutional debate was distorted by the disproportionate economic power of the Federalists. We cannot know for sure if the Constitution would have been rejected if the Anti-Federalists had access to the media on an equal level with the Federalists, but it does seem very likely given how narrow the Federalist victory was in several key states.

---

*Both the Federalist Papers and much of the work of the Anti-Federalists is available online. Some of the Anti-Federalist essays more directly resemble current newspaper columns and editorials and are written in a much plainer, and occasionally humorous, style.

The Anti-Federalists, while losing the battle over the Constitution, did win a key concession from the Federalists: a Bill of Rights. As part of the ratification deal, the Federalists had to agree to quickly pass a series of limits on the central government. When Madison and others began to write these protections of core liberties, the very first amendment to the Constitution guaranteed both free speech and a free press. Perhaps Madison, who wrote some of the most important Federalist Papers, had come to appreciate the power and necessity of a free press. In less than a decade, however, an American president would launch a frontal assault on free speech and a free press, imprisoning newspaper editors and shutting down printers. The Bill of Rights was a brave promise of freedom for American journalists, but it was not always a promise kept.

THE PARTISAN PRESS ERA: 1789–1860

As we have seen, early American newspapers had little conception of objective reporting. In the period from 1789 to 1860 the expectation was that newspapers would be formally or informally associated with a particular political party. In an era when the party system was just forming, newspapers often provided the necessary institutional glue for political movements. As historian Jeffrey Pasley put it:

> In nineteenth-century America . . . the newspaper press was the political system's central institution, not simply a forum or atmosphere in which politics took place. Instead, newspapers and their editors were purposeful actors in the political process, linking parties, voters, and government together and pursuing specific political goals. . . . From the 1790s on, no politician dreamed of mounting a campaign, launching a new movement, or winning over a new geographic area without a newspaper.[22]

The reader of a newspaper was typically a supporter of the political party that backed the paper. Advertisers expressed their support for a party by taking out ads in that party's paper. In part, the **partisan press** era in journalism was produced by the weakness of political parties. National and state parties typically had no permanent employees, no headquarters, no budget, and no building. Newspapers could offer all of these as well as a potent public voice.[23]

The Bill of Rights, passed shortly after the Constitution went into effect, granted to the press a privileged place among professions in the **First Amendment:**

> Congress shall make no law respecting an establishment of religion, or prohibiting the free exercise thereof; or abridging the freedom of speech, or of the press; or the right of the people peaceably to assemble, and to petition the government for a redress of grievances.*

No other nongovernmental occupation is mentioned in the first ten amendments to the Constitution save lawyers.

The guarantee that Congress shall make no law abridging the freedom of the press or of speech seemed to be an ironclad promise from the government that journalism would be untouched by hostile legislation. But the partisan affiliation of newspapers and the relative newness of the idea of a free press combined to produce the greatest attack on independent journalism in American history: the **Alien and Sedition Acts.** Passed by the Federalist Party during the administration of John Adams (1797–1801), the acts sought to punish the publication of "sedition," which was broadly defined as speech that was likely to induce disrespect for the president or Congress. The target of the legislation was clear: the Republican critics of Adams.

As they had during the debate over the Constitution, Federalists controlled the vast majority of newspapers when Adams was inaugurated. However, a number of fiery publications that opposed the Federalists had emerged during Washington's second term.[24] The Federalists were in grave fear of a popular revolt at this time because of the example of the French Revolution. Unlike the far more "tidy" American Revolution, the French upheaval had lasted for years and had resulted in the violent deaths of many aristocrats. The wealthy Federalists believed that French agents were encouraging similar social unrest in America and thus sought to rein in the media to prevent an uprising.

The federal government swiftly moved to enforce the act. Several Republican editors were sentenced to prison for seditious publication. Some Federalists went even further. One federal marshal threatened to beat a Republican editor "till he should not be able to rise from his bed."[25] Another Republican editor was brutally attacked

---

*A recent survey found that many more Americans knew the names of the judges on the TV show *American Idol* and the members of the Simpson's cartoon family than knew the five freedoms guaranteed by the First Amendment.

by a Federalist supporter, imprisoned under Adams's new laws, and had his presses destroyed by a Federalist mob.[26]

The response of Republican editors and their supporters was defiant. The number of Republican papers increased, and their circulation boomed. Rather than intimidating the opposition, Adams had caused many Americans to distrust his leadership. Virginia and Kentucky passed resolutions in opposition to the acts, and Jefferson, the leader of the Republicans, was encouraged by the public's anger at Adams. In the presidential election of 1800, Jefferson beat Adams, the man who had defeated him just four years earlier. For the Federalist Party, the attempt to prevent journalistic criticism backfired, and their party would slowly become extinct over the next two decades. It was America's great good fortune that the first attempt at widespread press censorship was such a crushing failure. Many other young democracies since then have had the opposite experience: a charismatic leader has successfully cowed the press through force and intimidation, at least temporarily. By contrast, when Jefferson took office, he pardoned all twenty-five publishers convicted under the act, and Congress refunded all fines plus interest.

The controversy over the Alien and Sedition Acts did little to stem the continuing alliance between papers and parties. A survey of 359 newspapers published in 1810 could find only 33 that had no party affiliation.[27] And the association of a newspaper with a party could still provoke violence. During the war of 1812, a Federalist paper in Baltimore was harshly critical of President James Madison and the war effort. Madison, the author of the Bill of Rights and an opponent of the Alien and Sedition Acts, was reluctant to ban any paper, but his followers had no such restraints. A mob of Republicans* destroyed the paper's offices and almost killed the editors. Undaunted, the Federalists resumed printing at another press in a more secure building with food to withstand a siege. Their first issue so disturbed Republicans that another mob gathered, this time armed with a cannon. Nine employees were savagely beaten by the victorious mob, one editor was killed, and the other was maimed for life.[28] In the partisan press era, passions could make a free press more a goal than a reality.

The same was true with the emerging controversy over slavery. As we have seen, the antislavery movement in America was given a great boost by journalist Tom Paine prior to the Revolution. Over the

---

*The "Republicans" of 1812 should not be confused with modern Republicans. They were actually Jeffersonian Republicans, later called Democratic Republicans, the party that went on to become today's Democratic Party.

ensuing decades, more and more Americans, particularly in the northern states, came to see the enslavement of African Americans as a moral evil. As with all political ideas of the day, those of strong opinions against slavery founded newspapers (see Box) and tried to mail them to the southern states. During the presidency of Andrew Jackson, southern leaders tried to limit the distribution of antislavery newspapers and magazines for fear that these would cause slave revolts or riots. Editors of abolitionist newspapers faced the threat of violence in advocating their views. It was even a crime to teach a slave to read in some southern states.

Presidents during the partisan press era were expected to select a **house organ,** a newspaper that would convey their views precisely. The house organ would receive a boost in prestige and circulation as well as lucrative printing jobs from the federal government. The editors could also expect to receive patronage jobs, which often required little or no work. Newspapers even played a role in diplomacy; European governments read the house organ of the president to anticipate policy shifts. At one point during Jackson's presidency, the Russian government was so angered by what appeared in "his" newspaper that they complained to the U.S. ambassador, who had to explain that the paper was not run by the government. However, this was a "diplomatic fiction" as little appeared in the pages with which Jackson disagreed.[29]

The partisan press era formally ended with the presidency of Abraham Lincoln. Lincoln was the first president to refuse to have a house organ. He believed it was important to maintain good relations with many papers rather than favor one. Lincoln also took a large step toward removing patronage from the newspaper business by founding the Government Printing Office. Previously, editors and publishers who wrote well of presidents could expect large contracts to print government manuals and documents.[30] Many historians end the partisan era in 1860, but the newspapers of America did not suddenly become nonpartisan. Editors remained key political figures in most political parties, particularly at the state level. One of the great journalists of the century, Horace Greeley, was nominated for president in 1872, continuing the tradition of journalists actually becoming politicians, a frequent occurrence in the first half of the nineteenth century.

The journalistic norm of objectivity was far from universal among newspapers well into the twentieth century. Most newspapers retained an affiliation, or at least an affinity, with one of the two major parties. Indeed, in most cities of average or greater size, two newspapers were sold, one appealing to Democrats and the other to

FREDERICK DOUGLASS

Hero of the Partisan Press

Humble as I am in origin and despised as is the race to which I belong, I have lived to see the leading presses of the country, willing and ready to publish any argument or appeal in behalf of my race I am able to make.

—FREDERICK DOUGLASS, in *Douglass' Monthly* August 1863[31]

Frederick Douglass was born in slavery in Maryland sometime in 1817. The son of a white father and a slave mother, Douglass was one of the few slaves taught to read. He escaped slavery in 1838 and traveled to the North. Fearful of discovery and a return to slavery, Douglass initially worked at anonymous manual labor, but in 1841 he began to speak in public, selling subscriptions to an abolitionist newspaper. Douglass would travel from town to town, giving speeches about the true experience of slavery, to induce white listeners to sign on to the abolitionist cause as well as to purchase newspaper subscriptions.[32] For many whites in the audience, it was their first experience listening to a black man lecture. Douglass saw his first publication in a newspaper in 1842 when a letter of his appeared in the *Liberator*, the leading abolitionist paper of the day.[33] Over the next five years, his essays appeared with regularity throughout the abolitionist press, and eventually he was printed in more mainstream newspapers.

In 1847 Douglass boldly struck out on his own, founding the newspaper *The North Star*. Many of Douglass's friends in the abolitionist movement warned him against starting a newspaper because of the harm he might do to the cause of black equality if he failed or produced a paper that was of low quality. Many doubted that Douglass, lacking any formal education, would be up to the task of producing an entire paper. Refusing to listen, Douglass committed himself to editing and selling the *North Star*, and journalism became his main occupation for more than a decade. As he later observed, looking back on a long career in public life, "If I have at any time said or written that which is worth remembering, I must have said such things between 1848 and 1860, and my paper was the chronicle of most of what I said during that time."[34]

Douglass's words were electrifying and powerful, and he wrote on subjects as diverse as the Missouri Compromise, John

Brown's antislavery raid, and Lincoln's inauguration. In his day, Douglass was justly renowned as a spell-binding orator, but his newspaper was at least as important in conveying his words to a broader audience. The very fact that the newspaper was edited by a black man challenged racist theories about black inferiority. Douglass's essays are among the most compelling ever penned by an American, each one demonstrating black equality in a fashion tough to deny. Douglass could also be witty and biting in his satire, as when he observed of South Carolina's secession from the Union over slavery that the state preferred "to be a large piece of nothing to being any longer a small piece of something."[35]

Like many papers of the day, the *North Star* made no secret of its partisan and ideological beliefs. The paper's motto symbolized Douglass's revolutionary views about sex and race: "Right is of no sex—Truth is of no color—God is Father of us all, and all we are brethren." Unlike a modern newspaper, Douglass's paper had a mission statement that was bluntly partisan:

> to attack slavery in all its forms and aspects; advocate universal emancipation; exalt the standard of public morality; promote the moral and intellectual improvement of the Colored People; and hasten the day of Freedom to the Three Millions of our enslaved Fellow Countrymen."[36]

No reader could expect that this newspaper would cover the emerging conflict over slavery in a neutral manner.

Douglass ultimately ceased publication of his paper, now named the *Douglass Monthly*, in 1863 to directly participate in the struggle against the Confederacy. Although he never went back to journalism full time, his writings frequently appeared in leading newspapers and magazines until his death in 1896. Douglass's story reminds us of a day when journalism was more than an occupation; it was a way of persuading others to take part in a revolutionary struggle for freedom. Later social movements did not found many newspapers although some such as *Ms.* for women's rights launched magazines, and Christian conservatives have launched several television programs and networks. With these exceptions, modern social movements led by blacks, women, conservative Christians, and homosexuals have largely had to rely on an allegedly neutral media to get their message out to other Americans. There are no more Frederick

Douglasses because activists are not expected to also be journalists today, and professional journalists cannot be activists. A gay
journalist is expected to cover a gay rights issue the same way a
straight journalist would, just as a born-again conservative journalist is expected to cover abortion with strict neutrality. Douglass
would be unlikely to approve of this type of neutral journalism;
for him, journalism was a passionate and opinionated endeavor,
a way to change the world and the minds of his fellow citizens.

Frederick Douglass wrote three autobiographies during his
long life: *Narrative of the Life of Frederick Douglass, an American
Slave* (1845); *My Bondage and My Freedom* (1855); and *Life and
Times of Frederick Douglass* (1881). Several collections of his articles and speeches are also available.

Republicans (with the exception of the south, which was becoming a
one-party state during this era). Papers were still deeply involved in
party politics after 1860. But the next era in journalism had already
begun with publication of a small, inexpensive newspaper called the
New York Sun in 1834. The real reason the connection between parties
and newspapers was waning was the rise of the mass media.

THE DAWN OF THE MASS MEDIA: SENSATIONALISM
AND MUCKRAKING, 1860–1920

In 1834 Benjamin Day published a newspaper that he sold for a penny,
the *New York Sun*. Traditionally, newspapers had averaged six cents, a
sizable sum in those days for many members of the working class.
Consequently, those papers' readerships were tilted toward the
wealthier classes. The press was not exclusively aimed at the mon-
eyed elite prior to Day, but little effort was made to woo working-class
readers, in part because of higher rates of illiteracy among workers.
Day's was the first of many **penny press** papers that depended on
newsstand sales and advertising for revenue. The readership of papers
rapidly expanded, and the subject matter changed as well. Moreover,
the pressure from advertisers and readers to be bipartisan or nonpartisan became increasingly strong. Advertisers wanted their ads to
appeal to as many people as possible. If a newspaper was read only

by Republicans or only by Democrats, large numbers of potential customers would not be reached.

In the mass media era, journalism became a legitimate career as opposed to just being a part of publishing and printing. Prior to the penny press, most newspapers did not have large staffs, and the concept of a "reporter" who spends his days searching for news stories was largely unknown. With the increased competition for readers fought out daily on the newsstands where young boys would hawk the latest papers, editors would pay more money to reporters who could deliver the hottest and freshest news. The concept of a "scoop," in which one paper beats a rival to a story, dates from this period.

The new mass media also focused on sensational and lurid aspects of life. The *Sun* differed from its competitors in avoiding lengthy political debates about complex national topics. Why read yet another series of editorials on the long-running nineteenth-century debates about tariffs or the gold standard when you could pick up Day's paper and read about juicy scandals? As advertising became more lucrative, competition for newsstand sales accelerated. Whereas previously an editor might have been able to count on partisan loyalty to retain subscribers, consumers now were making decisions about which paper to buy based on each day's headlines. A paper that got the interview with the jilted lover of an accused murderer from a disastrous high-society marriage was guaranteed sales for as long as they could string the story out. Standards of propriety fell, and the lurid coverage that began in the penny press moved up into the more mainstream papers, which were competing for advertising revenues and sales in a newly aggressive manner. The sensationalist trend in American newspapers came to be called **yellow journalism** during this period due to the controversy between two media magnates, Joseph Pulitzer and William Randolph Hearst (see Box), for control over a cartoon featuring the "Yellow Kid." Locked in a bitter circulation struggle in New York, both publishers claimed the rights to the cartoon and splashed yellow blotches on their papers to advertise that the wildly popular Kid was inside.

Hearst and Pulitzer were also excellent examples of another trend evident during the mass media era: media conglomerates of unprecedented size. Newspapers became more national in their ownership and in their coverage. Two developments aided this. First, the telegraph made possible rapid transmission of news

WILLIAM RANDOLPH HEARST
Publishing Titan of the Mass Media Era

There were many giants of the new corporate era in newspapers, including Joseph Pulitzer and William Scripps. But none rose so fast or achieved such a large role in national politics as William Randolph Hearst. At his peak, Hearst controlled twenty-eight major newspapers and many of the most important magazines, as well as owning radio stations and movie studios. Unlike other media moguls, Hearst was never reluctant to force all of his papers to take the same editorial line on the issues of the day, particularly foreign policy. Almost half a century after his death, Hearst remains the archetype for a media magnate.

Hearst was born to wealth in 1863 and got his first chance to run a newspaper when his father received ownership of the *San Francisco Chronicle* to settle a gambling debt in 1887. Hearst admired Pulitzer's media empire and set out to challenge it. The bitterest competition between the two came in New York City, the largest media market in the country. Hearst purchased the *New York Journal* in 1895 to take on Pulitzer's far more successful *New York World*.

In the midst of this nationwide struggle for dominance between Hearst and Pulitzer, the United States was arguing with Spain over its colony, Cuba. Hearst set out to convince Americans that Spanish atrocities in Cuba mandated American intervention on behalf of human decency and democracy. Hearst papers compared Spanish actions in Cuba to a recent genocide against Armenians in Turkey, in which hundreds of thousands, perhaps millions, were killed.[37] Sometimes Hearst acted as if his newspapers were actually part of the government itself; he paid for his own congressional delegation of three senators and two congressmen to go to Cuba to examine Spanish rule. After hostilities with Spain began, Hearst even considered

across the country and eventually the world. The telegraph produced the first association of newspapers working together to gather information, the Associated Press. In addition, larger and larger corporations began to be formed in the newspaper business. When newspapers were barely profitable, and owned by or affiliated with privately sinking a ship in the Suez Canal to block the Spanish fleet.[38] How many media owners today would even contemplate spending vast sums of their fortune engaging in clandestine military operations with global implications?

Why was Hearst so favorable toward war with Spain? Hearst claimed it was his love of freedom and democracy that prompted his numerous editorials: "No American can be true to the freedom of his own country without feeling such a sympathy for Cuba as will urge him to interfere for its liberation."[39] But war was also very good for Hearst's business interests. A war, particularly a war that was sometimes called "Hearst's War," boosted circulation of his papers. Hearst did not shy away from claiming credit either; his main paper asked its readers on its masthead, "How do you like the *Journal*'s war?" War with Spain ultimately came after a mysterious explosion on the Maine, an American battleship docked at Cuba. Both Hearst and Pulitzer papers immediately suggested the explosion had been caused by the Spanish, without proof.

Hearst's power declined in the decades after World War I, in part because of his support for isolationism on the eve of World War II. But his legacy in journalism remains strong. Hearst, founder of the most dominant media empire of his age, was a man with tabloid values and an instinctive sense of how to sell stories to the broad public. As he said in his 1933 Editorial Guidelines for all his papers, "Don't print a lot of dull stuff that people are supposed to like but don't." At one point during Hearst's life, more than one in five Americans read one of his papers. Seldom has one man had as much influence over information in the United States.

There are several good books on William Randolph Hearst, including *Citizen Hearst* by W. A. Swanberg. The movie *Citizen Kane*, directed by Orson Welles, is a thinly veiled portrait of Hearst. Many critics consider it the finest American movie ever made.

local party officials, a national conglomeration of papers was impractical or undesirable. As America underwent the Industrial Revolution, in which fewer and larger companies controlled more and more of the economy in a number of sectors, media empires began to appear. The telegraph contributed to this as well because it made sharing content among papers simultaneously possible, which gave a cost incentive for putting several newspapers under one owner.

Pulitzer founded the first major media empire, eventually owning dozens of newspapers across the country as well as other media outlets. Pulitzer, a Hungarian immigrant who rose from poverty to the highest ranks of American wealth, got his first media job working for a German-language paper in St. Louis, which he eventually took over. He moved on to purchase a controlling interest in the *St. Louis Post Dispatch* and then the *New York World*. At this point, Pulitzer began his epic clash with Hearst, who had expanded his media holdings from San Francisco to New York. The two titans of journalism fought to establish dominance over New York and other media markets, and Pulitzer's earlier emphasis on accuracy in reporting fell by the wayside. Hearst and Pulitzer's papers competed to appeal to America's jingoism, or blind patriotism, as a conflict with Spain over Cuba began to simmer.

But the competition between Hearst and Pulitzer could also be fought over which paper was more sympathetic to the common man against organized interests. Even though the media were becoming far more corporate during this era, both Hearst and Pulitzer responded to the emerging trends of populism and progressivism by using their papers to expose public corruption and corporate abuses. Indeed, the Hearst and Pulitzer empires contributed to two growing trends in the journalism of the day: the growing professionalization of the occupation of journalism and the rise of muckraking. Pulitzer called for establishing schools of journalism and, after his death, endowed both the Columbia School of Journalism and the Pulitzer Prizes for excellence in journalism, still today the most prestigious awards in journalism. The next major era in media would seek to formalize the neutrality of the press and to enforce increasingly standard norms of conduct for reporters and editors. As Pulitzer put it in a 1904 article arguing for the rigorous academic study of journalism,

> Our Republic and its press will rise or fall together. An able, disinterested, public-spirited press, with trained intelligence to know the right and courage to do it, can preserve that public virtue without which popular government is a sham and a mockery. A cynical, mercenary, demagogic press will produce in time a people as base as itself. The power to mould the future of the Republic will be in the hands of the journalists of future generations.[40]

The emerging mass media contributed to the next major era in print journalism, the professional press era, because it promoted a larger, more profitable media.

THE MUCKRAKERS: 1900–1920

In its heyday, muckraking was hugely influential on American journalism, politics, and society. To "muckrake" even today means to expose political or corporate malfeasance through investigative reporting. Certainly journalists had been exposing such things long before 1900. But in the past, exposés tended to be directed in a partisan fashion. Democratic papers exposed Republican misdeeds, and vice versa. Moreover, the new muckraking journalist did not wait for a scandal to be brought to the newspaper by some political gossipmonger. Rather, **muckrakers** tended to engage in months' long investigations, often going undercover in an industry to get at the real truth. Muckrakers were in many ways a response to the Industrial Revolution. As more and more power over American life was given to corporations, there was a need for accountability, which muckrakers sought to provide.

Muckraking as a movement emerged primarily from the magazines of the day. Between 1903 and 1912 more than two thousand muckraking articles were published in magazines.[41] Many historians date the official start of the muckraking era from 1902, with the publication in *McClure* magazine of Ida Tarbell's exposé of Standard Oil's brutal monopoly practices. A host of other magazines quickly began to print lengthy accounts of various problems and scandals in industries from meatpacking to steel. Printing at least some investigative journalism seemed to be an easy way to boost sales of newspapers and magazines. Among the most famous muckrakers of the day were Lincoln Steffens, Upton Sinclair, Will Irwin, Ray Stannard Baker, and Ida Tarbell (see Box).

The term *muckraker* comes from a 1906 speech by President Theodore Roosevelt. The word had a long history in English and originally meant a tool farmers used to distribute manure for fertilizing. It was later used in preacher John Bunyan's work *Pilgrim's Progress* as a pejorative term for someone who focuses on earthly things too much. Before the speech in which Roosevelt named investigative journalists, in effect, distributors of manure, Roosevelt had shared their agenda of attacking corporate interests. The shift came because Roosevelt, like many Americans, started to believe that the investigative journalism of the muckrakers had begun to hurt the public good. Too much bad news about important economic and political interests was corrosive to patriotism because it would lead Americans to believe that their system was fundamentally

IDA TARBELL
Muckraking Pioneer

Ida Tarbell was a trailblazing woman journalist and an early hero of the muckraking movement. The only woman who was prominent among the muckrakers in their heyday, Tarbell was famous for her fearlessness in covering corporate misdeeds.

Born in Erie, Pennsylvania, in 1857, Tarbell was the only woman in the graduating class of 1880 at Allegheny College. She gave up her desire to become a scientist when she got a job as an assistant at a small magazine. After seven years largely spent fact-checking and editing the work of male writers, Tarbell became a freelancer in Paris, an extraordinarily bold move for a single woman in her day. As more and more of her articles were published, she became a regular in *McClure's*, a magazine largely focused on human interest stories. While in France, she wrote a biography of Napoleon, which was critically acclaimed, and followed it with a hugely successful biography of Lincoln. Both biographies were serialized in *McClure's*, boosting sales so much that she was made managing editor.[42] She eventually convinced the publisher that there was a story in the oil monopoly of John D. Rockefeller. Following months of painstaking research, the first installment of Tarbell's exposé on Standard Oil was published in 1902. Over the next two years, every issue of *McClure's* featured a new article on Rockefeller and the shady tactics and illegalities he had engaged in to win dominance in the oil market.

The series on Rockefeller was a smash success, and circulation rose astronomically. Tarbell's portrait of Rockefeller and his company was a dark warning to the American public that power was passing from the hands of the many into the hands of the few. Standard Oil was depicted as a dangerous octopus, a monopoly on the most vital resource in the economy that had unfairly enriched a small group of ruthless men. Rockefeller himself, one of the richest and most private men in U.S. history, was outraged that Tarbell had discovered so many of his secrets. Even more outrageous, Tarbell had managed to find dozens of photos of the reclusive and camera-shy Rockefeller, as well as his top associates.

Representatives of Rockefeller fought back against Tarbell, recognizing the damage she was doing to their company. Hired publicists pointed out that she may have been prejudiced against Rockefeller from the start because her father was an independent oil producer bankrupted by Standard Oil's draconian tactics, and her brother went on to work for one of the company's few remaining competitors. As one hired gun of the company wrote:

> Ida Tarbell . . . is an honest, bitter, talented, prejudiced and disappointed woman who wrote from her own point of view. And that view is from the ditch, where her father's wheelbarrow was landed by a Standard Oil tanker. . . . She shot from cover, and she shot to kill. Such literary bushwhackers should be answered shot for shot . . . (her) method of inky warfare is quite as unethical as the alleged tentacled-octopi policy which they attack.[43]

Tarbell ultimately saw Rockefeller's monopoly reined in by legislation passed in large part because of the sustained furor her exposé caused. The government forced Standard Oil to break up into many of the oil companies we know today, including Aamaco, Chevron, and Exxon.

Tarbell left *McClure's* in 1906 to found the *American,* a magazine owned and operated by some of the most radical and famous muckrakers of the day. Tarbell, who had previously been almost scientific in her careful attention to fact and documentation, began to adopt a far more aggressive and critical style. Her anguish over the mixture of extraordinary wealth and devastating poverty produced by the Industrial Revolution comes through quite clearly in this excerpt from her 1909 attack on the Pittsburgh steel industry:

> Justice takes a terrible revenge on those who thrive by privilege. She blinds their eyes until they no longer see human misery. . . . She makes . . . a generation of men and women who day by day can pass hundreds of tumbled down and filthy homes, in which the men and women who make their wealth live . . . who can know that deadly fevers and diseases which are preventable are wiping out hundreds of those who do their tasks. . . . Little children may die or grow up stunted and evil within their sight and no penny of their wealth, no hour of their leisure is given them. . . . Wealth which comes by Privilege kills.[44]

Tarbell wrote into her eighties although the height of her celebrity was gone by the 1920s. As the only prominent female journalist of the muckraking era, Tarbell's legacy holds up well against any of her male counterparts. Every time a journalistic exposé leads to an improvement in U.S. laws or to an investigation into corporate abuses or social problems, Tarbell's example is being followed.

All in a Day's Work, Ida Tarbell's autobiography, has recently been reissued and is an excellent source on her life and work. Kathleen Brady's *Ida Tarbell: Portrait of a Muckraker*, resuscitated interest in this pioneering journalist.

flawed. As Roosevelt put it, "men with muckrakes are often indispensable to the well-being of society, but only if they know when to stop raking the muck."

What provoked such anger from Roosevelt? The rhetoric of the muckrakers had begun to boil, and the targets were expanding from corporations to politicians. Novelist and journalist David Graham Phillips had written a scathing attack on both parties entitled "The Treason of the Senate." He documented how several prominent senators were pocketing vast sums of money from corporations in return for legislating on their behalf. The articles, which ran in *Cosmopolitan** in 1906, caused a nationwide furor, not only over corruption but also over how far journalists should go in attacking America's institutions. Phillips certainly pulled no punches in the first lines of his powerful piece:

> Treason is a strong word, but not too strong, rather too weak, to characterize the situation which the Senate is the eager, resourceful, indefatigable agent of interests as hostile to the American people as any invading army could be, and vastly more dangerous: interests that manipulate the prosperity produced by all, so that it heaps up riches for the few; interests whose growth and power can only mean the degradation of the people, of the educated into sycophants, of the masses toward serfdom.[45]

Phillips argued forcefully that the only way to stop the continuing corruption was the direct election of the Senate, and the series was instrumental in finally changing the Constitution to require such

---

*This is, in fact, the very same *Cosmopolitan* magazine that today focuses mainly on fashion, sex, and makeup.

elections.[46] However, the mixture of solid documentation with gossip and innuendo, all gathered with novelistic force, gave many critics of muckrakers ammunition to discredit the movement.

Muckraking as a movement never really ended, but the intensity, frequency, and popularity of the attacks on business and government waned. An added strain on the muckraking movement was the increasing sophistication of corporate advertisers. They simply did not see a need to support magazines that achieved their circulation by trashing other corporations. Another explanation is that the economy of the 1920s was booming, and the average income was steadily increasing. Muckraking journalism, then and today, is most popular with readers when there is anger among the population, particularly about the economy.

KEY TERMS AND PEOPLE

Alien and Sedition Acts
First Amendment
house organ
muckrakers
Tom Paine

partisan press
penny press
yellow journalism
John Peter Zenger

DISCUSSION QUESTIONS

1. Of the eras discussed so far, which seems most similar to current U.S. journalism? What elements of each do you see in the United States today?
2. Would you prefer a system like the partisan press era, in which newspapers and television stations explicitly adopt a partisan viewpoint?
3. Some would say that the media became more sensationalistic because they became less elitist. In other words, to attract new readers who were less educated than the elite, the penny press had to cover more lurid and scandalous topics. Do you agree? Is this true today?
4. Do you know any modern journalists you would call "muckrakers"?
5. Neil Postman might observe that the great muckrakers, such as Ida Tarbell, wrote their exposés in complex accounts, sometimes involving hundreds of pages. Today muckraking exposés on

television have to be fully argued in just a few minutes. However, Walter Benjamin believed that new technology would show the viewer hidden aspects of life, including exploitation by corporations. This should make today's muckrakers more powerful, not less, if they can get compelling images of wrongdoing onto television. Who do you think is more correct about modern muckraking?

ADDITIONAL RESOURCES

Each of the journalist profiles contains a guide to sources on those individuals that typify their era.

NOTES

1. George Henry Payne, *History of Journalism in the United States* (Westport, CT: Greenwood, 1970), 3–6.
2. William David Sloan and Julie Hedgepeth Williams, *The Early American Press 1690–1783* (Westport, CT: Greenwood, 1994), 205–6.
3. Jeffrey L. Pasley, *The Tyranny of Printers: Newspaper Politics in the Early American Republic* (Charlottesville, VA: University Press of Virginia, 2001), 8–9.
4. Payne, *History of Journalism,* 67.
5. Sloan and Williams, *The Early American Press,* 78.
6. William Lowell Putnam, *John Peter Zenger and the Fundamental Freedom* (Jefferson, NC: McFarland, 1997), 11–12.
7. Quoted in Doug Linder, "The Trial of John Peter Zenger: An Account," Famous Trials Web site, 2001. www.law.umkc.edu/faculty/projects/ftrials/zenger/zengeraccount/html
8. Payne, *History of Journalism,* 52.
9. Ibid., 55.
10. Payne, *History of Journalism,* 32–33.
11. Willi Paul Adams, "The Colonial German-Language Press and the American Revolution." In *The Press and the American Revolution,* Bernard Bailyn and John B. Hench, eds. (Worcester, MA: American Antiquarian Society, 1980), 218–19.
12. Sloan, *The Early American Press,* 208.
13. Pasley, *The Tyranny,* 33.

14. Payne, *The Early American Press,* 99.
15. Ibid., 101–3.
16. Pasley, *The Tyranny,* 34.
17. Stephen Botein, "Printers and the American Revolution." In *The Press and the American Revolution,* Bernard Bailyn and John B. Hench, eds. (Worcester, MA: American Antiquarian Society, 1980), 32.
18. Pasley, *The Tyranny,* 41.
19. Jack Fruchtman, *Tom Paine: The Apostle of Freedom* (New York: Four Walls Press, 1996), 16.
20. Sloan and Williams, *The Early American Press,* 174.
21. Pasley, *The Tyranny,* 43.
22. Ibid., 3, 9.
23. Ibid., 11–13.
24. Ibid., 106.
25. Ibid., 172.
26. John Tebbel, *The Compact History of the American Newspaper* (New York: Hawthorne, 1963), 67–68.
27. Pasley, *The Tyranny,* 201.
28. Tebbel, *Compact History,* 81.
29. Ibid., p. 87.
30. Larry J. Sabato, *Feeding Frenzy* (New York: Free Press, 1991), 27.
31. Frederick Douglass, *The Life and Writings of Frederick Douglass, Vol III.* Philip S. Foner, ed. (New York: International Publishers, 1952), 375.
32. Frederick Douglass, *Life and Times of Frederick Douglass* (London: Collier, 1962), 217. (Orig. pub. 1892.)
33. Vernon Loggins, "Writings of the Leading Negro Antislavery Agents, 1840–1865." In *Critical Essays on Frederick Douglass,* William L. Andrew, ed. (Boston: G. K. Hall, 1991), 42–43. (Orig. pub. 1932.)
34. Quoted in Loggins, "Writings," 50.
35. Douglass, *Life and Writings,* 57.
36. Loggins, "Writings," 51.
37. Ian Mugridge, *The View from Xanadu: William Randolph Hearst and United States Foreign Policy* (Buffalo: McGill—Queen's University Press, 1995), 9.
38. Ibid., 16.
39. Ibid., 10.
40. www.pulitzer.org
41. David M. Chalmers, *The Social and Political Ideas of the Muckrakers* (New York: Citadel, 1964), quoted in *More than a Muckraker,*

Robert C. Kochersberger Jr., ed. (Knoxville, TN: University of Tennessee Press, 1994,) xxv.

42. Kathleen Brady, *Ida Tarbell: Portrait of a Muckraker* (New York: Seaview, 1984), 96–122.

43. Elbert Hubbard, *The Standard Oil Company* (East Aurora, NY: Roycroft Shop, 1910), 13–14, quoted in Kochersberger, *More than a Muckraker*, 66.

44. Kochersberger, *More than a Muckraker*, 90.

45. David Graham Phillips, *The Treason of the Senate*. George E. Mowry and Judson A. Grenier, eds. (Chicago: Quadrangle Books, 1964).

46. Abe C. Ravitz, *David Graham Phillips* (New York: Twayne, 1966).

CHAPTER 5

Journalism Goes
Electronic... and Corporate

Journalism was forever changed by the invention of radio and television. Even though print journalism remained the dominant form of media expression through most of the twentieth century, print journalism was increasingly affected by the growth of electronic media. Electronic journalism achieved greater and greater prominence, and by the end of the twentieth century television and the Internet were changing the content, norms, and ethics of all journalism.

THE PROFESSIONAL ERA: 1920–1972

During the professional era, journalism became both a widely studied academic topic and a profession that one trained for rather than simply learned on the job. This change is far more radical than it might at first appear. In becoming a true profession, journalism forever left behind the grubby roots it had in printing. The first journalists in America were typically working-class printers with little formal education. Journalism was a blue-collar profession for the most part, and many wealthy or highly educated young people were deterred from pursuing it. This social barrier lessened during the course of the nineteenth century, but the divide between journalism and elite professions such as medicine and law was still immense in 1920. Few journalists had advanced degrees, and most were without college educations. When a young Ernest Hemingway (later a Nobel Prize–winning novelist) became a junior reporter at the *Kansas City Star* after World War I, he had only a high school diploma and a love of language.

The creation of schools of journalism encouraged the development of rigid norms of conduct for the profession. It also led to greater respect and higher salaries. The most important change in journalism was separating the editorial pages from the rest of the paper. Readers gradually became accustomed to reading opinionated pieces in one section of the paper and "objective" news in the rest of the paper. Reporters were encouraged to keep their opinions out of the news. Publishers and editors had opinions; reporters were supposed to deal in facts. Independent columnists also emerged during this period. Previously, a newspaper might have run occasional pieces by authors who disagreed with the publisher or editor. But it was now possible for a reader of a paper to get three or four different viewpoints on the same issue in a single day. The paper's editorial might reflect one position, two columnists might take another, and the news coverage of the reporters might include yet another way of looking at the issue. During the presidency of Thomas Jefferson, it was said that you could know the attitude of the owners of any newspaper just by looking at what was on the front page. A paper that supported the president might not cover a presidential scandal at all, whereas one that opposed him might never write a positive word about a presidential initiative. Even during the professional era, some papers did not successfully separate their editorial views from their news coverage, but the norm was to at least make the attempt.

Journalistic writing became more standardized during this period. Newspapers wrote style manuals emphasizing certain common features. The **pyramid style of news writing** was taught to generations of reporters. In pyramid style the most important information is given first so the reader gets the "who, what, where, when" information in the first couple of sentences. The news story is written to make sense no matter how much an editor removes from the end of the piece. This was initially done because early telegraph transmissions were often unexpectedly truncated. If a reporter were covering a dramatic political event such as a riot or a battle and the outcome was left to the last few paragraphs—like the ending of a short story—the editor might not be able to run any story until the transmission was recovered.

The pyramid style persisted long after the telegraph ceased to be a vital part of the news business because it made the job of editing much more efficient and rapid. A reporter usually doesn't know how much space is available in the newspaper for each day's story.

Late breaking news of greater importance can mean that editors have to make sudden cuts. The pyramid style allows editing to be made at the very last minute. The pyramid style also rewards those who read only the headline and first few paragraphs of a story.

The pyramid style was one of the skills taught to aspiring journalists in the burgeoning academic field of journalism. Journalistic ethics were also formalized, and the boundaries of the profession began to be established. Journalism, much like law and medicine, developed its own jargon and vocabulary. A specialized and universal vocabulary, along with other norms, enabled journalists to move from paper to paper with greater ease.

Radio and television journalism also followed some of these guidelines. Given that most early electronic journalists began their careers as newspaper reporters, this is not surprising. By the closing years of this era, professionalization was becoming the norm in radio and television as well. Schools of broadcasting taught specialized courses in electronic journalism. Television and radio also developed their own norms, jargon, and style manuals. Roles in television journalism became more fixed and universal, such as station manager, news director, reporter, and anchor.

What was most distinctive about radio and television journalism during this period was the absence of bluntly partisan and editorial components. Radio and television were seen as public utilities whose limited bandwidth belonged in part to the public as well as to the owners. As discussed in Chapter 6, the legal environment of the electronic media has always been different, and thus there was less advocacy and opinion in the news coverage. The format of radio and television seemed to prevent much independent opinion. A thirty-minute radio broadcast simply has less room for two or three separate viewpoints on a given news subject. Thus, even as newspapers were beginning to adopt objectivity as a goal on the news page, and greater and greater diversity of opinion on the editorial page, their emerging electronic competitors often tried to avoid opinion and controversy.

Journalism's increasing professionalization took place as the size and profitability of media corporations continued to rise. The mass media era had seen the first truly national media corporations; during the twentieth century, this process accelerated. The electronic media played a role in exacerbating this trend. Radio and television stations and networks required much larger capital outlays than newspapers and were perceived as being much riskier. Fortunes

ARCHETYPE OF THE PROFESSIONAL ERA
Walter Lippmann, Journalist of the American Century

> For the newspaper is in all literalness the bible of democracy, the book out of which a people determines its conduct. . . . Now the power to determine each day what shall seem important and what shall be neglected is a power unlike any that has been exercised since the Pope lost his hold on the secular mind.[1]

For many decades Walter Lippmann was the most influential journalist in the United States, and he witnessed and participated in many of the vital changes in journalism during the twentieth century.

Several of his Harvard professors mourned when the young Lippmann chose journalism over academia or law because they considered it beneath a man of Lippmann's enormous talents. But Lippmann was part of the generation that treated journalism with a new respect. Indeed, one of his early causes was to campaign for professional training for journalists. Lippmann felt that most current journalists were "untrained accidental witnesses" and that journalism was "an underpaid, insecure, anonymous form of drudgery, conducted on catch-as-catch-can principles."[2] He wanted universities to train reporters to be "patient and fearless men of science."[3]

Lippmann wrote those words in 1919, when he was only thirty years old. What gave such a young man the credibility to make grand calls for change in his profession? By the age of thirty Lippmann had had a stunning career in journalism and politics. Upon graduating from Harvard, he worked as a reporter and then as an investigator for one of the leading muckrakers of the day, Lincoln Steffens. Their work together helped lead to the foundation of the Federal Reserve.[4] His first book, *A Preface to Politics,* was published to widespread acclaim when he was only twenty-four. On the strength of that book, he was invited to cofound the *New Republic,* which quickly became one of the most important magazines in the nation and is still published today.

Through his writings, Lippmann came to the attention first of former President Teddy Roosevelt and later President Woodrow

Wilson. He would go on to write speeches for and give advice to both men. Many observers read the *New Republic* to find out what President Wilson would do next because there was presumed to be such a close association between Lippmann's thoughts and Wilson's actions. Among Lippmann's main causes was to bring the United States into World War I on the side of Britain and France. When Wilson finally followed Lippmann and led America into war, Lippmann briefly gave up journalism to help Wilson's administration craft plans for a just peace. Lippmann was a main author of Wilson's famous Fourteen Points that helped end the war.

Lippmann also produced propaganda for the military during the war, an experience that forever changed how he felt about journalism. Lippmann's next book, *Public Opinion*, is still read for its keen insights into how politics is shaped by shifting public moods and how the press contribute to those moods. Citizens do not have the time nor the inclination to fully inform themselves about issues: they rely on the media to create a "pseudoenvironment" in which facts are seldom objectively presented. Truth is far too often the victim of propaganda, and most citizens never notice. Lippmann believed the only hope for democracy was for a special class of trained insiders to sift through the complexity of political realities and report back to the people.[5]

After the war, Lippmann returned to journalism, serving for six years at the helm of the editorial page at a leading newspaper and going on to become a nationally syndicated columnist. Although he never again worked directly in politics, he remained an insider, privy to special knowledge because of his access. He was also never afraid to inject himself into a political situation, offering advice to many presidents and their Cabinets.

By 1940 Lippmann was the most widely read columnist in America. So great was his influence that when the British desperately needed U.S. assistance as the Germans defeated France, Britain's ambassador to the United States turned to Lippmann. Together they devised the Lend-Lease plan, in which the United States would give Britain naval destroyers in return for use of British bases. Lippmann not only designed the plan, he helped create public support for it by secretly writing a speech in favor of it to be delivered by a war hero.[6] Today the program is recognized by historians as a key turning point in the war against the Nazis; without Lippmann's clandestine intervention, it is possible the British would have capitulated to or compromised with Germany in 1940–1941.

Lippmann's twice-weekly columns continued into the 1960s. At the very end of his career, he ventured into television commentary, and his occasional programs on CBS were widely watched. It is unlikely that Lippmann's career will be duplicated any time soon. Professional norms today do not permit journalists to intervene in politics as frequently or as casually as Lippmann did and still remain journalists. Professionals are expected to belong entirely to journalism or politics, although they can move between the two occupations. George Stephanopoulos went from being a top White House aide to Bill Clinton to hosting ABC's *This Week*. More recently, President Bush selected Fox News host Tony Snow as his press secretary. This was Snow's fourth change of sides; he had started as a journalist, worked as a speechwriter in the first Bush White House, and then gone back to journalism. While some criticize this revolving door between reporting on politics and practicing politics, Lippmann's habit of advising the politicians he reported on would probably be more objectionable today.

The definitive biography of Lippmann is by Ronald Steel, *Walter Lippmann and the American Century*. Among Lippmann's ten books, the most important remains *Public Opinion*. Several collections of his columns are also available at most good libraries.

were won and lost on Wall Street as radio and television ventures flourished or foundered. For the first time, nonmedia conglomerates began to see media companies as profitable acquisitions. Although Hearst and Pulitzer had gotten very rich running media empires, they remained newspapermen to the day they died, and their companies remained centered around journalism. Television, in particular, opened the door to the integration of media companies into larger corporations in which journalism was only a fraction of the company's holdings. The implications of this were not fully realized for decades, but the seeds were planted during this era.

Among the other developments in journalism during this period was the rise of **access journalism.** This can be seen as a coping strategy by politicians overwhelmed by the new power of the media. Visionaries such as H. L. Mencken and **Walter Lippmann** (see Box) had seen in the early twentieth century that the alliance between political parties and newspapers was breaking down. The vanishing of the partisan press tradition, in which a politician knew which papers were for and which were against him, was disorienting for many politicians. Muckraking, in which politicians were the direct targets of media hostility that seemed to follow no party or consistency, was even more alarming. Now journalism, armed with its new status and the power of radio and television, seemed to be an even greater threat to politicians. In response, politicians began to use access as a weapon to maintain their power over the media.

Perhaps the most important pioneer of this technique was President Franklin Roosevelt. Roosevelt understood journalism's new norms. Journalism was a business that ran on certain rules, such as the need for scoops. Politicians "made" news, which was a commodity that journalists "sold" to their editors to receive their salaries. Fresh news was more valuable than old news. News that was exclusive to one reporter was even more treasured. Roosevelt cultivated particular journalists by doling out exclusives or interviews. A reporter was then expected to portray Roosevelt in a favorable light. Friendly journalists were granted access, which gave them the reputation as "in the know" and connected. Journalists who were perceived as hostile by the Roosevelt White House could be frozen out. If a newspaper's Washington correspondent was always a day behind other journalists and never got any scoops, he might well lose his job. Access journalism created a symbiotic relationship between individual reporters and the politicians they covered. Republican publishers sometimes lamented that their reporters were simply charmed by Roosevelt's sunny personality. But it was also his deft management of access that led to more favorable stories.

A professional journalist was expected to get close to his subject, to uncover the real truth, and if the subject was politics, this meant being on a first name basis with politicians. This was true at the municipal and state level as well as at the national level. The tight relationship between entire newspapers and political parties was sometimes replaced by an even tighter relationship between specific reporters and specific politicians. Getting "access" could evolve into becoming corrupt; payoffs to reporters from corporations and politicians were not unknown during this era.[7] Even when payoffs were not involved, many reporters ended up working as press secretaries for the politicians they had previously covered so closely. Although the professional norm of objectivity was increasingly widespread, politicians and corporations found other ways to get favorable coverage from specific media outlets.

Roosevelt may have been the first king of access journalism, but the technique reached its apotheosis with the presidency of John Kennedy. Kennedy's narrow victory in the 1960 presidential election may be attributed to his cultivation of the press. His opponent, Vice President Richard Nixon, had a hostile relationship with the media and seldom gave reporters covering his campaign access to him or scoops on his latest policy proposals. Kennedy, by contrast, wooed the press.[8] Perhaps because he had worked briefly as a reporter for Hearst International, Kennedy understood how the press operated in a way Nixon never would. Kennedy enjoyed joking and arguing with the press, both in private and in his entertaining press conferences. He adroitly allocated access to friendly reporters and guided his White House and Cabinet secretaries to reward them with scoops. One of Kennedy's slyest techniques for getting reporters to side with him was to make extremely risky and politically unwise statements to them privately. Without establishing that a conversation was off the record, Kennedy would say something so scandalous about an issue or another politician that the reporter felt admitted into Kennedy's circle of intimates.[9] By drawing the media in, Kennedy probably got more favorable coverage.

Professional journalism also meant that most reporters did not report on the personal lives of politicians. During the partisan press era, politicians were investigated quite extensively by writers working for opposition papers. Thomas Jefferson, Andrew Jackson, Alexander Hamilton, and Abraham Lincoln found that their private lives were subjected to scurrilous and degrading speculation in the media. In the professional era, however, journalists tended not to report on personal scandals unless there was an arrest or official investigation, or if another politician of some stature brought up the matter. Politicians could appear drunk in public or hide their medical status from the public with the active cooperation of journalists.

The degree to which the media collaborated in hiding important truths from the public is inconceivable in today's journalistic environment. From 1932 to 1945, the press corps hid from the public the truly crippling nature of Roosevelt's polio. Roosevelt was unable to walk from early middle age and spent the remaining decades of his life almost entirely in a wheelchair. He traveled the country in a long convertible car but never got out to greet the crowds who gathered to see their president. When necessary, he gave the appearance of walking by leaning on assistants and using stiff leg braces. Journalists were well aware that he was a cripple, but they never reported the extent of his handicap. Indeed, thousands of press photos of FDR were taken during his lifetime, but only three show him in a wheelchair, even though that was where he spent more than 95 percent of his waking hours. Perhaps more troubling was that during his last campaign for the presidency in 1944 it was clear to journalists who got close to him that he was gravely weakened and probably near death, but they never told the American people that they were reelecting a man unlikely to serve out his term (in fact, he died a few months after his inauguration).[10]

Professional journalists felt it was beneath them to report on the personal lives of politicians. Congressmen who put their beautiful mistresses on the public payroll were a subject of much jocularity among reporters, but little of this made it into their newspaper reporting. In 1956 presidential candidate Estes Kefauver, known to many reporters as a brilliant, iconoclastic senator, was also known by many to be a drunk who sometimes groped women when he was under the influence.[11] The reluctance to report on philandering and harassing politicians was in part a product of the all-male nature of the press corps. No other politician benefited as much from this aspect of the era than did John Kennedy. Reporters were well aware of his reckless infidelities, although the extent of it as well as his drug use, secret health problems, and affair with a Mafia don's mistress would come out only many years after his death. But as for the president's infidelities, many members of the media knew and chose not to cover the story. At one point, the landlord of a young paramour of Kennedy's paraded in front of the White House with a sign implicating the president in adultery and offering photographic evidence to any journalist who wanted it. One reporter took the pictures to his editor and was told, "no story there."[12] It is difficult to imagine a journalist today refusing to run photographic evidence of ongoing marital infidelity committed by a sitting president.

Professional journalism which put access over accuracy, was perhaps inherently unstable. If a free press is a requirement for a healthy republic, then a press that was too supine and too willing to be wooed by crafty politicians was unhealthy. The twin crises of

Watergate and Vietnam would lead to the development of a new type of journalism in which reporters should not be seduced or cowed by politicians.

RADIO: THE IGNORED MEDIUM IN POLITICAL NEWS?

Radio emerged during the professional era as an exciting new medium for political news. Journalists such as Edward Murrow, who broadcast from London during the intense German bombings of 1940–1941, became household names. Radical political figures such as Father Coughlin, a neofascist Catholic priest, used radio to make their views sound more acceptable to the masses. Politicians like FDR used radio to speak directly to the people in his famous "fireside chats." For both political figures and journalists, radio made their voices and their personalities hits with the public.

So why doesn't radio merit an era all its own? Radio was influential in certain specific circumstances, but it never became the dominant medium for political information. During the era of radio's greatest popularity, the major newspapers were still more influential in setting the nation's agenda. Radio's importance was as a precursor to television. The warm friendliness that made FDR popular over the radio signaled that electronic media would personalize politics in ways that print media had never done.

In the late 1980s and on through the current era, radio has reemerged as a vital "new" media, a rather odd term for a technology that is significantly older than television. Talk radio with hosts such as Rush Limbaugh, Sean Hannity, and Laura Ingraham have become popular ways for conservatives to present their take on the day's news. Initially they began with a rebel aesthetic, believing that the mainstream media were inherently liberal and unwelcoming to their views. Thus conservatives were forced to go to talk radio. After 2002, when Republicans gained control over all three branches of government and at least one major network, and with the top-ranked cable news programs reliably conservative, the idea of right-wing talk radio hosts as dangerous dissenters from a liberal orthodoxy is rather ridiculous.

In 2004–2005 a few less conservative national voices began to be heard on radio. First, syndicated and wildly popular radio talker Howard Stern endorsed John Kerry for president. Stern, who is more of a libertarian (if not a libertine) than a liberal, was angry at the Bush administration for cracking down on obscenity and did not really endorse Kerry's views on many issues. Second, Air America, an avowedly liberal radio network, began to attract listeners. Neither Stern nor Air America as yet outweigh the national market share of Rush Limbaugh, but they represent a crack in the monolithic conservative nature of talk radio.

WATCHDOG JOURNALISM: 1973–1991

The close relationship between journalists and politicians that characterized the professional era produced a backlash in the 1970s: watchdog journalism. The roots of this movement came earlier though. One of the key causes of watchdog journalism was the Vietnam War. In 1964 Lyndon Johnson told Congress and the nation that naval forces of North Vietnam had attacked U.S. ships. The American media reported the incident with much less skepticism than did foreign correspondents, some of whom doubted that anything had happened at all. However, a popular incumbent president, sailing toward reelection, convinced the American media to report his version of a murky event almost without question. Based in part on the media's unwillingness to question the president, Congress gave Johnson the authorization to expand the war in Vietnam.

Throughout the Vietnam War, Johnson worked hard to maintain the support of the media in general and of certain powerful columnists and reporters in particular. When Saigon fell to the victorious communists in 1975, there were many who blamed Johnson and other politicians for misleading the public into America's greatest defeat. At the same time, many journalists felt a sense of personal responsibility for failing to effectively investigate the early claims of the Johnson administration and the later conduct of the war. We know now that LBJ himself doubted that there was an attack by North Vietnam on U.S. forces at the onset of the Vietnam conflict. The skeptical European media got the story right while the professional U.S. media accepted what they were given by the president.

Just as the Vietnam War was winding down in tragedy and disappointment, America's greatest constitutional crisis since the Civil War caused a sea change in journalistic attitudes. **Carl Bernstein** and **Bob Woodward,** two junior reporters at the *Washington Post* (see Box), almost single-handedly exposed how Nixon's aides had engaged in

ARCHETYPE OF THE WATCHDOG ERA

Bob Woodward

Bob Woodward, of Wheaton, Illinois, graduated Yale in 1965 and then spent five years in the Navy. He began his journalistic career on a small paper in suburban Maryland in 1970 and was hired by the *Washington Post* in 1971 to cover local news. When he broke the Watergate story, Woodward had been a journalist for less than two years. Within a year, Woodward was one of the most famous reporters in the United States because of a front page story in the *Washington Post* that began:

> One of the five men arrested early Saturday in the attempt to bug the Democratic National Committee headquarters is the salaried security coordinator for President Nixon's reelection committee.[13]

For many months the *Post* reported on the emerging Watergate scandal, facing considerable derision from the very popular and powerful Nixon White House. Most of the rest of the media initially treated the Watergate break-in as a minor political caper, unconnected to the White House. As Woodward and Bernstein continued to dig throughout 1972, 1973, and 1974, their reporting uncovered a host of illegal activities by agents linked to the White House, including spying on Democratic politicians and their families, compiling dossiers on their personal lives, sabotaging Democratic campaign events, infiltrating radical groups and encouraging them to engage in illegal acts, raising illegal campaign funds, and many other acts of political skullduggery.[14] Eventually, when Nixon was forced to resign in August of 1974, many gave the credit for pushing him out to Woodward and Bernstein.

The stories that exposed the truth about Watergate involved the controversial use of an unnamed source, identified by the reporters as "Deep Throat." The use of unnamed sources requires the readers to trust that the reporters have correctly assessed the credibility and integrity of their sources. As detailed in their bestseller *All the President's Men,* Woodward and Bernstein did not have the entire story handed to them by one secret source; rather, along with other reporters working at the *Post* and other papers, they used public documents, court proceedings, and hundreds of interviews to establish the tawdry truth. Still, the single most important break in their investigation was Woodward's chance meeting a few years before Watergate with Mark Felt, a top FBI official. Felt became "Deep Throat" when he felt that the FBI was being used to help Nixon cover up Watergate crimes. When Felt finally identified himself as Woodward's source in the summer of 2005, the greatest secret of late twentieth-century political journalism was finally revealed, and a new round of questions about the propriety of leaking and using anonymous sources began. Some conservatives pointed out that Felt's true motivation in bringing Nixon down may actually have been his resentment in not being selected to run the FBI. Should reporters assess the motives of anonymous sources as well as the quality of the information given?

Breaking the Watergate story put Woodward into the first rank of journalists. Since 1979 he has been an editor at the *Post* while continuing to break stories as a reporter. Moreover, he is the only living author to have eight nonfiction books hit number one in sales. Among his many books are *The Commanders,* on the first Persian Gulf War, and *The Maestro,* on Alan Greenspan and the Federal Reserve. The Woodward interview technique, as critically described by Clinton aide George Stephanopoulos, involves talking to as many top officials as possible and looking for discrepancies and disagreements in their accounts of meetings and controversies.[15] Why do they talk to Woodward, given his reputation for exposing misdeeds, mistakes, and secrets? Often, they believe they can guide the story, or "spin" Woodward's coverage, whereas if they remain silent, their political rivals will be the ones guiding the story. The portrait of the disarray and chaos within Clinton's White House was so devastating that Clinton remained furious at Stephanopoulos and others for exposing so much about his White House.

Bush at War, a recent book by Woodward that covered the White House from 9/11 to the end of the initial phase of the Afghan war, faced even more criticism because it was so reliant on insider accounts. The Bush White House, with its extraordinary message discipline, may have been able to spin Woodward's book in Bush's favor. For some it seemed that the quintessential watchdog journalist had come to resemble the access journalists of old, trading favorable coverage for inside information. Perhaps in response to such criticism, Woodward's next book, *Plan of Attack,* which covered the Iraq War from inception through its first months, was much more balanced in its treatment of the president.

a pattern of criminal conduct, which Nixon certainly helped cover up and probably approved. But **Watergate** was bigger than the exposure of the scandal itself. Part of what was discovered during the course of the investigation was that the Nixon White House had an "enemies list" on which journalists were very prominent. This seemed to represent the dark underside of access journalism; those who didn't play the game, and reported skeptically or negatively about Nixon, would not just be denied scoops. They might face unspecified government actions from wiretapping to IRS auditing. Once the tide turned, however, it became a badge of honor among Washington journalists that they were on Nixon's enemies list.

Watergate changed the heroes of journalists and aspiring reporters. The icon of the professional journalism era was Walter Lippmann, a man on a first name basis with presidents, senators, Cabinet secretaries, and foreign kings and prime ministers. The new icons were the shaggy haired duo, Woodward and Bernstein. Far from being wooed by presidents, the new journalists took an instinctively hostile or at least doubting attitude toward nearly everything politicians said. Access journalists who had promised they would deliver the truth by getting close to the men in power now seemed to be collaborators with the powerful to prevent truth from being exposed.

In some ways, the watchdog journalism era was a return to muckraking values. The difference was that watchdog journalism tended not to focus on broad social and corporate questions but on specific statements and actions by politicians. Candidates for president, in particular, were subjected to intense scrutiny. The example of Nixon seemed instructive. Nixon's flaws were seen by some to be innate to his personal character.[16] Why hadn't journalists done a better job of reporting the flaws in his psychology? Journalists began to dig ever deeper into the character and background of presidential candidates. Eventually, the focus of journalists turned to sexual matters, which previously had been largely off limits. In 1987 questions about Senator Gary Hart's infidelity to his wife forced him out of the race for the Democratic presidential nomination, which he was leading at the time. This was a turning point in watchdog journalism. The line between public and private conduct eroded entirely when a reputable journalist asked a presidential candidate at a press conference if he had ever in his life committed adultery.

Following Hart's withdrawal, the *New York Times* sent a questionnaire to all the remaining candidates requesting the following:

complete medical records, academic transcripts from high school and college, employment files, tax returns (state and federal) for the preceding five years, birth certificate,* marriage and driver's licenses, accounts of any civil or criminal cases involving the candidate, and access to all FBI and law enforcement files. Candidates were also asked to provide a list of their closest friends in high school and college, plus current friends, business associates, advisers, and fundraisers.[17] The request for raw FBI files was particularly disturbing because they often include hearsay and unsubstantiated allegations. Although public outcry forced the *Times* to withdraw the request, no candidate for president can expect that any item from that list will remain private. Even the refusal to provide such information can create a story. The change in the norms of American journalism has been breathtakingly rapid. In 1967 President Johnson appeared drunk in front of several reporters, and this was never reported. In 2007, if a candidate were rumored to have been publicly drunk years before entering politics, it would be reported and discussed because it might indicate a problem with alcohol that citizens should know about.

It was during the watchdog era of journalism that television replaced newspapers as the main source of information for most Americans. One reason for this transformation was that television did a better job of covering the personal characteristics of politicians than newspapers did. When the focus of journalism was on the issues of the day, newspapers were better suited to convey their complexity. When the focus became the men and women in government, their backgrounds and character, this played to television's strengths. It is also possible, of course, that the focus of journalism changed because of the growing power of television. It was television, more than any other medium, that led the way into the next era of journalism: infotainment.

THE RISE OF THE NEW JOURNALISM

The standardized format of journalism, so recently established in the professional era, came under sustained attack during the watchdog era. The **new journalism** emerged in the 1960s as a rebellion

---

*Among the minor matters that consumed the media in 1987 and 1988 was that Hart had changed his name and might have lied about his age. Since then, a surprising number of revelations have come out from journalists investigating birth certificates, including the existence of unknown close relatives in the background of presidential candidates Bill Clinton and Wesley Clark.

against the style and content of mainstream journalism. Rather than attempting to neutrally observe events, new journalists entered into the event and made their very personal opinions and actions part of the story. Some utilized styles more appropriate to novels and short stories, including wild speculation and biting satire amidst serious reporting. Writers such as Terry Southern, Tom Wolfe, Hunter S. Thompson, Norman Mailer, and other new journalists tended to write for magazines rather than newspapers, and even at the height of their popularity their work seldom appeared in influential newspapers.

But new journalism had, and continues to have, an influence on mainstream print journalism. If you have ever read a news story in which the reporter's personality or role in the story comes through, that's an example of new journalism. New journalism interacted quite well with the increased emphasis on character and personal qualities. Mainstream journalists looked for clever, novelistic details to capture the character of a politician. New journalism's personalized reporting also began to appear on television news, with quirky segments in which reporters took an active role in investigations of corporate fraud or other malfeasance.

THE ERA OF INFOTAINMENT: 1992–PRESENT

A presidential candidate, hounded by a watchdog media about allegations of marital infidelity and drug use, appears on a late night talk show and plays the saxophone. One could find many events to date the ascendance of infotainment journalism, but surely the appearance of candidate Bill Clinton on the Arsenio Hall late night show during the 1992 campaign qualifies as a seminal moment. Wearing hip shades, Clinton played a competent sax solo as Hall's young audience whooped in support. It is difficult to picture Harry Truman or Franklin Roosevelt or most previous presidents taking part in such an event.*

---

*To be sure, candidate Richard Nixon in the 1960s did appear on the satirical program *Laugh In,* which was very similar to the modern *Saturday Night Live.* But his appearance was extremely brief, and it was part of an effort by Nixon's campaign to convince Americans that the notoriously stiff and unpersonable Nixon was much more fun than they thought. Today these appearances have become standard fare, whereas the Nixon appearance was a risky and unusual gambit.

Infotainment journalism describes a period in which the lines between entertainment and journalism blur, when celebrity gossip and political reporting begin to resemble one another. The line between late night talk-show host and journalist begins to fray as well. Who, in fact, is a journalist in the infotainment era? Recall that the professional era began to require advanced degrees for journalists at elite media outlets. Clearly, the anchor of the evening news is a journalist, subject to the modern standards of impartiality and objectivity. What about the host of a network morning show such as the *Today* show? Was Katie Couric a "journalist" during her years on morning television before she was picked to anchor the evening news? Many of the tasks she performed were journalistic, such as interviewing politicians. On the other hand, much of the time she spent in the studio was clearly entertainment: interviewing celebrities, commenting on in-studio fashion shows, cohosting a cooking segment, or flirting with cohost Matt Lauer.

One might suggest that journalism has always mixed fun with news. After all, newspapers often include gossip, salacious stories, movie reviews, and a sports section. But one important difference is inherent in the medium: the viewer of television "news" can't determine the mix of ingredients and has to accept viewing a segment on a new diet alongside the Iraqi War coverage. As Neil Postman observed, such placement cheapens the serious news by making it equal with the ephemeral and silly. All that separates the suffering of thousands of victims of a South Asian tsunami and tonight's lottery winner is an insincere segue. Another difference is that often the person who covers a celebrity scandal also anchors a serious story about politics. At most newspapers, by contrast, the gossip columnist isn't covering the president's new tax plan. As political journalism comes to resemble entertainment news, is it any wonder that more and more sports heroes and movie actors have become politicians? If journalists can't seem to tell the difference, how can the voters?

Entertainers are becoming journalists as well. Most Americans would not consider Jay Leno, Jon Stewart, or David Letterman to be journalists, but some studies suggest that many Americans become aware of political events or developments through the monologues of these late night comics. The Pew Research Center found that 47 percent of eighteen- to twenty-nine-year-olds received some of their information about the 2000 presidential race

ARCHETYPE OF THE INFOTAINMENT ERA

Katie Couric

Raised in Arlington, Virginia, former high school cheerleader **Katie Couric** was told during her stint as a producer at CNN in the early 1980s that she was "too cute" to be a broadcast journalist. Rejecting this sexist advice, Couric persevered and became a reporter for a local news station. Rising quickly through her drive and perky charm, in 1991 Couric was named cohost of NBC's *Today* show. The show quickly won the ratings war, emerging as one of NBC's reliable moneymakers.

Couric has interviewed many world leaders and every major presidential candidate since 1992. She has also won most of the major awards in televised journalism, including a Peabody, six Emmys, a Sigma Delta Chi award from the Society of Professional Journalists, and the Associated Press Award. But symbolic of her stature as a media icon in an infotainment age, Couric also wins accolades more appropriate for a movie star, such as the 2002 "Wow Woman of the Year" award from *Glamour*, a women's magazine of fashion, sex, and celebrity. Couric has also won a place on the list of "most popular TV personalities" as measured by an annual national poll. Along with right-wing TV host Bill O'Reilly, Couric was one of two news stars to appear

from late night talk shows.[18] If you watch Leno set up a political joke, it is clear he is teaching the public about politics. Typically, he starts out by saying, "Did you hear about" a certain political event: he then summarizes it in a sentence or two, followed by the joke. This format is used so those in the audience who don't follow the news as carefully as Leno's writers will still get the joke. Inadvertently, Leno is also educating the public about politics. For some Americans, watching Leno is all the political news they will get, which makes his jokes vitally important in shaping public opinion.

Because of the power of Leno and Letterman, political campaigns follow how their candidates are treated by these shows. If we define journalists as those who inform the public about politics, then on a list mostly populated by comedians and entertainers.[19] Couric's love life is also followed in the tabloids and celebrity magazines as avidly as those of A-list Hollywood starlets.

In an infotainment era, journalists are clearly celebrities, and this leads to a new, and more personal, style of journalism. When Couric's husband died of colon cancer, she launched a national campaign to increase awareness of this preventable disease. Because her emphasis was on early detection and treatment, Couric agreed to undergo a colonoscopy on air. Her aim was to demystify the uncomfortable procedure and to encourage viewers to get checked. Viewers were treated to a close-up view of the inside of Couric's colon as her doctor looked for signs of cancer. So effective was this show in increasing awareness of the disease and the procedure that screenings for colon cancer leaped by 20 percent, a response researchers called "the Couric effect." It is inconceivable to imagine staid journalists such as Walter Lippmann going through such a process, but surely many lives were saved by Couric's act.

In 2006 Katie Couric was selected to anchor the *CBS Evening News.* The woman who had been told she was too cute to be a television reporter had been chosen to fill the most prestigious spot in television journalism—the position once held by the legendary Walter Cronkite.

for many Americans these comics have to be considered journalists. Moreover, late night comics help set the nation's political agenda by what they choose to emphasize. In 2000 Letterman and Leno pounded Bush and Gore for their perceived personal shortcomings. Each joke that portrayed Gore as boring and duplicitous or Bush as ignorant and stupid helped set in stone those questionable characterizations. In an era in which politics is more personal than ever, such agenda setting can be decisive.

Television news heads sometimes go out of their way to convey the message that journalism is only for entertainment. To the extent that Couric is a journalist, Leno briefly became one in 2003 when he and Couric switched jobs for a day. Couric hosted Leno's program, and Leno took on Couric's morning job. The highlight of Leno's morning was his interview with then Secretary of State Colin Powell. The surreal spectacle of a stand-up comic posing questions about Middle East politics to one of the most powerful men in the world in front of a national television audience scarcely raised an eyebrow.[20] Meanwhile, Couric's time on Leno's show featured a segment about the shapely nature of her legs. When celebrities are journalists, and journalists are chosen in part for their sculpted bodies and sexy visages, entertainment values have become dominant in journalism.

As Neil Postman and others have argued, much of television journalism brings the values of Hollywood into the newsroom: titillation, simplification, and cheap drama. Although many attribute the rapid rise of the Fox News Network to its unabashed endorsement of conservative values, the network has also shown an adroit sense of show business. The network's director, Roger Ailes, began his career as the host of a celebrity talk show, the *Michael Douglas Show.* He went on to produce several successful Broadway plays as well as serving as a famous political consultant for Republican candidates.

Ailes leads a network that often feels like a tabloid newspaper brought to television.* Its leading talent, Bill O'Reilly, first achieved prominence as the host of *Inside Edition,* a sleazy Hollywood gossip show that was classic infotainment. Fox News does things that the more staid network news organizations would never consider; O'Reilly conducted a long interview with Jenna Jameson, a world-famous porn star. It is inconceivable that Brokaw, Jennings, Rather, or any mainstream network anchor would have given a sex performer twenty minutes of prime time. The morning show on Fox News features three "journalists": a former sports reporter, a former host of children's shows, and a sexy female journalist who tends to wear extremely short skirts. A frequent guest is "Mancow" Muller, a radio shock jock whose diatribes against liberal political figures and television journalists on other networks often border on the obscene, and who often makes appearances with strippers and other adult entertainers. Fox's coverage of politics merges titillating sex, patriotic violence, lurid coverage of crime, and conservative politics. Except for the final ingredient, much the same could be said of many

---

*Given that the network is owned by Rupert Murdoch, a conservative media mogul who owns some of the raunchiest tabloids in Britain, featuring nudity and scandal, this should not be a surprise.

other news programs, but no network has turned up the volume as much on tabloid news as Fox.

The infotainment era could just as easily be labeled the "corporate media era." During most of television journalism, news divisions at media companies were not expected to make a significant contribution to the profit of a network. News was seen as something television stations did to promote the public good. Today, however, the news division is expected to turn a significant profit because almost all major media outlets are owned by vast corporate empires. Emblematic of this shift was the debate in 2002 over whether to replace *Nightline,* a popular news program ABC had been broadcasting for many years, with David Letterman's more popular late night comedy/talk show. *Nightline* had always turned a profit, but the profit margin was only 5 to 10 percent, whereas a successful comedy show might get higher ratings and a return of 20 percent. The profit pressure is directly tied to ratings, which determine advertising revenues. Advertisers want to buy time on programs with many young and wealthy viewers. Older Americans have already formed loyalty to certain products and poorer viewers don't have the disposable income to make large purchases. News programs are pressured to get not just high ratings but high ratings from the right demographic.

Second, as media companies became ever larger (and fewer), they were often led by corporate CEOs, many of whom had never worked in journalism in their lives. The distinction between entertainment and news divisions at media companies began to fall. To Disney, ABC's parent company, replacing a news program with an entertainment one was nothing more than an effort to attract a younger and larger audience.[21] The idea that owning the airwaves implied an obligation to inform the public about politics and current events has become passé. Infotainment stems in part from corporate control of journalism.

Finally, the proliferation of cable television helps spread infotainment values. When there were only three network evening news programs, usually at the same time, Americans had little choice but to watch the news or turn off the television during the broadcasts. Now, even during national crises like 9/11, there are choices, and journalists have to fight to keep the public's attention. Thanks to twenty-four-hour news channels, Americans don't have to wait for the evening news to find out what happened during the day. They can tune in to CNN and find out in virtual real time. To get and keep viewers, news stations are forced to inject entertainment and humor into journalism.

Infotainment and Agenda Setting

Infotainment alters every aspect of journalism. Recall from Chapter 2 that one of the key functions of journalists in a democracy is to set the agenda. Infotainment has radically changed the media's sense of what is important for citizens to know. When a young, attractive, white female is missing, this is seen as highly newsworthy by cable news networks. Lurid stories of child and teenager abduction, murder, and rape that would once have been merely local are now made national by CNN and Fox. Should such stories be judged more newsworthy, on a daily basis, than developments overseas, the progress of congressional legislation, rulings by the federal courts, and actions by the president? The search for ratings may cause the news media to deeply mislead the public. One could argue that even if these stories are somewhat worthy of national news coverage, placing them so high on the agenda creates the impression that the problem is growing worse. Even though child abductions declined by 14 percent from 1997 to 2001,[22] the perception has grown that children are in terrible danger in the United States today. Parents report higher levels of fear, and children are far more closely supervised today than at any point in the past. The fact that the danger may be no worse or even reduced compared to 1990 or 1980 is irrelevant to the level of fear. Given the need to fill twenty-four hours of cable news, the networks run stories of child abduction, creating the mistaken impression that children are in graver danger now, when the truth is just the opposite. As one local television executive put it:

> If you look at the facts, there hasn't been a rash or inordinate number of actual cases, but in the news more prominence is given to kidnappings. It gives a distorted picture to the public. . . . One of the problems is news agencies are focusing on these issues [but] . . . . The general populace needs to be aware of significant issues. We are sacrificing coverage of significant events.[23]

Of course, the attempt to make journalism profitable through entertainment did not begin in 1992. In 1976 Paddy Chayefsky wrote *Network*, a movie that depicted television news as an entertainment-saturated medium where money-crazed corporate heads did whatever was necessary to increase ratings, even if it meant turning journalism into "a goddamn amusement park!" And some of the same criticisms leveled against infotainment today were used against the penny press in the nineteenth century. Those who see television journalism as inevitably getting worse should remember that the first host of NBC's *Today* show, back in the early 1950s, was a congenial former radio disc jockey who often cohosted with a chimpanzee. Perhaps Postman and others who worry about the intrusion of entertainment values into political journalism are overly pessimistic about the present, and overly rosy about the past.

Indeed, even if it can be shown that infotainment is on the rise, there remains a positive aspect of infotainment—it brings politics to the masses. Americans are not reliable voters compared to citizens in most democracies. Political scientists as early as the 1960s worried about citizens with little information about politics and even less interest in government. If politicians appear on *Oprah* or *The Tonight Show* and become celebrities, perhaps this is not entirely a bad thing if it makes just a few Americans pay more attention to candidates, issues, and elections. In the early nineteenth century, President Andrew Jackson changed U.S. elections by giving many lower income Americans a new sense of efficacy and involvement in politics. Many in the elite strata complained about Jackson's perceived crudeness and the unwashed nature of his backers. Is it possible that some of the opposition to "infotainment" journalism that is seen among the political and academic establishment is snobbery?

Maybe. Yet the critique of infotainment remains worthy of consideration. Perhaps infotainment journalism has made politics more relevant to the daily lives of Americans who might otherwise be less informed, but what have they learned from watching politics on MTV or Letterman or by watching endlessly repetitive segments about tragedies that affect individual attractive, young, white women? Infotainment journalism may be to real journalism what fast food is to healthy meals. Just as fast food is popular, easy, cheap, and gives the consumer a sense of being full while providing little nutritionally, infotainment journalism may give Americans the illusion of being informed about politics when all they have really learned are superficial irrelevancies about sensational crime stories and politicians' sex lives.

The Rise of the New Media and Infotainment

One of the most intriguing aspects of the infotainment era is the prevalence of "new media" outlets as conveyers of political infor-mation. **New media** include not just the late night comics but all nontraditional media outlets. As defined by media researchers Richard Davis and Diana Owen, the new media include "talk radio and television, electronic town meetings, television news maga-zines, MTV (music television), print and electronic tabloids, and computer networks."[24] The new media have become popular avenues for politicians who seek to speak more directly to the American public than they can through traditional media. *Larry King Live,* a talk show on CNN, became a very popular place for politicians once H. Ross Perot chose King's show to announce his candidacy for the presidency in 1992. Why did Perot and so many other politicians choose Larry King as a venue? One simple reason is that King has a well-earned reputation for asking softball ques-tions about feelings and family rather than difficult questions about policy details or controversial decisions.

During the 2004 presidential campaign, both candidates and their wives spent time with Dr. Phil, a pop psychologist renowned for his "tell it like it is" style when dealing with all types of sex-ual and family problems. When the president was on, he was asked whether he spanked his daughters and how he felt about one of his daughters making a rude gesture to reporters.[25] Both candidates were guaranteed that the focus of the interview would be on their families and not on politics. Traditionally, respectable journalists do not allow such limits to be placed on questions, but in the new media such limits are often assumed. No one expected Dr. Phil to ask President Bush difficult questions about the occu-pation of Iraq.

There is a symbiotic relationship between the new media and politicians. Politicians like the new media outlets because they get to reach potential voters who may not be paying attention to tradi-tional media. They also get to speak around the sophisticated, and some might say cynical or negative, political beat reporters. New media like appearances by politicians because they have historically done very well in the ratings. When Bush appeared on Letterman's show in 2000, it gave the show some of its best ratings in years. When Governor Arnold Schwarzenegger of California appeared on Leno's show, ratings went through the roof. When Gore and Bush went on *Oprah* separately in 2000, her viewership spiked upward by several million.[26]

At some point, perhaps the novelty of new media appearances by politicians will fade, the ratings of such shows will drop, and politicians will get fewer invitations. Or perhaps one politician will take it one step too far and be subjected to ridicule for a new media mistake. But so far this seems unlikely. Politicians such as Senator John McCain have even been guest stars on one of the most irreverent and raunchiest shows on television, *Saturday Night Live* (SNL). In 1975, when Gerald Ford's press secretary appeared on SNL, he was widely and harshly criticized inside and outside the White House. Today politicians such as McCain, Mayor Rudy Guiliani, and even (briefly) the presidential candidates appear on SNL with nary a word of criticism. There is perhaps no better example of the age of infotainment than shows on which politicians are indistinguishable from the actors whose job it is to mock politicians.

Of all the new media, the newest is the Internet. Given the growth in the number of Americans who get their news from the Internet, it is likely that we are about to enter the Internet era. The implications of that for political journalism are discussed in Chapter 11.

KEY TERMS AND PEOPLE

access journalism	new media
Katie Couric	pyramid style of news writing
infotainment journalism	Watergate
Walter Lippmann	Bob Woodward and Carl
new journalism	Bernstein

DISCUSSION QUESTIONS

1. Do you think the media should report personal details about the private lives of politicians? Is there anything you wouldn't want the media to cover?
2. Do you think of journalism as a highly skilled profession for which going to graduate school is almost mandatory?

3. Do you agree with Neil Postman that infotainment is dangerous to democracy? If no, why not? If yes, what can be done about it by government or by citizens?
4. Do you favor the more entertaining news sources for your political information? Do you think that has affected your political views? How?
5. Do you listen to talk radio? How does it differ from the mainstream television news? Which is more accurate, in your opinion? Which is more entertaining?

ADDITIONAL RESOURCES

Amusing Ourselves to Death, by Neil Postman, remains the best single book on the infotainment era.

Walter Lippmann and the American Century, by Ronald Steel, is a penetrating portrait of the professional era in journalism.

American Journalism: History, Principles, Practices, by W. David Sloan and Lisa Mullikin Parcell, is an edited volume in the style of a textbook, covering a wide range of historical and current topics in American journalism.

The movies *Network* and *Broadcast News* are both critical portraits of how television has cheapened journalism. *All the President's Men* is a reasonably accurate account of how Woodward and Bernstein exposed Nixon's crimes. (A more humorous recent take on it is the movie *Dick*). Finally, *Good Night, and Good Luck,* directed by and starring George Clooney, is a heroic portrait of one of the stars of the early days of television news, Edward R. Murrow. It includes a passionate critique of some aspects of television journalism.

ONLINE RESOURCES

If you find the history of American political journalism intriguing, you may want to read *Media History Monographs,* an online publication affiliated with the American Journalism Historians Association: http://facstaff.elon.edu/dcopeland/mhm/mhm.htm

NOTES

1. Walter Lippmann, *Liberty and the News* (New Brunswick, NJ: Transaction, 1995), 44–45. (Orig. pub. 1919.)
2. Ibid., 71.
3. Ibid., 74.
4. Ronald Steel, *Walter Lippmann and the American Century* (Boston: Little Brown, 1980), 36.
5. Ibid., 181–84.
6. Ibid., 384–86.
7. Larry Sabato, *Feeding Frenzy* (New York: Free Press, 1994), 29.
8. Theodore H. White, *The Making of the President 1960* (New York: Atheneum, 1988).
9. Sabato, *Feeding Frenzy,* 39.
10. Stephen R. Graubard, *Command of Office* (New York: Basic Books, 2004).
11. Author interview with Arthur Schlesinger Jr., New York City, August 1999.
12. Thomas C. Reeves, *A Question of Character* (New York: Prima, 1997).
13. Carl Bernstein and Bob Woodward, "GOP Security Aide Among Five Arrested in Bugging Affair," *Washington Post,* June 19, 1972: A1.
14. Carl Bernstein and Bob Woodward, "FBI Finds Nixon Aides Sabotaged Democrats," *Washington Post,* October 10, 1972: A1.
15. George Stephanopoulos, *All Too Human* (New York: Little Brown, 1998).
16. James David Barber, *Presidential Character,* 4th ed. (Englewood Cliffs, NJ: Prentice Hall, 1992).
17. Sabato, *Feeding Frenzy,* 151.
18. Pew Research Center for the People and the Press, "Audiences Fragmented and Skeptical: The Tough Job of Communicating With Voters" [Press release]: February 2003.
19. "Drew Carey Recaptures Top Spot as Nation's Most Popular TV Personality, Followed by Regis Philbin." Harris Poll Survey [Press release]: January 23, 2002.
20. Robert P. Laurence, "Monkeying Around with 'Journalism': It's No Big Deal; It Is Just Show Biz," *San Diego Union Tribune,* May 12, 2003.
21. "Letterman Re-ups with CBS: Nightline to Stay Put," CNN, March 27, 2002. http://www.cnn.com/2002/SHOWBIZ/News/03/12/letterman.nightline/

22. Robert S. Mueller, "Remarks." White House Conference on Missing, Abducted, and Exploited Children [Press release]: 2002.

23. Joseph Hadfield, "Child Kidnappings Down Despite Increased Media Coverage," BYU Newsnet. September 2, 2002. http://newsnet.byu.edu/story.cfm/39653

24. Richard Davis and Diana Owen, *New Media in American Politics* (New York: Oxford, 1998), 3.

25. Jennifer Frey, "Dr. Phil's Advice to Candidates: Come on My Show," *Washington Post,* September 29, 2004: C01.

26. Ibid.

The Media and the Law

Congress shall make no law . . . abridging
the freedom of speech, or of the press.
—First Amendment, U.S. Constitution

*A*fter the 9/11 tragedy, television networks across the United States broadcast video and audio messages from Osama bin Laden, the terrorist mastermind of al Qaeda. Although the Bush administration worried that bin Laden might be encoding hidden messages to terrorists in the United States, the government had no power to stop the broadcasts. In many other nations, the idea that the government would permit such access to a sworn enemy would be entirely foreign. Even a very democratic nation, Great Britain, made a different choice in combating domestic terrorism. Confronted by terrorists opposed to British policies in Northern Ireland, Britain banned the broadcast of their faces or voices. Does this mean that the United States is less serious about defeating al Qaeda than the British were about winning the war against the Irish Republican Army?

Of course not. The difference is that the United States has a very strong—indeed, perhaps the strongest—constitutional barrier preventing government censorship of the media in all but the most extreme circumstances. The media have always occupied a special legal status in the United States, but even here the media are not free to print or broadcast anything. There are limits and exceptions to the liberty of the media. This chapter outlines how the media and the law intersect in the United States.

Beyond simply outlining the state of the law, deeper questions are considered. Both Postman and Benjamin saw video as intrinsically different from print media. Most U.S. regulations on the media treat broadcasting as radically different from publication. If Postman is right, and television poses inherent dangers to democracy, perhaps this higher level of regulation is justified.

EXCEPTIONS TO FREEDOM OF SPEECH

The First Amendment announced the broadest freedom of speech and press ever granted by a government to its citizens and the media. Even so, this didn't stop the federal government from quickly attempting to ban criticism of the president and Congress through the Alien and Sedition Acts (see Chapter 4). Although this attack on the First Amendment was defeated, our current understanding of free speech is of a very recent vintage. For much of American history, the First Amendment was not even seen as applying to state and local government regulation of the media.

Several key exceptions to the freedom of speech and of the press remain: national security, clear and present danger, presidential threats, obscenity, libel/slander, privacy, and commercial speech. The strongest action the government can take is to forbid publication or broadcast of certain material; this is called **prior restraint.** The principle that prior restraint can be exercised only in extreme circumstances was established in the Supreme Court case *Near v. Minnesota* (1931). A tiny circulation newspaper had been publishing allegations that the mayor of Minneapolis was linked to a Jewish mobster. The articles were both obscene and defamatory, and the police shut it down under a state law forbidding "malicious, scandalous, or defamatory" newspapers. The publisher appealed, and the Supreme Court ruled that with very rare exceptions neither state nor federal police could shut down a printing press. They outlined the types of exceptions that might be permitted:

> No one would question but that a government might prevent actual obstruction to its recruiting service or the publication of the sailing dates of transports or the number and location of troops. On similar grounds, the primary requirements of decency may be enforced against obscene publications. The security of the community life may be protected against incitements to acts of violence and the overthrow by force of orderly government.[1]

Since *Near,* it has been almost impossible for a government official to use prior restraint against the media. The default assumption is always press freedom.

National Security

Even though *Near v. Minnesota* recognized the possibility of prior restraint to prevent direct damage to national security, the applicability of that principle remains unclear. Several "First Amendment absolutists" such as Supreme Court justices Hugo Black and William O. Douglas still believed that the government could never take such actions. According to First Amendment absolutists, the government's job is to maintain secrecy in the rare instances when secrecy is warranted; the press's job is to ferret out the truth as much as possible, regardless of the consequences.

In the 1971 **Pentagon Papers case**, the Nixon administration tried to stop the *New York Times* from publishing stolen government documents outlining the history of U.S. involvement in Vietnam.[2] The government argued that publication would damage U.S. security. The Supreme Court reviewed the documents rapidly and decided that they could be published. In this case, the media won and prior restraint was not allowed. Yet the Court was deeply split about what they had done. The absolutist justices felt that even the review of the material was inappropriate because it implied that prior restraint was possible in some future case.

Other justices argued that prior restraint of the press was only allowable if the government could demonstrate that direct, irreparable, and serious damage would be done to national security if the material were published. Because the Pentagon Papers were not that dangerous, they voted with the absolutists against Nixon. Finally, the three dissenters felt that the government had made its case and that the press should be prevented from publishing the government's secret history of the war in Vietnam.[3] After more than two hundred years of history, it is still not entirely clear when the government may use national security to rein in the press, or even if such power exists.

Suppose someone wanted to publish the secret of the hydrogen bomb? Would that merit prior restraint? In 1978 freelance writer Howard Morland, in a protest against government secrecy, tried to publish an article in a left-wing magazine that outlined the bomb's inner workings. The article was not a "how to build it" manual, but it did describe exactly how a thermonuclear bomb worked,[4] which could be of great use to nations seeking to develop hydrogen bombs. A federal court issued an injunction. While the case was on appeal, it became clear that parts of the secret to the hydrogen bomb's creation

WHAT IS CENSORSHIP, EXACTLY?

A newspaper publisher has almost complete freedom to control what appears in the paper's pages. When a newspaper fires a columnist or refuses to run a letter to the editor or an advertisement that offends the owner of the newspaper, this is sometimes called **censorship**. In fact, this is not censorship in the strict definition of the term. Censorship should properly be applied only to government actions limiting speech. Censorship occurs when a government shuts down a newspaper or controls what is broadcast on television. If a newspaper gets a reputation for speaking with only one voice, never allowing dissenting views on key issues to be heard, it will eventually suffer a loss of readership, or, at least, so most free market advocates believe.

It is much more difficult to identify an act of censorship on the airwaves. Television and radio stations, like newspapers, retain the power to reject any advertisement they find offensive, improper, or even disagreeable. But this power is controversial because broadcast media use "our" public airwaves. If you want to say something politically important, and every television station in your area rejects your ad as offensive, the most important medium of political discourse has been taken away from you. In fact, this has happened in recent history. In 1996 New Hampshire's only major television station refused to air two ads by a fringe candidate for president because they graphically depicted gay kissing and the use of hypodermic needles. The fringe candidate was running in the Democratic primary against overwhelming odds to bring attention to HIV prevention and gay rights. The FCC later admonished the station for rejecting the ads,

were already available to the public, and the case was dropped.[5] The legacy of the Morland case, like that of the Pentagon Papers, is therefore unclear, but it does suggest that the government will not hesitate to employ prior restraint when it deems it necessary.

Clear and Present Danger

The most stringent protection of free speech would not protect a man in falsely shouting fire in a theatre and causing a panic. . . .

but the message remained unviewed by voters and did not attract national attention. Was this message a victim of censorship?

Similarly, many television stations have rejected graphic depictions of bloody fetuses in ads that pro-life groups wish to run. Television stations argue that depictions of gay sex or aborted fetuses might disturb their sensitive viewers so much that the station would suffer economic harm. Free speech advocates counter with the argument that the public airwaves should be open to political messages because there really is no alternative for such dissident voices.[6]

Most recently the liberal advocacy group Moveon.org was outraged when CBS refused to air its anti-Bush television ad during the 2004 Super Bowl. The Super Bowl is almost unparalleled in terms of audience and is among the most prestigious media events in the United States. Any ad run during the Super Bowl attracts national attention, even ads for mundane household products. According to Moveon.org, CBS labeled the ad and another by People for the Ethical Treatment of Animals "controversial." CBS, which counts on the Super Bowl for immense ad revenue, probably feared that such an ad might detract from the usual national celebratory mood of the event, which highlights athletics, patriotism, sexy cheerleaders, and consumerism. Yet the Super Bowl can hardly be labeled nonpolitical; President Bush made a courtesy appearance in the broadcast one year, and his administration was allowed by CBS to run a very controversial ad linking marijuana use by American teenagers to terrorism. Should the FCC allow broadcast companies to pick and choose which political messages to air? If it does regulate political advertising, how can it define a "political" message?

> The question in every case is whether the words used are used in such circumstances and are of such a nature as to create a clear and present danger.[7]

In 1917, when the United States was in the midst of World War I, the Socialist Party published a pamphlet calling on young men to resist the draft. The federal government arrested the general secretary of the party, Charles Schenck, and charged him with violating the newly passed Espionage Act. He argued that the pamphlet was protected by the First Amendment. Supreme Court Justice Oliver Wendell Holmes ruled that Schenck's acts represented a **clear and present danger.** According to Holmes, when speech is linked so directly to conduct (in this case, obstructing the draft), it ceases to be protected—like falsely shouting "Fire!" in a crowded theater.* The standard is admittedly a murky one. Moreover, it has changed since 1919. Today speech that violates the clear and present danger test must intend to incite lawless activity, the activity must be imminent, and the speech must be likely to succeed at inciting it.[8] This is a very high standard to meet.

Threatening the President

Could a newspaper publish an editorial calling for the assassination of the president? It is inconceivable that a mainstream media outlet would do such a thing, but it is not an irrelevant question. Radio talk show host and convicted felon G. Gordon Liddy bragged to his audience that he used pictures of then President Bill Clinton and his wife as targets on his shooting range.[9] "Gonzo journalist" Hunter S. Thompson told a crowd of college students that then Vice President George H. W. Bush "should be killed. He should be stomped to death, and I'll join in!" Unlike Liddy, Thompson was briefly investigated by the Secret Service, which enforces the ban on any threats to the president, written or spoken. More recently, college journalist Glenn Given, managing editor of the *Stony Brook Press*, wrote a sarcastic editorial calling on God to "smite" George W. Bush.[10] A week later Secret Service agents descended on the newspaper's offices, searched Given's home, acquired his medical records, subjected him to a psychological profile, and allegedly confiscated thousands of copies of the paper.[11]

The law about threatening the president was intended to make the president safer by making conspiracies difficult to even discuss, but does it limit the freedom of the press to criticize the president in passionate and perhaps violent terms? Pat Robertson, host and founder of the Christian Broadcast Network, recently called for

---

*The analogy that Holmes uses is one that modern students may find odd. When Holmes wrote, there were no fire codes, sprinklers, or clearly marked exits. Fires spread extremely fast, and often as many people died in the crush of the crowd as in the fire itself. Therefore, falsely yelling "Fire!" could result in the deaths of many innocents, who would trample each other to death to get out of the building. In those days, the difference between life and death in a fire was often a matter of mere seconds.

placing a nuclear device in the State Department during a televised interview with a critic of the State Department. Since this would also clearly threaten the president's life, should the Secret Service investigate broadcasters like Robertson, who claimed that the comments were somehow humorous? The Secret Service even looked into an unreleased song by rapper Eminem that allegedly contained a threat to shoot the president. How far should the government go in making assassination of the president impossible to discuss?

Commercial Speech

One way to think about the First Amendment is that its protections differ depending on the type of speech under consideration. The most protected speech is speech with a political or religious message, and among the least protected is **commercial speech** designed to sell products. Thus the government cannot review a newspaper editorial and assess whether it is factually accurate, but the ad right next to the editorial is held to a different standard. False claims about a product or offer can be investigated and punished. In the past, states could also freely regulate advertisements for tobacco, alcohol, prescription drugs, and many other products and services. Today, however, the courts hold such regulations to a higher standard, and the rights of citizens to learn about new products is broader.[12] Even so, commercial speech is far more subject to regulation than political speech.

Libel

If the media print or broadcast something false about a person, this is called **libel**.[13] Thanks to *Near v. Minnesota*, the media cannot be stopped in advance from distributing falsehoods (that would be prior restraint), but they can face penalties in court later, usually fines. Does this mean that everything you read about celebrities in the *National Enquirer* is true? Hardly. Since 1964 the standards for libel have been radically different for public figures than they are for private citizens. If a newspaper printed something false about a private citizen that damaged his reputation, the paper could be sued in a civil court by the citizen. But a public figure would have to show that the newspaper acted with "actual malice" or a reckless disregard for the truth.[14] This makes it very difficult for public figures, such as politicians and entertainers, to win libel cases in the United States.

Why did the Supreme Court protect the right of journalists to be inaccurate about public figures? Primarily, they did so because they felt that the right to criticize public officials was so vital that it was worth the cost of occasionally damaging the feelings or even the reputations of those who enter the public arena. If newspapers faced huge lawsuits every time they made an error about a public figure, this would have a **chilling effect** on political speech, according to many scholars. The term "chilling effect" is frequently used in free speech and press cases. Punishing one media outlet for inappropriate or illegal speech will result in other outlets hesitating before they print or broadcast anything even near the borderline of the punished speech.

Public figures are also not protected against rough satire by the media. As dramatized in the movie *The People vs. Larry Flynt,* the Reverend Jerry Falwell was the subject of a bitter political cartoon in the pornographic magazine *Hustler,* edited by Flynt. The cartoon suggested Falwell, a leader of the religious right, had conducted an incestuous affair with his mother in an outhouse while intoxicated. *Hustler* also depicted Falwell as preaching while drunk. Falwell sued Flynt and initially won damages, not precisely for libel but for intentional infliction of emotional distress.[15] On appeal, however, the Supreme Court ruled that satire of public officials was even more protected than usual criticism; in order to win, a public figure would have to show that beyond actual malice the satire was of such a nature that someone might believe the false allegation. The Court also assumed that a public figure like Falwell, unlike a private citizen, has media access to answer false allegations.

Certainly, public debate is freer because journalists do not worry so much about libel suits. But it is also possible that this freedom comes at a significant cost to public figures and to the country as a whole. Perhaps some Americans don't enter politics, even though they have the desire and the ability, because they fear the scathing nature of unrestricted press criticism. Some American public figures have even resorted to bringing lawsuits in British courts against British papers that print exactly the same stories American papers have printed because the law there is less protective of the media's "right to be wrong."

Privacy

Sometimes the media are denied access to information because it would violate the privacy of citizens who are not public figures.

One recent Supreme Court case involved the autopsy photos of former White House aide and close presidential friend, Vince Foster. Foster, who committed suicide in a Virginia park in 1994, has been the subject of numerous conspiracy theories, even though several independent investigations have established that he killed himself due to depression. Allen Favish, a conservative anti-Clinton activist, sued the government to receive ten gruesome autopsy photos to investigate what he believed was a government cover-up of Foster's killing by associates of President Clinton. Favish filed a **Freedom of Information Act (FOIA)** request, an official document that forces the government to give out information or assert legal grounds why it should not. FOIAs are frequently used by journalists to investigate the government, and consequently several media organizations joined Favish's case, arguing that the family's privacy rights were minimal and the public's need to know, in this case and others, was great.[16] The Foster family, joined by the Bush administration, opposed the request because they feared the horrific photos would quickly appear on the Internet, causing further pain to a deeply anguished family.[17] In the past the widespread distribution of the postmortem photos of famous people such as John Lennon and John F. Kennedy has caused great distress to their families, and it is not as uncommon a situation as you might imagine. Among those filing in support of the Foster family was the family of Dale Earnhardt, the race car driver who died during a race in 2001. His family has been fighting a long legal battle against several media companies to keep his autopsy photos private as well.

Should the government be allowed to keep information from the media out of concern for the privacy of individual citizens? Remember that the amount of information the government has about Americans increases every year. We might agree that such matters as arrest records should be available to the public and the media, but the government also has medical records, income history, and divorce court proceedings. And, of course, any death that is at all suspicious is likely to result in an extensive series of autopsy photos and reports. Where should the government draw the line between the media's right to know and a family's desire not to have the image of their deceased loved one widely distributed?

So far, both the Earnhardt and Foster families have won their cases, denying the media access to gruesome autopsy photos.

ANONYMOUS MEDIA IN THREE FORMATS?

Should your right to put ideas about politics out to the world without attaching your name to them be protected? **Anonymous speech** has a long and respected tradition in America. The debates over passage of our Constitution were often conducted by writers using pseudonyms to shield their identities. The Bill of Rights itself, of which freedom of the press is a part, was suggested anonymously by critics of the Constitution. The Supreme Court has recently reaffirmed that citizens possess the right to publish anonymous newspapers and pamphlets, particularly those that address political questions.[18] Unlike many nations, in this country it is perfectly legal for someone to print a newspaper anonymously, although for obvious reasons this right is seldom exercised by large media corporations.

Political ads on television and radio are sometimes purchased by shadowy groups of mysterious origin and ownership. In the 2000 Republican presidential primary, several vicious attack ads appeared that demonized Senator John McCain (R–AZ). Campaign laws in effect at that time did not require the group to immediately disclose who was purchasing the airtime. Long after McCain was defeated by Bush, it was revealed that the funding for the smear ads came from major Bush supporters.[19] Also in 2000, a group affiliated with the National Association for the Advancement of Colored People (NAACP) ran a brutal ad

Obscene and Indecent Speech

Of all the exceptions to the First Amendment, perhaps none has inspired more court cases than obscenity. This may be because of the eternal war between the human fascination with matters of sexuality and the belief among many that sexuality is both sacred and potentially dangerous. Of course, only the broadest definition of "media" would include X-rated movies and pornographic magazines. But the ban on obscene materials has also been used to stifle political speech.

Newspapers that veered into harsh invective and obscene language in their political criticism were not rare in the early American experience. Occasionally such papers were attacked accusing Bush of indifference to the horrendous lynching of a black man in Texas.[20] Again, it was impossible for Republicans to know who was funding this unfair assault on their candidate. The Federal Election Commission (FEC) continues to study the question of whether to permit anonymous groups (or even groups that are temporarily anonymous until reporting deadlines are met) to put out political messages during campaigns. The Supreme Court has not yet addressed the question of whether anonymous communication is permitted on the airwaves.

The Internet poses anew the question of anonymous political commentary. At least in the case of e-mails, it is increasingly possible to "remail" anonymously so that rumors, untruths, and other potentially damaging political information can be distributed under the radar of the national media. For much of the Clinton presidency, crank Web pages and anonymous e-mails detailed various sinister allegations against Clinton that were never covered by the national media. Such rumor campaigns were not unknown in days long before the Internet, of course. In 1920, while running for vice president, Franklin Roosevelt cheerfully passed along the rumor that Republican Warren Harding had black blood somewhere in his ancestry, a very dangerous allegation in those racist times.[21] But the Internet allows anonymous, potentially libelous content to be distributed worldwide in seconds.[22]

by the authorities as "public nuisances" or sued for libel. Today, however, the major newspapers are limited in their use of obscenity primarily by market forces. If the *Wall Street Journal* or the *Washington Post* suddenly started using four-letter words to criticize politicians and their programs, it is unlikely they would face any legal ramifications; instead, they might lose readers (and advertisers).

Obscenity and indecent speech are highly regulated in the broadcast media. The exceptions to free speech outlined so far apply equally to print and broadcast media, but regulations regarding electronic media are much more extensive and require separate consideration.

SPECIAL RULES FOR BROADCAST MEDIA

The electronic media have always been treated differently by our government. The simple explanation is that even in the early days of radio, politicians realized that the airwaves had a limited bandwidth. Publication of one more newspaper might not hurt the other newspapers directly, but there are only so many spots on the radio dial for stations. When the first national radio conference was convened by the Commerce Department in 1922, government regulators wrestled for the first time with how to allocate frequencies among competing groups, such as amateur radio operators, commercial stations, merchant shipping, and the government.[23] Today that is just one of the tasks taken up by the **Federal Communications Commission (FCC),** an independent government regulatory agency created in 1934 that oversees radio and television. Indeed, the FCC oversees not only broadcast media but every device that emits a broadcast or wired signal, including cell phones, telephones, satellite communication, cable television, microwave ovens, home alarm systems, wireless computer networks, and even radio-controlled children's toys. This broad range of responsibility makes the FCC among the most powerful agencies in the United States.

The FCC is charged with upholding communication laws passed by Congress, writing additional regulation as permitted by Congress, licensing the broadcast industry to make sure laws and regulations are observed, and investigating violations. The commission has five members, appointed by the president to five-year terms, conditional on approval by the Senate. No more than three members may be of a single political party. Those who created the FCC believed that the nation's airwaves were a public trust. However, suiting America's free market traditions, the airwaves were not directly owned by the government but were merely regulated by government. Many other democratic nations have government-owned radio and television networks, although today in many of those countries privately owned media empires are growing.

Licensing and Fining

Want to start your own newspaper or magazine? All you need is a computer, a printer, and a copier. It requires no permission from anyone in government at any level. Newspapers are not regulated except for laws that apply to all companies and organizations equally. However, if you want to start a radio or television station in your basement, you will need a license from the FCC for any broadcasting that has significant range.

Perhaps the most important function of the FCC is to oversee the licensing of radio and television stations and networks. Suppose that a parent hears salacious or inappropriate material on a car radio while traveling with a child. The organization that receives the parent's complaint is the FCC, which can impose a fine on the station if an investigation confirms that the radio station broadcast adult material in a family time slot. In extreme cases the FCC could take away the license of such a station, but it is more likely that the station's parent company would simply face more difficulty getting approval for future purchases. Control over licensing of stations is what allows the FCC to impose its will on the media across a broad spectrum of activities.

Obscene and Indecent Broadcast

Legendary stand-up comedian George Carlin used to deliver a monologue called "Filthy Words" about the seven words that could not be broadcast. Ironically, when a left-wing radio station broadcast Carlin's words at 2 p.m., it led to a test of the FCC's power to regulate indecent broadcast speech. The Supreme Court ultimately ruled that the FCC had the power to regulate indecent speech even though Carlin's speech was not obscene (because it did not intend to arouse the audience, merely make them laugh) and the station was broadcasting it as part of a news program on censorship.[24]

In recent years radio hosts have gotten increasingly clever at broadcasting indecent speech that avoids using banned words. The FCC eventually responded to listener complaints by fining radio hosts such as Howard Stern millions of dollars.

Yet the popularity of indecent radio programs continues to rise, and Stern's competitors took it even further. In 2001 two "shock jocks" for Infinity Broadcasting ran a public sex contest in which listeners in teams of two were encouraged to have sex in various public places around New York City. When two contestants were arrested for having anal sex in St. Patrick's Cathedral, the FCC became involved, ultimately fining Infinity more than a quarter of a million dollars.[25] At the same time, standards for broadcast radio and television have become much looser. Sexual situations as well as words such as "damn," "penis," "ass," and "bitch," which would have led to major fines in decades past, now appear regularly on prime time television. The FCC is currently examining whether to reinvigorate its indecent speech enforcement following thousands of complaints from concerned parents and other citizens.*

Why is indecent speech regulated so differently in electronic media? The key is not only that the networks were envisioned as a public trust but that electronic media are uniquely burdened with the problem of the "unwilling" listener or viewer as well as vulnerable minors. A pornographic magazine will not suddenly appear in the home of a conservative Christian, but a radio or television program does just that. Some argue that the solution to offensive broadcasting is for sensitive citizens to change channels. Others feel that at least in the case of minors the government has an obligation not to allow the broadcast of indecent material. It is impossible for a parent to monitor a child's consumption of the media at all times, and a child could be educated in an instant about matters a parent would rather keep silent. To address this issue, the FCC has promulgated "safe harbor" rules, in which speech standards are different during hours when children are likely to be listening or viewing.

Broadcasters are under increasing commercial pressure to include "edgy" material. Not only are such broadcasts often very profitable, but cable television has very few restraints under current FCC guidelines. Cable stations like HBO are gaining popularity with programs like the *Sopranos* and *Sex and the City*, which include nudity and words that could not be used on network television. Similarly, satellite radio, which requires a special receiver and a monthly fee to hear, currently faces no FCC regulation. Tired of years of fines and limits, Howard Stern moved to Sirius Satellite Radio in 2005.

Public Interest and Children's Programming

Because the airwaves are a public trust, the FCC requires television stations to broadcast at least three hours a week of educational or socially responsible programming for children. The FCC also limits the number of commercials in all children's programs. Behind both of these acts is the idea that children are particularly vulnerable to poor programming. Stations are also required to air local news and political issues to maintain their licenses.

---

*It was later discovered that a very high percentage of the complaints came from one social conservative watchdog group. Few actual viewers independently complain about sex on television and radio.

These rules generally apply only to broadcast channels. Cable television raises fundamental questions about the necessity and workability of these regulations. Entire cable channels are now devoted to children's programming and local news. Does it still make sense to require broadcast outlets to take on these tasks?[26]

Equal Time

Comedian Craig Kilborn was about to tape his popular late night talk show in August of 2003 when lawyers for his network killed several bits involving candidates for California governor in a recall election, including incumbent Gray Davis, actor Arnold Schwarzenegger, and porn actress Mary Casey. The lawyers worried that if Kilborn gave any airtime to these candidates, the network would be required by FCC rules to give "equal time" to all 135 candidates running in the election. The FCC requires that free airtime be made available to all candidates on an equal basis. Newscasts are largely exempt from the **equal time** provision; if coverage is given to one candidate because he or she has engaged in activity that is legitimately newsworthy, the FCC does not require that all other candidates receive the same amount of time. Presidential debates are also exempt, so even though Ralph Nader was excluded from the free television time granted to Bush and Kerry in the 2004 presidential debates, he did not receive comparable time. However, other broadcasts are not exempt. If a candidate is a former actor, showing his movies on television can trigger the equal time provision. What truly irked Kilborn in 2003 was that the rules apply only to broadcast television; cable networks are exempt from the equal time doctrine.[27]

Why does the FCC require equal time? It worries that if a station or network supported a particular candidate for office, he or she could appear on the air so often, and in such a favorable light, that the independence of our electoral system would be threatened. The FCC also requires that stations make advertising time available to candidates at equal, low rates.[28] This is to prevent a station from favoring one party or candidate over another.

Ownership Limitations

The FCC also monitors the number of media outlets that are owned by a single corporation. If one individual or company controls every newspaper, radio station, and television station in a single area or state, the entire concept of a free media is threatened. To prevent media monopolies, the FCC uses its licensing authority to stop media conglomerates from dominating specific areas. However, a 1996 bill passed by Congress relaxed those standards and radically altered the media markets in several ways. For example, one company is now allowed to own up to eight radio stations in a local area. Critics of the relaxation felt that this opened the door for abuse of media power, particularly in small communities with few choices. Perhaps the most famous example was Minot, North Dakota, which was served by six different commercial radio stations, all owned by the largest radio corporation in the country, Clear Channel. Many of the stations ran nationally syndicated programming that required no actual human presence in the station for broadcast. In January of 2002 a dangerous gas leak after a train wreck required an emergency broadcast, but local officials were unable to get anyone at a Clear Channel station to respond.[29]

The Minot case is used by critics of media conglomeration to demonstrate that the current standards are not strict enough and that locally controlled, independent media are quickly becoming a thing of the past. Yet advocates for even lighter controls point out that larger media companies are not always bad for news coverage. One study by the Project for Excellence in Journalism suggests that television stations that are owned by newspaper companies actually provide more in-depth news than pure television companies do. Others point out that the Internet and cable television have made the entire idea of a lack of media diversity ridiculous. As conservative columnist Jay Ambrose put it:

> In the recorded history of the human family, there has never ever been a time and place with as many information outlets as there are now to be found in the 21st century in the United States. The Internet alone provides the possibility for virtually all of us to possess the equivalent of a printing press. Then there is cable TV, which provides hundreds of channels . . . of course, there are newspapers, and there are magazines and books and newsletters.[30]

The issue of media concentration erupted nationwide in the summer of 2003 when the FCC voted to lower the 1996 standards even further, allowing large media conglomerates to control more television companies, radio stations, and newspapers* across the

---

*The FCC has no independent regulatory power over newspapers and cannot directly regulate a company that owns newspapers in every city, for example. It can regulate only the intersection of newspaper ownership and broadcast media ownership.

country. More than 100,000 citizens filed comments with the FCC through various means, almost all of them opposing the shift, but it passed regardless with the three Republicans outvoting the two Democrats on the commission.

In a bipartisan effort, Congress—including conservative Senator Ted Stevens (R–Alaska) and the conservative National Rifle Association—tried to reinstitute the old standards. In particular, they focused attention on the new regulation that would allow one media network to own stations reaching 45 percent of Americans, up from 35 percent. Because President Bush supported the new standards for larger media corporations, a compromise was reached setting the permissible level at 39 percent, perhaps not coincidentally roughly the percentage that Viacom and Fox already owned.

Critics of the FCC's latest moves, however, feel that the more important changes have to do with allowing one media company to dominate a local market. Media companies want to make these changes, in part, to make the media industry more efficient. Much of the work that a newspaper and local television news division perform is similar; if the same company can own both outlets, costs go down and profits go up.

THE MEDIA GO TO COURT: PRIVILEGES AND RESTRICTIONS

No discussion of the intersection of the media and the law would be complete without examining the complicated question of what happens when journalists go to court, either as witnesses in trials or as reporters covering trials.

Reporters as Witnesses: Protecting Sources or Hiding the Truth?

The modern journalist often uses confidential sources who are guaranteed anonymity by the reporter. If sources did not trust that they would remain anonymous, many would not speak to reporters, and the quality of journalism might decline. The Watergate story, among many others, relied on confidential sources. But what if a journalist learns of illegal activities that become part of a trial? If the journalist is subpoenaed and asked to name his or her source, does the "freedom of the press" promised in the Constitution protect the journalist's right to refuse to testify?

MAJOR MEDIA COMPANIES

Should you be worried about media concentration? Scholar Ben Bagdikian feared for our democracy in 1983 because approximately twenty major media companies controlled most of the news.[31] Today Bagdikian and others count about six to eight such companies, some owning hundreds of newspapers, radio stations, television stations, movie studios, cable networks, Web sites, and magazines. Many liberals would like to see the FCC or Congress take action against the escalating concentration of media power in fewer and fewer hands. Libertarians and conservatives argue, by contrast, that the media have never been more open and free because of cable television and the Internet. They want the FCC to loosen the limits on media concentration. However the debate turns out, it is unquestionable that the size and diversity of today's media empires are unprecedented. Here are seven major companies and their primary holdings.[32] This list does not include the nonmedia holdings of these conglomerates, holdings that may affect how media outlets cover certain political issues. It should also be noted that with the speed at which the media conglomerates merge and alter their holdings, any such list is quickly outdated.

Disney
ABC broadcast network
ESPN and Disney cable networks
10 TV and 26 radio stations
Disney and Touchstone studios

News Corp
Fox broadcast network
Fox News and FX cable networks
35 TV stations
The *New York Post* newspaper
20th Century Fox studio
(also owns many media enterprises overseas)

Viacom
CBS and UPN broadcast networks
MTV and Nickelodeon cable networks

39 TV stations and 180 radio stations
Paramount movie studio

GE
NBC and Telemundo broadcast networks
MSNBC, CNBC, and Bravo cable networks
14 TV stations

Time Warner
WB broadcast network
Turner Broadcasting cable channel
Warner Bros and New Line movie studios
Time magazine
America On Line

Tribune Co.
WGN cable network
26 TV stations
LA Times, Chicago Tribune, and 10 other daily
    newspapers

Clear Channel
More than 1,200 radio stations
36 TV stations

A "network" refers to a company that provides content to broadcast and cable stations across the country. Most local broadcast stations have a network affiliation but are not directly owned by a network. Some of these media companies also own large cable providers, which have been the cause of some of the bitterest fights among media giants. If your local television station is owned by Fox, this doesn't hurt ABC's ability to broadcast on another local television station. However, if Fox owns the local cable provider, Fox could choose not to run one of ABC's cable affiliates. Because most cable operators are already monopolies, the viewers would have little choice in the matter.

Federal courts have spoken to this issue several times, and the Supreme Court acknowledged in *Branzburg v. Hayes* that the press do occupy a special position under the Constitution. However, the Court ruled that reporters must testify if subpoenaed about criminal conduct:

> we cannot seriously entertain the notion that the First Amendment protects a newsman's agreement to conceal the criminal conduct of his source, or evidence thereof, on the theory that it is better to write about crime than to do something about it. . . . The crimes of news sources are no less reprehensible and threatening to the public interest when witnessed by a reporter than when they are not.[33]

Although some federal courts have recognized a limited right of refusal, there is no consistent national protection for reporters in such circumstances. Forty-nine states and the District of Columbia have laws that offer journalists some protection from forced testimony, but standards differ. Many of these laws allow compelled testimony if the reporter's testimony would be directly relevant to a criminal case and there is no other way to acquire the necessary evidence.[34]

Over the years journalists have been convicted of contempt of court for refusing to name their sources, some even going to prison instead of breaking the promise they made to a source. Others have testified under the threat of imprisonment. There have even been cases in which the criminal conduct the reporter is shielding is the act of talking to the reporter. In 2003 conservative columnist Robert Novak identified a woman named Valerie Plame as a CIA operative in his column. Plame had in the past been part of a special division within the CIA that is provided with fake jobs and undertakes missions of the deepest secrecy. According to Novak, he was given the information about Plame by two senior Bush administration officials.

Why would someone at the Bush White House illegally release such information? Plame's husband, retired diplomat Joseph Wilson, was a critic of President Bush's claims that Iraq possessed large quantities of weapons of mass destruction, and he had publicly revealed that a key Bush statement was untruthful. Several other Washington journalists were also called with the information about Wilson's wife at the same time as Novak. Had the White House attempted to punish Wilson for his criticism of the president by revealing his wife's secret occupation? If so, they had potentially violated a strict statute that makes such revelations a serious crime.[35] A Justice Department investigation was eventually begun to track down who at the White

House had given out this sensitive information, and several reporters were subpoenaed about their contacts with the White House. Novak swore that he would never divulge a source under any circumstances, and many journalists supported his decision. Ultimately, one journalist was sent to prison for refusing to name her sources, and another relied on waivers issued by his sources that allowed him to testify. Eventually both testified before a grand jury.

In addition to the Plame case, a number of leaks have occurred during the Bush presidency that have angered and embarrassed the administration. In just the period from 2002 to 2006, government sources have leaked information about alleged torture and murder of terrorism suspects, illegal arrests and detentions, unauthorized wiretapping, planting pro-American stories in the Iraqi media, kidnapping terrorism suspects in foreign countries and delivering them to governments that practice torture, and the operation of secret prisons by the CIA in more than seven countries. In response, the Bush administration has subjected many employees, particularly at the CIA, to polygraph examinations, hoping to uncover leakers. President Bush has called the leaking of his wiretapping program a "shameful act" that aided al Qaeda terrorists and damaged American security.[36]

Should journalists have special privileges because of their profession? If any other citizen witnesses a crime, he or she can be subpoenaed and forced to testify. A precedent does exist for such privileges. Some states, federal laws, and federal courts recognize various immunities from testifying, such as the right of a spouse not to testify against his or her partner or the right of priests or therapists to keep confessions to themselves under certain circumstances.

Gag Orders: Can Courts Command Media Silence?

Imagine you are falsely accused of a heinous crime. While you are in custody, stories about the case continue to leak out from prosecutors and police officers—stories that tend to make you look guilty. Your attorney, concerned that the pool of potential jurors will be "tainted" by the sensational and sometimes false information, asks the judge to impose a **gag order** on all parties in the case. A gag order typically prevents all public comment on a case, under penalty of contempt of court. In rare cases, a gag order may apply not only to those involved in the trial but also to the media themselves.[37]

Most gag orders originate from the concern that trials should not be conducted in the media and in the court of public opinion.

There are many reasons to fear such media trials. For one thing, courts have rules about what evidence is admissible. In most rape trials, for example, the past sexual history of the victim is not admissible. Research shows that juries are more likely to acquit if the accuser has a promiscuous past. Because rape shield laws now prevent sexual history from being brought to jurors' attention during the actual trial, some defense attorneys try to get it into the media before juries are selected. Extreme, sensationalistic media attention can make it very difficult to find enough jurors who still have an open mind about a particular case.

The number of gag orders issued by judges has been increasing rapidly according to one study.[38] Some judges seem to impose them almost without a second thought, and most don't hold a hearing before the gag order is imposed. Sometimes a gag order has been applied in cases decided by a judge, in which the danger of tainting a jury is nonexistent. Critics of gag orders point out that if journalists can't talk on the record to any of the parties, they will be forced to rely on leaks and rumors, which may be far less accurate than public statements.

Behind the conflict over gag orders lies the deeper issue of the appropriate balance between the needs of the legal system and the freedom of the press. A trial can be characterized as a battle not only over what the truth is but over which truths are relevant and admissible. The media, on the other hand, often take the attitude that they will circulate as much information as possible and let the public figure out what the truth is. These two attitudes toward information are inherently in conflict. In addition, the modern media's emphasis on appearance and emotion is at odds with traditional court standards of credibility and evidence. Many lawyers believe that news cameras in the courtroom have changed litigating attorneys, judges, and juries—and not for the better.

Perhaps because of this, the legal system remains the most secretive branch of our government (with the possible exception of the military and the intelligence agencies). We know less about how the Supreme Court makes its decisions than we do about the National Security Council's processes or about any aspect of Congress. The Supreme Court does not allow cameras in its hearings, let alone its internal debates. The same is true for jury deliberations across every level of the judiciary. If you were an unpopular defendant, would you want news cameras in the jury room during the debate over your fate?

The media are getting closer to such practices today. Jurors in high-profile criminal cases can expect to appear on national television shortly after the verdict is handed down. Even if jurors in a case involving Michael Jackson or Martha Stewart won't face a camera in the jury room during debate, they know that whatever they say could end up being reported by a fellow juror on *Larry King Live* as soon as the trial ends. This knowledge must affect jury deliberations in ways that are damaging to the cause of justice. There is no easy resolution to the conflict between the needs of the legal system and the needs of the media.

Emblematic of this ongoing debate is the controversy over secret detentions and military tribunals as part of the war on terror. One of the constitutional guarantees that every American possesses is the right to an open criminal justice system. Secret detentions, arrests, and trials have not been part of our history. Yet after 9/11, thousands of citizens and aliens were held by federal authorities, in diverse locations, on uncertain charges and often for lengthy durations. The government denied the media access to the vast majority of detainees or even knowledge of their names. The media also were not allowed to witness the military tribunals at Guantanamo Bay, Cuba. Should the government be allowed to maintain media silence about these detentions, or should it be legally obligated to disclose some minimal information? Should the media have fought harder to find out the names and the conditions facing these prisoners?

INTERNET MEDIA AND THE LAW

Should a news Web site be the same as a newspaper under the law, or should it be considered more like a television station? As we have seen, the law treats broadcast media quite differently from print media. In some ways, the Internet resembles broadcast media; it requires electricity and either a wireless or wired connection. As with television, which is supported by satellites, cable distribution networks, and broadcast towers, a massive infrastructure of servers and cables, some government subsidized, is required to support the Internet. Yet in many ways the Internet resembles a newspaper or even a letter among friends.

Unlike traditional broadcast media, there is practically no limit to the number of Web sites. Because there is no scarcity on the Internet, there is less fear of corporate dominance. Yet the most popular news sites remain those affiliated with major media orga-nizations. So far Internet readers tend to favor sites sponsored by names they know and trust. Of course, there are exceptions, such as the Drudge Report, essentially a one-man operation that gets mil-lions of hits every year from readers. Most "bloggers" (a neologism created from "web log" or an Internet diary) don't get that many readers, but the success of Drudge, Andrew Sullivan, and others suggests that the Internet isn't in danger of speaking in one voice.

Much of the regulation by the FCC, designed to prevent monop-olistic control of the media, does not seem to apply to the Internet. Yet many social conservatives believe the Internet is particularly in need of regulation. They argue that children are frequent users and that it is easy to find hard-core pornography on the Internet. In addi-tion to shielding children from indecent content, regulators seek to protect children from those who use the Internet to distribute child pornography. Congress has attempted several times to regulate indecent and obscene material on the Internet, but the courts so far have not upheld most regulations. In this sense, the Internet is being treated much more like print media.

What about libel on the Internet? Dozens of courts have already addressed questions arising out of alleged libel on the Internet. Internet communications are often full of fiery personal attacks, known as flames. Personal e-mail full of inaccurate venom would probably not qualify as libelous because it is not publicly distrib-uted. However, e-mails posted to public bulletin boards have been the subject of libel suits against both the author and the host of the bulletin board as well as the owner of the server. The outcomes of these cases have varied widely, but in general false public state-ments on the Internet that defame or damage a private citizen or business are actionable.

Perhaps the most famous case of Internet libel occurred when the Drudge Report ran an item in 1997 alleging that new Clinton aide Sydney Blumenthal had violently abused his wife. While Drudge posted a retraction two days later, Blumenthal launched a thirty mil-lion dollar lawsuit over the alleged pain that Drudge's story caused. Drudge admitted that he had been lied to by a Republican source out to damage Blumenthal, but he refused to apologize to Blumenthal for the error. The case was ultimately settled by Blumenthal paying a token amount to Drudge for his court fees.[39] It was unlikely that Blumenthal, a public figure, would have been able to win the case against Drudge because the Internet reporter claimed at least one credible source. However, unlike a more mainstream journalist, Drudge made no effort to verify whether there was a shred of evidence to support the allegation against Blumenthal before distributing it around the world.

One limit on any attempt to regulate the news media on the Internet is the international nature of the Web. It is very easy to jump to Web sites far outside the territory of your own country, and it is difficult to see how national governments can effectively regulate the content of the Internet. The Internet may pose the greatest challenge so far to governments that seek to censor and control their journalists because the Internet gives citizens immediate access to journalists all over the world. Unfortunately, the same is true of child pornographers, gamblers, and others who seek to violate U.S. law.

THE FEDERAL JUDICIARY AND THE MEDIA

Most of the key decisions touching on media law have been made in one place, the Supreme Court. Perhaps not surprisingly, the Supreme Court's own relationship with the media has been highly contentious.

In December 2000, the Supreme Court took an unprecedented step: It allowed the media to immediately broadcast an audiotape of its hearing in *Bush v. Gore,* the case that ultimately decided who won the presidential election of 2000. That the most hidden and secretive branch of our government would take such a step is illustrative of how high the public's attention to politics was at that moment of indecision and doubt. Even under the white-hot scrutiny of a worldwide media frenzy, the Court moved only marginally toward letting journalists into its inner workings. The media were absolutely forbidden to photograph or videotape the proceedings. Most important, journalists and the public were permitted to witness only the oral arguments before the Supreme Court. Much like many floor speeches in Congress, these arguments do not decide the outcome but rather just air key issues in the case. Even some Supreme Court justices consider these hearings mostly show without effect on the ultimate ruling. The most important parts of the story, the actual deliberations, debates, and votes in the inner chambers of the Supreme Court, are always off limits to anyone but the nine justices themselves.

Historically, justices of the Supreme Court have not sought media attention; indeed, just the opposite. There are two main reasons. First, unlike members of Congress or first-term presidents, federal judges will never face the electorate; they serve for life unless impeached by Congress, which happens very rarely. They do not need to maintain their personal popularity through the media as politicians do. Second, one of the firm principles of American jurisprudence is judicial objectivity and impartiality. To the greatest extent possible, competing parties in a case should have no reason to think that any judge is biased for or against them or their positions. If justices agreed to regular interviews and profiles with the media, they would be accused far more frequently of having prejudged important issues and cases. On the rare occasions when sitting federal judges speak out in the media, they can find themselves forced to recuse themselves from a future decision. This happened to Associate Justice Antonin Scalia in 2004. Speaking to a conservative group, he criticized the attempt to get "under God" removed from the pledge of allegiance. When his comments were widely circulated in the media, Scalia had to remove himself from hearing a case dealing with just that situation. Judicial impartiality was also breached when liberal federal judge Guido Calebresi spoke out intemperately against the Bush administration in a speech to a liberal judiciary group. Legitimate questions about Judge Calebresi's impartiality are certain to arise the next time he rules on a case involving President Bush.

The secrecy surrounding the Supreme Court has only occasionally been breached by the media. In the most famous example, reporter Bob Woodward, along with coauthor Scott Armstrong, got access to the personal papers of a number of justices and interviewed many former clerks. Based on those sources, they wrote *The Brethren*, a best-selling account of the inner workings of the Supreme Court, which angered and embarrassed some justices with its raw portrayal of the politics and personalities involved in specific decisions. Much later, a former clerk exposed secrets of the Rehnquist Court's inner deliberations in the book *Closed Chambers*. Both of these books were excerpted in the mainstream press in ways that damaged the Court's reputation according to some observers. The Supreme Court responded to these rare intrusions by forcing future clerks to sign strict nondisclosure agreements in the hope of preserving the Court's low profile and secrecy. Both of these were print exposés: so far, there has been no video intrusion into the Court's sanctity.

Another reason the Court doesn't appear on television is due to the well-known biases of television for simplicity. Court rulings are often so complex that no one without a law degree can grasp the reasoning. Major national newspapers like the *Washington Post* and *New York Times* assign a full-time reporter to cover the Court, and those reporters immerse themselves in the legal issues of each session. Most cable networks hire a few attorneys as needed but don't devote the same level of expertise to the federal judiciary. Sometimes it shows. When the *Bush v. Gore* decision was handed down, several television reporters tried to interpret the dense ruling on camera, with very mixed results.

The Court lacks almost every aspect that would attract television news: the justices are largely anonymous, there is little human drama and conflict, and even still pictures of justices in debate are lacking. When the most important Supreme Court decision in modern U.S. history was handed down, the video media were stuck with the picture of the Clerk of the Court handing out the *Bush v. Gore* ruling to a horde of waiting reporters.

Has the Supreme Court been damaged by its media avoidance? It is clear that Congress felt that it had to get on television to compete with the media power of the American presidency. Yet the same forces are not at work in the federal judiciary. In fact, surveys reliably show that the judiciary is the part of the federal government that Americans trust most and know the least about.[40] There is no public groundswell calling for television cameras in the courtrooms of the federal judiciary. However, more and more Americans are getting used to watching state court cases on television. An entire cable network, Court TV, relies for much of its content on courtroom cameras. The presence of cameras in the O. J. Simpson courtroom taught generations of Americans the basics of criminal law procedure (although it may also have taught them some rather unsavory lessons about the inequality money introduces into the legal system). Regardless, it will be a long time before the federal judiciary joins Congress and televises its hearings. As Associate Justice David Souter put it recently, they will get cameras in the Supreme Court only "over my dead body."

CONCLUSION: NECESSARY INSTITUTIONS IN CONFLICT

The media and the legal system have deeply divergent goals. The legal system pursues justice, whereas the media seek to broadcast information. They may share an interest in the truth, but even this is perceived differently. The legal system often seeks to prevent hearsay and other questionable information from intruding into cases, whereas the media often broadcast stories that they know are incomplete or emerging.

Friction between the law and the media is not uncommon. Reporters seek the utmost extent of First Amendment privileges and resist judicial questioning about sources. Media corporations resist ownership regulation and lobby Congress and the FCC for ever looser rules. It may also be no accident of history that the televised media are the most tightly regulated. The government, aware of the potential power of video to shape political ideas, has historically placed tighter restrictions on television than on print media. If the Internet emerges as the dominant medium in the next decade, how will government regulators respond?

KEY TERMS

anonymous speech
censorship
chilling effect
clear and present danger
commercial speech
equal time
Federal Communications
  Commission (FCC)

Freedom of Information Act
  (FOIA)
gag order
libel
Near v. Minnesota
Pentagon Papers case
prior restraint

DISCUSSION QUESTIONS

1. Do you think prior restraint is ever justified?
2. Do you worry about media consolidation in which fewer and fewer companies own more and more of the media?
3. Should reporters have the right to keep their sources secret?
4. Should reporters honor "gag rules" that judges issue during high-profile trials?
5. Should radio and television stations be forced to take any nonobscene political ad on the theory that the public, and not the stations, actually own the airwaves?
6. Do you believe the government is doing enough, not enough, or too much to regulate indecent and obscene material in broadcast media?

ADDITIONAL RESOURCES

The Media Monopoly, by Ben Bagdikian, is a seminal text, newly revised, on how media conglomerates are increasingly in control of what Americans read and watch.

Mass Media Law, by Don R. Pember and Clay Calvert, is an excellent textbook covering all the major media cases in American law.

ONLINE RESOURCES

www.fcc.org.gov is the official Web site of the FCC. You can read about recent cases, study profiles of the commissioners, and get an overview of the commission's functions.

http://foi.missouri.edu is the Web site of the Freedom of Information Center, run by University of Missouri's Journalism School. It analyzes government openness, monitors enforcement of secrecy laws, and advocates for greater press access to information.

NOTES

1. *Near v. Minnesota* 283 U.S. 697 (1931).
2. John MacKenzie, "Court Rules for Newspapers, 6–3," *Washington Post,* July 1, 1971: A1.
3. *New York Times v. U.S.* 403 U.S. 713 (1971).
4. Howard B. Morland, *The Secret That Exploded* (New York: Random House, 1984).
5. *U.S. v. Progressive* 467 F. Supp 990 (1979).
6. ACLU Newswire, "NH Primaries, HIV Prevention and Free Speech." December 23, 1996. Archive.aclu.org
7. Oliver Wendell Holmes, in *Schenck v. U.S.* 249 U.S. 47 (1919).
8. *Brandenburg v. Ohio* 395 U.S. 444 (1969).
9. Howard Kurtz, "Clinton Long Under Siege by Conservative Detractors," *Washington Post,* January 28, 1998: A1.
10. Josh Green, "Be Careful What You Pray For," *The American Prospect,* April 9, 2001.
11. Reporters Committee for Freedom of the Press, letter to Secret Service, 2/15/01. Available at rcfp.org
12. *Central Hudson v. New York* 477 U.S. 557 (1980).
13. A related term, "slander," refers to verbal falsehoods.
14. *New York Times v. Sullivan* 376 U.S. 254 (1964).
15. Rodney A. Smolla, *Jerry Falwell vs. Larry Flynt* (New York: St. Martin's Press, 1988).
16. Charles Lane, "Privacy Case Goes Before Justices," *Washington Post,* December 4, 2003: A04.
17. *Office of Independent Counsel v. Favish* (02-0954).
18. *McIntyre v. Ohio Elections Commission* 63 Sup. Ct. 4279 (1995).
19. Laura Meckler, "Secret Money Enters Political System," *Laredo Morning Times,* June 7, 2000: 10A.

20. Jeremy D. Mayer, *Running on Race* (New York: Random House, 2002).
21. Geoffrey Ward, *A First Class Temperament* (New York: Harper Collins, 1992).
22. A. Michael Froomkin, "Anonymity and Its Enmities," *Journal of Online Law* (1995): 4.
23. Radio Service Bulletin. May 1, 1922: 23–30.
24. *FCC v. Pacifica* 98 S Ct. 3026 (1978).
25. John Maynard, "Near-Record Fines for Radio Indecency: 'Elliot,' 'Opie & Anthony' Cited by FCC," *Washington Post,* October 3, 2003: C03.
26. F. Leslie Smith, Milan Meeske, and John W. Wright II, *Electronic Media and Government* (White Plains, NY: Longman, 1995).
27. Craig Kilborn, "My Couch Is Too Small for 135 Candidates," *New York Times,* August 30, 2003.
28. Ford Rowan, *Broadcast Fairness: Doctrine, Practice, Prospects: A Reappraisal of the Fairness Doctrine and Equal Time Rule* (New York: Longman, 1984).
29. Dan Kennedy, "Mad as Hell," *Boston Phoenix,* June 6–13, 2003.
30. Jay Ambrose, "Limiting Freedom for the Public 'Good,'" *Washington Times,* June 8, 2003.
31. Ben H. Bagdikian, *The Media Monopoly,* 6th ed. (Boston: Beacon Press, 2000).
32. Frank Ahrens, "FCC Eases Media Ownership Rules," *Washington Post,* June 3, 2003: A1.
33. *Branzburg v. Hayes* 408 U.S. 665 (1972).
34. Douglas Lee, "Press Shield Laws." First Amendment Center, 2003. firstamendmentcenter.org
35. Vicky Ward, "Double Exposure," *Vanity Fair,* January 2003.
36. Dan Eggen, "White House Trains Efforts on Media Leaks," *Washington Post,* March 5, 2006.
37. Gag orders that apply to the media directly were largely ruled unconstitutional in *Nebraska Press Association v. Stuart* 427 S. Ct 529 (1976).
38. Lucy Daglish, "The News Media Must Keep Fighting the 'Gag Instinct,'" *The News Media and the Law,* Spring, vol 24 (2000): 2.
39. Anthony York, "Drudge vs. Blumenthal," *Salon,* May 2, 2001.
40. John R. Hibbing and Elizabeth Theiss-Morse, *Congress as Public Enemy: Public Attitudes Toward American Political Institutions* (New York: Cambridge University Press, 1995), 32.

CHAPTER 7

The Personalized, Image-based Media Presidency

*I*nside the White House lives one of the most recognizable persons in the world. The modern global media have made the U.S. president a public figure in almost every country on earth. As the last remaining superpower, the United States is the focus of more media attention than any other country. The president personifies the nation and receives the lion's share of this attention. With rare exceptions, people at home and abroad learn about this most powerful person through the prism of the media.

Every president attempts to manage the media using the formidable powers of his office. Does the president sit atop the media like a man holding the reins of a horse, confident and in charge; or is the president perched precariously atop a hungry tiger, always on the verge of falling off and being eaten? Do the media determine whether a presidency is successful? Can the media be managed by the president and his staff? Should the media be managed?

THE PRESIDENT'S POWER AND THE MEDIA

The media have empowered the president in the last hundred years, increasing the president's ability to persuade citizens and overpower Congress. When Thomas Jefferson was president, he wrote a friend that he hoped "to avoid attracting notice and to keep my name out of newspapers."[1] Such sentiments would be ludicrous today, and were unrealistic even then as Jefferson, the victim of scurrilous rumors and sordid stories, already knew. Yet the expectation that the media would focus more on Congress was not entirely wrong. For most of America's history, Congress had the dominant role in policy making; today the president is the mover of the agenda. There are many reasons for this change, but the media's focus on the presidency provides both cause and effect of the president's rise to preeminence.

The media projects the president into the homes of Americans on a daily basis while often ignoring Congress and Cabinet secretaries. This shows the power of images and narratives. The presidency is a simple story of struggle, of identifiable successes and failures. The Congress, the bureaucracy, the courts, the political parties—other institutions of power that compete with the president for control of the nation's agenda—appear so complex by comparison that the news media have a difficult time conveying much about their struggle. In truth, the presidency is also a complex institution with thousands of employees and difficult internecine battles. But unlike most other political institutions, the presidency can appear to be the story of one person. This empowers the president.

One example is the media's attention to the president's family. Does anyone recognize the spouses or children of the leaders of Congress? How often are they profiled in the mass media? The focus on the presidential family, which has been a staple of television news coverage of the presidency since at least Kennedy, humanizes the president. The First Lady is usually among the most admired women in America in almost every national survey. The media make her a star, and this gives the president an additional boost in the polls and even in political fund-raising because First Ladies now hold independent political events to raise money for their husbands' campaigns.

Of course, the media's appetite for White House family news can hurt a president as well. President Clinton was embarrassed by his brother's troubles with the law and by his brother-in-law's questionable dealings in Eastern Europe and elsewhere. The first president Bush saw one of his sons pilloried in the media for his involvement in the savings and loan scandals of the late 1980s, and the second president Bush saw global coverage of his brother's involvement with prostitutes. Even such family embarrassments may serve to further humanize the occupant of the White House. Many Americans can sympathize with a man embarrassed or troubled by the behavior of his close relatives.

An American president receives more coverage from his nation's media than do most other chief executives because the president plays so many roles in our system. Germany, the United Kingdom, and most other democracies split the function of "head of state" from "chief executive." In the U.K., the monarch is the head of state, and the prime minister leads the government. The president of the United States is both king and prime minister. The president's family become for our media what the royal family is for the British press. Sometimes, as with the Kennedys and the Reagans, the media glare lasts long after the president has left office.

Because he is the head of state, the president has immediate access to sacred icons of our nation in a way that no other political actor does. The White House itself is a potent symbol of the nation, and the president can display it at will whenever he feels the need to enhance his personal gravitas. The White House is the most frequently used symbol, but presidents can pick any one of dozens of settings for policy announcements and photo opportunities, each laden with emotion and history. Arlington National Cemetery, Mount Rushmore, Yellowstone National Park, Monticello, and the Statue of Liberty are some of the venues presidents have used. Leaders of Congress or political opponents of the president have a much more difficult time gaining national media attention during a visit to one of these sites. The president's opponent for reelection cannot easily deliver a partisan speech at a national park or monument, but the incumbent president can by simply scheduling it.

Whenever national tragedy strikes, the nation and the media look to the White House for a statement or for a comforting speech. In 1995, when the Oklahoma City terrorist bombing occurred, President Clinton was at a weak point in his presidency. His magnificent speech at the site of the bombing helped remind Americans of his gift for communicating and deftly allowed him to criticize the antigovernment radicalism of certain Republican figures. When the *Challenger* space shuttle blew up in January of 1986, Ronald Reagan delivered one of the great speeches of the last thirty years, reminding Americans of his fundamental decency and charismatic leadership. The president also has international prestige that no other U.S. politician can harness. A trip abroad gives the president access to media images of foreign capitals, American flags, and the stirring sounds of "Hail to the Chief," the president's official song. Suffice to say, the leaders of the House, the Senate, and the Supreme Court lack a well-known anthem that the media could play on the rare occasions when they travel abroad.

BUSH'S DISCIPLINED IMAGE MANAGEMENT

The Bush White House has been justly famed for its discipline. Unlike President Clinton's administration, which was notorious for its inability to keep secrets and prevent staff leaks, the Bush team has developed a "passion for anonymity" that helps it serve the president better. Clinton staffers relished their media appearances, but Bush staffers tend to brag about not calling reporters back.[2] This discipline has allowed Bush to craft a much more targeted and successful media strategy.

The Bush White House has been very careful to place positive messages in text around the president at every public event. If he is speaking on education, education slogans are put at every possible angle around him. If it is the economy, upbeat words about jobs and employment will be displayed in the background.[3] Regardless of what the media say about a speech by Bush on education, his message of "No Child Left Behind" will have a chance of escaping the media filter and reaching the viewer because that exact phrase is embedded in every media image shown. Similarly, because Bush wants to convey an image of support from average Americans, at some speeches wealthy Republican supporters on the stage behind the president have been asked to remove their neckties so they will look more like working-class Americans.[4] The attention to image is total, as Bush's top image adviser told the *New York Times:*

> We pay particular attention to not only what the president says but what the American people see. . . . Americans are leading

CHALLENGES FOR THE PRESIDENT

One of the biggest challenges facing the president comes not from the other institutions of political power, such as the Congress, but from the infotainment cacophony of the media. A presidential policy announcement competes with the latest movie news, celebrity gossip, sports stories, and pure entertainment such as sitcoms, reality shows, and soap operas. If a presidential speech doesn't even make cable news, does it really matter? In 1996 President Clinton and his busy lives, and sometimes they don't have the opportunity to read a story or listen to an entire broadcast. But if they can have an instant understanding of what the president is talking about by seeing 60 seconds of television, you accomplish your goals as communicators.[5]

Bush is hardly the first president to manage his image. Indeed, historians claim that George Washington was extremely vigilant over his dress, bearing, and overall appearance because he believed that it was vital to leadership.[6] But the Bush White House has gone to greater lengths than most administrations to avoid ugly pictures. Prior to the president's visit to troops in Iraq over the Thanksgiving holiday in 2003, the military made sure that troops who did not support the president would be left out of the ceremony.[7] Under the claim of presidential safety, the White House has also prevented protesters from getting within half a mile of Bush during his visits around the country, an unprecedented level of security that some attribute to the desire to avoid clouding the positive themes with images of dissent.[8] Unlike President Clinton, who engaged in townhall meetings early in his administration in which nonsupporters of the administration were given a chance to interact with the president, sometimes with very negative outcomes, the Bush White House rarely puts the president in situations where he will be confronted by angry constituents, and very few in which he will face unexpected questions. As a consequence, the media have very few unappealing images of Bush to run, even if we assume that they want to do so.

staff worried that the State of the Union address, one of the premier media events on the presidential calendar, would be dwarfed by the release on the same night of the verdict in the O. J. Simpson civil trial. Although the worst case scenario—a verdict delivered in the middle of the speech—did not occur, much of the coverage put Simpson's verdict ahead of the president's proposals.

The media also create expectations that must be met, or the president may pay a heavy price. In 1993 *Time* magazine portrayed President Clinton on its cover as a miniature figurine, labeled the "incredibly shrinking presidency." In part, this was because Clinton had failed to convince the media that he was still atop events and controlling the nation's agenda. The media that make a president can swiftly tear him down.

Presidents must satisfy the media, which has been called "feeding the beast." At the most fundamental level, the media expect the president to make news, the commodity that they sell to the public. If a president fails to make news about his positive agenda, the media may be forced to write negative stories in an effort to have stories. The president must respond, and quickly, to important developments throughout the world; otherwise, the media may well report that the White House is befuddled or adrift. In late 2004, when President George W. Bush waited four days to speak on camera about the disastrous Asian tsunamis, he faced criticism in the press. Presidents no longer have the luxury of taking a few days to consider their response. The media won't allow it.

Of course, presidents must also understand when they cannot comment on a matter, regardless of how much the media desire it. In 1994 and 1995 President Clinton was pressured to make some statement about the "trial of the century," the O. J. Simpson case. Politically, anything Clinton could have said would have hurt him, given that some of his strongest supporters, the vast majority of African Americans, believed Simpson to be innocent, but the majority of the nation thought the former football star was guilty. Wisely, Clinton avoided giving his own views. "Feeding the beast" by commenting on every controversy in the media is not the path to presidential success, although this would make the White House press corps very happy.

Luckily for them, presidents don't face the challenge of the media alone. Some of the best minds in public relations and media politics are available to help a president navigate the difficult terrain of presidential–journalist relations.

THE WHITE HOUSE MEDIA STAFF

The growth of the office of the presidency in the last hundred years has been extraordinary. The number of people who worked directly for the president was a few dozen late into the nineteenth century. Today thousands labor for the executive office of the president (EOP), the apex of the executive branch. Many of them spend all or part of their time doing media relations. The influence and prominence of the press secretary and other communications staffers have also grown over time. Each president organizes his White House differently; the discussion here follows the broad outline of the George W. Bush White House.

Communications Office

The **Communications Office** takes primary responsibility for handling the media. In the Bush White House, Communications is in charge of speechwriting, the office of the press secretary, global communications, and media affairs. The current director of communications, Nicole Devenish, helps craft the president's overall message and image, along with top political advisers in and out of the administration. Working with pollsters and other consultants, the Communications Office decides how to sell the president's policies to the nation and how to position him on emerging events and issues.

Among the responsibilities of the Communications Office are to decide when and how to expose the president to the press. Each day brings new issues and events and new opportunities for the president to make an impression on Americans. The media staff has to determine what venue will show the president in the best light. The Communications Office also monitors how the president is doing. In many administrations, weekly reports on the coverage in television and print media circulate among top staff. In Clinton's White House a pollster kept careful tabs on each White House story on network news: where did it appear in the newscast, how long was the story, and was it positive or negative?[9]

In most White Houses the communications director also plans media appearances for the entire administration.[10] A Cabinet secretary who gets booked onto the Sunday talk shows without at least notifying the White House is likely to find her- or himself in deep trouble.

Here are the other specific offices that the Communications Office oversees.

Office of the Press Secretary The **press secretary** is the person most Americans think of when they imagine the staff the president assigns to handle the press. The press secretary has several major responsibilities, most involving managing the White House press corps. To do this, the secretary holds two types of briefings, at least one almost every weekday. The first, called **the gaggle,** usually happens without cameras. The White House press corps gather to ask the press secretary questions. The briefing typically begins with a dry recitation of the president's scheduled activities for the day.

By contrast, televised briefings in front of cameras from all the major networks can often be contentious and confrontational. Some attribute this to the television cameras, which first appeared at some briefings in the 1980s. The cameras were usually allowed only to record images, without sound, unless a major announcement was taking place. Since 1995, briefings have been routinely televised with sound. Former Clinton press secretary Mike McCurry believes this has led to a decline in their usefulness:

> In retrospect . . . as much as it made me famous, it was a mistake. It became this kind of theater of the absurd, with people braying their questions and the press secretary with sweat pouring down his forehead taking all this incoming fire.[11]

Press secretaries are often pushed to defend presidential policies that seem contradictory or unpopular. Their job is particularly hard when the president they serve is avoiding the press corps. When McCurry worked for Clinton, there was a long period when Clinton refused to answer questions about the Lewinsky scandal that eventually led to his impeachment. Clinton, who had enjoyed many press conferences prior to the scandal, now left it to McCurry to respond to each development in the various scandals Clinton was tied to. But even when the president is regularly answering questions from the media, the press secretary faces an almost daily barrage of questions on almost every imaginable topic.

Briefing reporters is only the most visible aspect of the press secretary's job. From dawn to midnight, a press secretary finds himself tracking down various stories, keeping in close touch with reporters from the White House beat. Often, a press secretary tries very hard to affect how a story is covered, even if he can't stop a particular storyline from emerging. The office of the press secretary also handles all interview requests for the president and top officials and, working with the White House Travel Office, helps make sure travel arrangements are made for the media when the president leaves the White House.

Speechwriting   Every recent president has had a team of wordsmiths who author the dozens of speeches a president must give each week.

Because these speeches often become news, they must be carefully vetted by the Communications Office. Major addresses to Congress or the nation undergo a lengthy process of review involving senior staff and relevant Cabinet secretaries. Presidents vary in their own level of participation in speechwriting, with some writing large parts of important speeches themselves and others simply giving positive or negative feedback at various stages of the scripting process.

Speechwriting has changed due to the influence of modern media norms. Given that the television news grants an average of only seven seconds to comments by a politician, speeches are now sound-bite delivery systems. They don't have to hold together as coherent narratives or sustained works of poetic images and rhetoric. Today's speeches are often a series of unrelated ideas, each section intended to deliver to the cameras a short sharp slogan: "Read my lips—No new taxes" (Bush I), "The era of big government is over" (Clinton), "Axis of evil" (Bush II). These sound bites have to work with the overall themes established by the Communications Office.

Another big change in speechwriting that the media has caused is the decline of ad-libbing by the president. During JFK's presidency, speechwriters concentrated on major addresses, and the president would often interact with groups with no prepared remarks. In part, this was because of Kennedy's glibness and ease in public speaking. However, it was also because the media were not in twenty-four-hour "gotcha" mode. Today the press corps cover every public utterance of the president, looking for a video clip showing an error, misstatement, mispronunciation, gaffe, or inappropriate remark. Speechwriters now prepare for almost every interaction between the president and the public.[12]

Media Affairs Office   This office handles all of the media that aren't included in the White House press corps. This includes local news, almost all radio outlets, Spanish-language media, the religious press, and any other special interest press that occasionally needs White House access, such as sports reporters covering the traditional visit to the White House by victorious athletic teams. The Media Affairs Office also designs and administers the White House Web page, an increasingly important part of the public face of the administration.

Global Communications   This small office is responsible for handling much of the international media. The president is news around the globe, and the White House has to address the concerns of international journalists as well. This office also provides advice to other government agencies that communicate with international audiences and helps plan for foreign media interactions during overseas trips.

Other White House Offices with Media Responsibilities

Although the Communications Office controls all the major offices that directly deal with the press, a number of other parts of the White House inevitably interact with the media. The First Lady and the vice president have separate press offices to handle media relations. The Communications Office must also work very closely with the Presidential Advance Office, which interacts with local authorities when the president travels. Before the president arrives on a stage to give a speech or attend a conference, hundreds of small decisions made by communications and advance staff have to be carefully made. What color should the podium be? How tall should it be? Where should the news cameras be placed? Who should be on the stage behind the president? Who will make sure that the president gets to shake hands with an appropriately diverse group of constituents? For the Bush administration's townhall meetings, the questions are particularly exact: Which audience member is authorized to ask a question? What will the question be? How should it be phrased? How should the president answer it? All of these decisions go toward making the president look good on television so that regardless of what the media may say about the president's speech or visit, the pictures and sound bites will be flattering to the president and advance his agenda.

The White House Press Corps

Although they don't work for the president, the **White House press corps,** the correspondents who cover the president, have offices at 1600 Pennsylvania Avenue. Their relationship with the White House media staff is both symbiotic and contentious, intimate and distant. As happens in many presidencies, the press have expressed great frustration with the information control exerted by the Bush White House. Many believe that Bush and his press office are particularly effective at message discipline. As Bill Plante, a CBS News White House correspondent since 1980, put it: "In this administration, the controls on information are tighter than in any other one I have covered."[13] Among the complaints that are frequently heard is that

Bush punishes those who write critically about his administration, and that White House staffers tend to use exactly the same talking points on the few occasions reporters have access to them. If the administration didn't have a unified message on important questions, however, the press would be the first to label this a controversy and a problem of management by the president. As former Bush press secretary Ari Fleischer points out, it may not be possible to please the press, regardless of what the White House does.

> I think there is a difference between the press's demand for information and the public's demand for information. . . . Sometimes I think the press won't be satisfied until there's Oval Cam, and people can watch the president 24 hours a day in the Oval Office.[14]

It also seems possible that the Bush White House has a low regard for the press as an institution. Members of the White House Staff have gone so far as to describe the media as just another "special interest" instead of how the media prefer to see themselves—a voice for and representative of the public.

Who are the members of the White House press corps? They are usually promising prominent journalists who have competed very hard to get the plum post at the White House. Every national network and cable news network has a reporter working the White House beat, and the major newspapers do as well. The prestige of the assignment has varied over time, declining in recent years because Bush seldom held press conferences in his first term. **Presidential press conferences** are opportunities for the whole nation to watch the White House press corps challenge the president with tough questions. These are rare moments in American politics. In Great Britain, by contrast, prime ministers face weekly questioning from their political opponents in Parliament. The dialogue is often sharp and critical, and prime ministers and their supporters must be deft speakers, atop many facts and political situations. The American president is much more insulated from harsh questioning; the only time a president faces anything like "Question Time" is when he holds a press conference in front of the White House media, and even then the questions are usually much easier than those faced by the British prime minister.

Press conferences were begun in the last century, with the first (depending on how we define "press conference") occurring during the presidency of William Howard Taft (1909–1913). Presidents from Calvin Coolidge to Harry Truman (1923–1953) averaged five press conferences a month.[15] When technology first made it possible for press conferences to be televised during the Eisenhower administration, they became far more staged and formal events. They also became less frequent.

Televised presidential press conferences had become institutionalized by the 1960s, a part of the job that few thought a president could avoid. In fact, they were seen by some journalists as essential to our democracy.[16] Some presidents, such as Kennedy, were at their best during press conferences and held them frequently. So deft was JFK at answering questions that his staff allowed the conferences to be televised live, which Eisenhower had avoided. When Presidents Nixon, Reagan, and Clinton went through extended periods without press conferences because of scandals, the media became critical. Early in the George W. Bush administration, conservative columnist William Safire warned that Bush's failure to schedule press conferences was dangerous to his presidency:

> If the Bush administration fails to set and adhere to a regular schedule of televised meetings with the press, he will be disserving the public and weakening his governing discipline. . . . The whole bureaucracy convulses to come up with specific policy decisions lest the top man go off half-cocked. Those suggested answers are studied, and often amended, by the president. That's how he finds out if his administration is marching in the direction he desires.[17]

Many in the media agreed with Safire that the press conference was a vital way for a president to communicate with the American people, and that presidents would pay a substantial price for avoiding them.

Bush is known to keenly dislike press conferences, however. He seems to perceive them as "gotcha" exercises where the media try to trip him up or reveal gaps in his knowledge. Consequently, in his first year in office Bush held fewer press conferences than any president in almost one hundred years.[18] Instead of facing a barrage of press criticism for avoiding press conferences, Bush was often praised by the press for the disciplined nature of his media strategy. Avoiding press conferences was part of that success in his first term. As former Bush communications director Dan Bartlett put it, "if you have a message you're trying to deliver, a news conference can go in a different direction." Even when Bush agrees to take questions from the press corps, he tends to announce these sessions with little advance warning, a tactic intended to keep the media from preparing carefully.

Bush does interact almost every day with at least a few members of the White House press corps. The president is usually involved in several photo opportunities each day, but the ground rules established by the Communications Office often forbid questions. Sometimes selected print and television journalists get to throw a couple of questions at the president. The president can choose which of several questions he wants to answer, or he can use the visiting dignitary or prominent guest to dodge difficult questions. If the president is hosting the king of Saudi Arabia, a question might come up about a particular controversy in domestic politics. If the president feels unprepared, he can easily say, "I'm here today to talk about what we are doing to help the people of the Middle East, with my good friend, the king of Saudi Arabia."

Reagan's communications staff found an ingenious way to give him limited but positive exposure to the press corps. As Reagan walked down the long path to the presidential helicopter, the press corps would shout questions at him, struggling to be heard over the noisy propellers. If Reagan heard one that he wanted to answer (perhaps one his staff had anticipated by giving Reagan a comic line or tart response), he would get just close enough to answer it. If a follow-up came on a subject that he didn't want to discuss, Reagan could hold his hands up to his ears and point at the helicopter as if to say, "I'm so sorry, I'd love to answer that, but I can't hear it over the chopper." So effective was this method that White House journalist Sam Donaldson became famous for literally bellowing his questions to Reagan in an effort to be heard over the chopper.

Should we be concerned about a president who seldom holds formal press conferences? Some feel that it allows Bush to avoid tough questions about the economy, the war in Iraq, and other matters. Yet Bush may well have had a point about the press being a "special interest." Reporters may lament the decline of the press conference because so many prominent journalists, particularly television broadcasters, rose to prominence by asking tough questions at nationally televised presidential press conferences (Donaldson, Dan Rather, and Wolf Blitzer, to name just a few). Moreover, doing well at a press conference may demonstrate presidential glibness, wit, charisma, and mastery of facts and details. Are these the most important traits for a president to possess? Certainly some great American presidents, such as Thomas Jefferson, would have been unlikely to do well at a modern press conference.

TABLE 7.1   Presidential Press
Conferences for Recent Presidents
(*First two years and 45 days in office*)

President	Number of Press Conferences
Lyndon Johnson	52
Richard Nixon	16
Gerald Ford	37
Jimmy Carter	45
Ronald Reagan	16
George H. W. Bush	58
Bill Clinton	30
George W. Bush	8

Source: Research by Martha Joynt Kumar as reported by
Mike Allen, "Bush's Distaste for News Conferences
Keeps Them Rare," *Washington Post,* March 7, 2003: A20.

Perhaps in response to those who criticized Bush for avoiding conferences, or in reaction to persistent low approval ratings in the early
months of his second term, Bush began to hold press conferences
almost every four weeks. However, later in his second term, Bush
returned to his previous pattern of few press conferences. See Table 7.1
for a list of presidential press conferences for recent presidents.

Asking the president questions at press conferences and photo
opportunities is only a small part of the job of a White House correspondent. They also work the entire White House beat, getting the
administration's reactions to world events and congressional legislation. They travel with the president all over the nation and the world.
Although the glamorous aspects of the job may have declined under
Bush, the daily drudgery of the **body watch** must still be performed.
The body watch is the assignment of a small number of reporters to
closely accompany the president each day so that if anything newsworthy happens, a pool report will be immediately available to all
the media. "Newsworthy" events can range from a presidential fall
off a bicycle to witnessing historic moments such as assassination attempts or presidential reactions to sudden unexpected international
events such as invasions or terrorist attacks. Most of the time the
body watch is exceedingly boring but necessary work.

The White House Correspondents Association hosts an annual
dinner that most presidents and vice presidents attend. The comic
evening is one of the premier events on the Washington social

calendar, and for some critics it symbolizes the incestuous nature of the relationship between the president and the reporters who cover him. Rather than having an adversarial relationship, some feel that the modern White House press corps are far too cozy with the president and his staff. Like many presidents before him, Bush has tried to cultivate certain members of the White House press corps, giving several of them memorable nicknames. Bush has always enjoyed teasing journalists and bantering with them in a lighthearted way, as shown in the campaign film *Journeys with George*. In that documentary, filmed on the Bush campaign plane by a young television journalist, we see Bush turning on the charm for the reporters who cover him.

MEDIA TACTICS FOR GOOD NEWS: POLISHING THE POSITIVE

Tactics refer to the methods each White House adopts for handling specific issues. Even good news can't just be released. The timing, method, and style of the announcement of good news is a highly complex matter.

Good news typically has several characteristics. First, it is often something for which the White House can plan ahead. If a particular program is having great success in one of the Cabinet departments, the president's staff will know ahead of time and can plan an event around an announcement. Second, there is often an information monopoly; in many good news situations, the White House is the only voice of authority. When the Bush White House informed the world that they had captured Saddam Hussein, there were almost no other sources of information about the manner of his capture or his current whereabouts. The executive branch, through the Pentagon, was running the story.

Here are some common ways the communication staff of the president handles good news.

The Press Release or Announcement

The White House issues thousands of press releases every year. The communications staff has to decide which type is appropriate for each piece of good news. The simplest form is a document, frequently distributed to the media electronically. This is appropriate for minor public events of the president: meetings with low-profile groups or celebrities, signing relatively obscure congressional legislation, or issuing symbolic proclamations about "Broccoli Week." Such a tactic signals to the media that this "good news" is not even worth the time it takes to make it part of the press secretary's briefing. Of course, specialized media that are particularly concerned with this event will be able to make news out of this release, so it is not wasted effort by the staff. A presidential meeting with a group of high school seniors from a small Midwestern city isn't news—except in the students' hometown where the press release will make the front page.

Slightly higher profile events and announcements are made by the press secretary or his deputy at the gaggle or the full televised briefing. If the staff thinks the topic merits greater attention, a Cabinet secretary or other senior official might be invited to join the press secretary at the podium. This creates a picture that is more appealing to the media, giving them a new face for the televised news to broadcast. The heat is turned up even more if the president drops by the briefing room. Particularly if there have been few recent press conferences, a chance for reporters to see and ask questions of the incumbent will attract much more attention to the topic of the announcement.

Presidential Events and Photo Ops

If the good news is sufficiently good, the White House can work it into the president's schedule as a full-fledged event. Good news announced in person by the president in a dramatic setting almost guarantees positive press coverage. This is particularly true if the president travels from Washington to make the announcement. The local media will surely cover the event with lavish attention. If celebrities or other politicians can be brought to the event, all the better. Attention to every aspect of the announcement is crucial to ensure maximum positive press.

The difficulty with scheduling an event is the finite nature of the president's time and the relatively limited budget for White House travel and advance work. The president can't spend all his time making announcements of minor successes. Also, there is a limit to how often the media will cover the president in any given week absent a crisis. So presidential events must be used sparingly. The easiest to do is a simple photo op in which several White House photographers are permitted to take pictures of the president with a guest.

Timing

When should good news be released? Obviously, at a time that will ensure maximum press coverage. In 1997 Clinton press secretary Mike McCurry was given some good news: the FBI and CIA had apprehended Mir Aimal Kansi, who had brazenly murdered two CIA employees in Virginia four years earlier. McCurry was asked when the arrest should be announced and responded without hesitation—8 p.m. This would lead to the greatest amount of positive coverage in the nation's newspapers due to the nature of modern news cycles. Reporters would have only a couple of hours before their final deadlines to throw a partial story together, almost entirely based on the White House's version of the facts. Because the story would be somewhat brief and incomplete, without the usual responses from experts and other political figures, the papers would be forced to run another story the next day, thus producing two days of good headlines for Clinton.[19] The same logic used to apply to network television news, although now that twenty-four-hour cable news is in the mix, timing is less important for television news.

Scoop Service

If a bit of good news is leaked as an exclusive to one media outlet, it is likely to get very large coverage in that outlet.[20] This tactic can be part of a larger strategy of cultivation. It does have the downside of potentially alienating other reporters, but few journalists can resist the thrill of getting a scoop on all their competitors in the press.

Theme

Good news can be made the White House "theme of the day." Communications staff used to have thematic goals linked to months and weeks. Although they still make these decisions, most of the attention is now paid to daily talking points that are often distributed to all White House staff and political allies around Washington. With leaders in Congress and the president's own staff all giving essentially the same answers on the same issue, the media are forced to give full voice to the White House's view of a topic. A bit of good news on the economy can fit into a daily theme such as "Fighting for Working Families."

BUYING GOOD PRESS?

**Secret Media Subsidies
and the Bush Administration**

You are watching the local news one night and see a news clip
from Washington about the new prescription drug benefit plan
signed by President Bush. The reporter, Karen Ryan, seems remarkably positive about the program. The brief story ends, and
the local anchor moves on to the next story.[21]

According to some media analysts, you just became a victim of government propaganda. Although the news director
who put the clip on the air knew that it came from the Bush
administration, viewers around the country assumed Karen
Ryan was a legitimate reporter and not a paid government
contractor. Eighteen organizations of journalists, representing
more than 25,000 reporters, issued a statement lambasting the
use of government funds to create propaganda disguised as
journalism. The Government Accounting Office, a nonpartisan watchdog on misdeeds by the executive branch, declared
that the Video News Releases (VNRs) by the Health and
Human Services Department were likely illegal. Although no
one was prosecuted, the Bush administration did promise to
cease the practice.

Themes also allow the communications staff to set goals and
evaluate their success. If the media aren't picking up on their chosen themes, they can analyze why this is so. Did unanticipated bad
news blow the positive news out of the headlines? Did the media
choose another angle about the selected topic? Themes are often attempts by the White House to impose a frame on the media's coverage (see Chapter 3). If a medal ceremony is held for soldiers who
fought in Iraq, the event might be linked to several antiterror
initiatives in an attempt to frame the conflict in Iraq as part of a
broader war against terrorism. If the media choose a different frame
and ignore the White House's theme, the media staff will have to
ask themselves what went wrong.

During President Bush's first term, it was also discovered that the Department of Education had spent hundreds of thousands of dollars on contracts with journalists and commentators to get them to promote the administration's education reforms. After much criticism from the press and from Democrats, administration officials, including the president, admitted that these actions were wrong.[22] As with the VNR's, the danger came not from a columnist agreeing with the administration but rather from television shows and columns promoting the administration's viewpoint that never told readers and viewers that they were subsidized views paid for with their own tax dollars.

Such actions are taken so seriously by journalists because they threaten to directly erode the trust people have in the independence of the media. Congress had banned such practices because they realized that if government secretly purchases the news the free marketplace of ideas itself is endangered. Of all the innovative tactics adopted by the Bush administration to support the president's popularity and his programs, buying good press was recognized by both the administration and the media as outside the bounds of acceptable practice.

MEDIA TACTICS FOR BAD NEWS: DAMAGE CONTROL

No matter how successful a presidency is, bad news is inevitable, and the media staff of the president must have tactics ready for these occurrences. There are days when the press is in a "feeding frenzy," and the president's policies appear to be ineffective, contradictory, or deceptive.

Bad news can be particularly challenging when certain conditions are present. First, the media staff often does not have any warning about the onset of bad news. It can occur at any time and is usually immune to scheduling efforts. Second, the White House will usually be one voice among several when bad news occurs. Third, the fundamental facts may not be known to the communications staff. During the Whitewater scandal, many bits of information were held by the president's lawyers, or by the president and the First Lady, and the president's communication staffers were unaware of what the actual facts were. How could they manage a story that they didn't completely understand or grasp?

Squelching

The best way to handle bad news is to prevent the media from covering it at all by convincing the media that there is no story. Because the media are the filter through which Americans perceive their president, if a story isn't played in the major media, it doesn't exist for most Americans. Sometimes the communications staff has to press hard to prevent a number of media organizations from covering a story by rapidly discrediting the source of the bad news. In 1996 a disgruntled FBI agent who had been stationed at the White House wrote a book that portrayed President Clinton as rude and sexually indiscreet. The agent made a number of unsubstantiated claims about Clinton's personal life and the conduct of senior staff. The author, Gary Aldrich, was initially scheduled to be on ABC's *This Week* (a Sunday news talk show), *Larry King,* and *Dateline NBC.* Presidential adviser (and now host of *This Week*) George Stephanopoulos called numerous reporters, editors, and producers, outlining a number of falsehoods and errors in Aldrich's book. Although Stephanopoulos failed to convince ABC to cancel its interview with Aldrich, the White House's tactics did succeed in keeping the book and its explosive, incredible allegations out of most mainstream media outlets.[23] Aldrich's error-ridden book went on to become a bestseller, but it sold mostly to those already convinced that Clinton was an immoral president.

At other times a White House can prevent coverage by refusing to comment. In 1996 a London newspaper reported that a disgruntled White House staffer was passing rumors about Clinton having sex with a member of his staff (not Lewinsky) and that Hillary Clinton had an affair with another staffer. The press secretary decided that even a denial of the story would make it bigger news. The story was covered in right-wing newspapers, but it failed to get mainstream coverage, a success for the administration.[24] A similar strategy was adopted during the elder Bush's administration when the mainstream British media identified a woman as his longtime mistress. No major American media outlet covered Bush's alleged lover. If the White House communications staff can convince the media that a story is groundless, irrelevant, or illegitimate, that's the best outcome. However, most bad news cannot be brushed off quite so easily. That's when other tactics have to be adopted.

Change the Topic

No political actor in the world can set the news agenda with the speed and precision of the U.S. president. The release of good news at the right moment can overwhelm bad news. A bold president can even wipe away bad news through deliberate misdirection of the press. In 1964 President Johnson was watching network coverage of the Democratic Convention, which was about to nominate him for president. Johnson had worried for weeks that black protesters would expose the divide in the Democratic Party between southern white racists and liberals who advocated integration. When Fannie Lou Hamer, an outspoken, charismatic black activist, gave extremely emotional testimony about beatings, murders, and other tactics used by white supremacist Democrats, the media put her live on three networks. Johnson, realizing how damaging Hamer's speech could be to his hopes of portraying a unified Democratic Party, made a sudden unscheduled appearance on the floor of the convention hall. Even though LBJ had no news to announce, the spectacle of an American president being cheered by the surprised delegates was enough of an appealing visual to convince the networks to switch to the positive pictures of LBJ's welcome.

Presidents retain the ability to take action in the hope that it overwhelms the bad news or at least prevents it from dominating the media. As Clinton went through the early days of his impeachment, he launched an attack on Afghanistan and Sudan. Many Republicans accused him of trying to distract the nation from his sexual problems. Similarly, when damaging information began to come out about the second Bush administration's alleged failures in preventing 9/11, the Bush administration announced a long-planned radical reorganization of homeland security agencies. Some felt the timing of this good news, as well as later leaks on the arrest of the alleged al Qaeda operative, was too beneficial to the White House to be coincidental.

Friday Evening Releases

Just as there is a right time for good news, there's also a great time for bad news: Friday evening. Readership of Saturday papers is lower than the rest of the week, and the same holds true for the ratings of the network news. The media have a preference for the hottest and the freshest news. If the White House releases bad news on a Friday, by Monday, when the nation is back to paying more attention to politics, it could be "old news." Of course, if the story "gets legs" and continues to develop and grow, then the **Friday evening release** may not work. But much of the time, the White House still makes the attempt.

Spread Blame, Center Credit

Suppose you are communications director at the White House. The Secretary of the Interior has called to inform you that she has excellent news: Studies now show that the government's efforts have led to an unprecedented increase in the number of bald eagles in the lower forty-eight states. As soon as you get off the phone with her, the Treasury Secretary calls you with bad news: The national debt is set to grow again, this time to a record figure in the trillions of dollars. You go to work to **spread blame** and **center credit.** You tell the Treasury Secretary that he'll have to make the announcement himself (or better yet, get a faceless bureaucrat from inside Treasury to give the press conference in the hope of minimizing coverage even further). Whereas you ask the Interior Secretary to hold the good news on the eagle as long as possible and wait for a moment when the president can fit a visit to a bald eagle sanctuary into his schedule and into his political needs.

As communications director, you want to spread blame to other departments and keep the president as far away as possible while associating the president as much as possible with the good news. George W. Bush has been remarkably successful at convincing the rest of the executive branch to work with the White House on media management. The centrifugal forces of Washington bureaucracies and the personal ambitions of Cabinet secretaries often defeated such efforts in the past.[25] To combat these tendencies, the Bush administration has appointed loyalists throughout the communications offices of the various agencies and departments.[26] Bush is also the first president to require that Cabinet secretaries spend a few hours each week at the White House whenever possible, to make sure all departments are working for the White House's main goals. As the old adage goes, success has many fathers, but failure is an orphan. In the modern White House, success is a child of the president, but failure belongs to the bureaucracy.

Local News Preference

Local news preference is one option used by many White Houses during difficult times. This strategy puts the president before the much less sophisticated reporters of the local media. For local reporters, a five- or ten-minute interview with a president can be the highlight of their career, a moment they will put on their résumé. Not only are such reporters prone to treating a president with awe and great deference, they are also much less likely to be informed about current White House troubles. For conservative presidents, there is the added appeal that some research suggests that local reporters are less liberal than national reporters. For all these reasons, presidents like to deal with local news media, particularly during periods of bad news.

The More-Bad-News-Is-Better Tactic

Sometimes the best tactic for handling bad news is to pile more bad news on. This tactic has many varieties. First is the "document dump." If the media have been clamoring for details on a particular controversy, the White House suddenly releases hundreds or thousands of pages of documents, many of them of only peripheral relevance. In fact, the more documents, the better. Reporters will spend days sifting through these, trying to figure out if anything can be made of them. Rather than releasing one memo with bad news, it is often better to release four hundred memos along with the bad-news memo. It gives the appearance of openness, and sometimes the media will miss the bad news or become confused. Even when the media quickly find negative information in the document dump, many times it is better to have one or two days of negative headlines than have bad news come out day after day, drop by drop. Each day of negative coverage hurts the positive themes the communications staff is trying to get across.

If the White House gets wind that a very negative story is about to break in a major media outlet, they have one last tactic to use: go

A MEDIA BLITZ ON
THE ANNIVERSARY OF WAR

In March of 2004 the Bush White House media team launched a major effort to sculpt the news using almost every available tactic. With the one-year anniversary of the invasion of Iraq looming, the Bush team realized that the media would be focusing on retrospectives on the invasion and the prospects for peace and success in occupied Iraq. The overall theme Bush wanted to convey, according to a White House staffer, was that the nation is more secure because of the attack on Iraq. To promote saturation of the media with this message, the White House planned at least one major event for each day:

Sunday: Three war Cabinet members appear on all three network Sunday talk shows with similar talking points. By sending three of the most prominent defenders of the war (Secretary of Defense Rumsfeld, Secretary of State Powell, and National Security Adviser Rice) with similar talking points, the White House hoped to set the mood of the anniversary week.

Monday: The Secretary of Energy holds a press conference with Libyan nuclear materials to demonstrate one of the claimed by-products of the Iraqi invasion.

Tuesday: A swarm of radio talk-show hosts and reporters are given live interviews at the Pentagon from Rumsfeld, Rice, and others.

Wednesday: Two American-controlled networks in Iraq cover memorial ceremonies for victims of a chemical

public before the story is released. This again gives the appearance of openness and simultaneously takes the exclusive scoop away from the investigative reporter.[27] This tactic puts the press corps in a tough bind. If they think they have a great story of White House scandal, and they check it out fully with the press secretary, they can lose an exclusive that they have worked months to develop when the press secretary releases it to the general media. But if they don't check it out, they will be accused of treating the White House unfairly.

attack on Iraqi Kurds to demonstrate that Saddam Hussein had once possessed weapons of mass destruction. Also on Wednesday the House Republicans introduce a resolution claiming the invasion of Iraq made Americans more secure.

Thursday: The president and the First Lady visit troops at Fort Campbell, Kentucky, where the president gives a rousing speech endorsing the invasion and visits with bereaved military families.

Friday: The president visits Walter Reed military hospital and spends time with wounded soldiers from Iraq.[28]

The list of activities is impressive and was largely successful in garnering positive attention from the media. Several of the events were "must cover" for the media; it would be impossible for the media not to report on a president's speech to troops in such a dramatic setting or to fail to broadcast pictures of the Secretary of Energy before Libyan nuclear equipment.

The unified positive message was momentarily thrown off track when Rumsfeld was caught in a lie on an appearance on *Meet the Press.* Rumsfeld, who claimed that neither he nor the president ever used the phrase "immediate threat" in regard to Iraq during the period leading up to the war, was confronted seconds later with proof that he used that precise phrase in testimony before Congress on September 19, 2003. However, the unflappable secretary proceeded with his talking points, and most of the media failed to cover the incident, instead focusing on the planned events of the week.

CONCLUSION: THE IMAGE PRESIDENCY

Presidents today rely on popular support to maintain their political power much more than did past occupants of the White House. Daily tracking polls of presidential popularity make the president more or less powerful in his negotiations with Congress or other powerful institutions. More and more White House time and effort go into making sure the image of the president as portrayed in the media is a positive one. Former Secretary of the Treasury Paul O'Neill, who had served in three other White Houses, felt that the biggest change when he returned to the White House in 2001 was the dominant role of political concerns in every internal policy debate.[29] O'Neill blamed the Bush administration for the change, but it is possible that any White House would have made similar adjustments because of the relentless media glare.

The role of the media in the presidency has grown in part because the public role of the president has expanded. Since the 1970s, numerous presidential scholars have argued that successful modern presidents have to "go public" to win support for their agenda.[30] Through televised speeches and by using new media outlets such as talk shows, presidents can speak over the heads of the media and engage the public directly. Although some, such as presidential scholar George Edwards, believe that **going public** is less successful than "staying private" and negotiating with Washington elites, the Bush administration shows no sign of lessening its emphasis on public relations.[31]

The centrality of image to the American presidency is likely to grow. We may only be at the dawn of the era of the "short attention span presidency," in which substantive policy proposals become props in the pursuit of effective image conveyance. It is difficult to think of a countervailing political, technological, or cultural force that could stop the increasing salience of images to the voting preferences of the American public. In this sense, the gloomy lament of Postman and other communication scholars appears to have been confirmed in the decades since his baleful predictions were first written.

Is it inevitable that modern presidents will pursue their gossamer and ephemeral image at the expense of long-term historical accomplishments? Consider Truman and Eisenhower, the last two presidents before image became the dominant means of political communication. No American president has been lower in the polls at the point of leaving office than Truman was in 1953.[32] Yet despite the image of a country bumpkin too small for the presidency, which Truman took with him back to Independence, his stock has risen in the esteem of historians in every poll on presidential greatness since 1953. Eisenhower was apparently content to let the public think he was less sharp than he actually was in order to achieve substantive policy goals of moderate conservatism. One might observe that Truman and Eisenhower correctly put their time and efforts into matters of substance. Yet their presidency is not the one George W. Bush was sworn into on January 20, 2001. Image is so directly linked to the ability to achieve substantive policy goals that tactics such as Eisenhower's may no longer be feasible. Even a president committed to achieving substantive goals will have to follow the logic of image management.

Yet there is another possible future, in which substantive concerns will not be lost even as images become more and more powerful in the American presidency. One of Benjamin's key claims for the virtues of film may be as applicable as Postman's dark predictions: film would free the masses from elite filters because of its immediacy. In the case of one iconic image of George W. Bush, we can see evidence of Benjamin's prescience: the aircraft carrier landing in the spring of 2003 after the end of the initial Iraq War hostilities. Although widely viewed at the time as a brilliant exploitation of Bush's victory over Saddam Hussein in May of 2003, by April of 2004 many more Americans had died in the occupation of Iraq than in its liberation. Unlike the largely positive pictures that came out during the initial war in Iraq, the images of Americans massacred and humiliated in March and April of 2004 were very tough for the Bush White House to spin; their immediacy was far less subject to elite filtering as Benjamin would have anticipated. Perhaps Postman is wrong: the triumph of image over substance, of spin over reality, may be less inevitable than he believed.

For presidents, it is enough to conclude that both the media's role in determining the success of a presidency and the power of presidential image have grown during the era of television media.

KEY TERMS

body watch	presidential press conferences
Communications Office	press secretary
Friday evening releases	spread blame, center credit
going public	the gaggle
local news preference	White House press corps

DISCUSSION QUESTIONS

1. Do you think the good news/bad news tactics discussed in this chapter are manipulating the public? Are these examples of spin tactics troubling to you or just what you would expect?
2. How vital do you think presidential image is to presidential success? Do presidents today spend too much time on image and not enough time on substance?

3. Do you think a physically attractive president will be more effective than one who is not attractive? Why or why not?
4. Do you think press conferences are important moments for the public to see how their leader handles tough questions?
5. Who is your favorite White House correspondent? What makes that person better than the rest?

ADDITIONAL RESOURCES

Spin Cycle, by Howard Kurtz, a top *Washington Post* reporter, is a provocative insider account of how Bill Clinton's press secretary interacted with the White House press corps.

Who Speaks for the President? The White House Press Secretary from Cleveland to Clinton, by Dale Nelson, provides a careful look at each press secretary, with discussion of how the office has evolved.

Spin Control, by John Maltese, is a careful and thoughtful academic exploration of the White House's efforts to manage the media.

The Image-Is-Everything Presidency, by Richard Waterman, Robert Wright, and Gilbert St. Clair, is very sympathetic to the Postman view of the media and has great examples from recent presidencies of how image has come to dominate the presidency.

POTUS Speaks, by Michael Waldman, is an entertaining account of what it was like to write presidential speeches during the Clinton years.

Journeys with George, a film by Alexandra Pelosi, is a very personal portrait of George W. Bush and the journalists who covered him during the 2000 presidential campaign.

ONLINE RESOURCES

www.whitehouse.gov/news/briefings is the official press briefings Web site of the White House. It has transcripts from all the daily press gaggles and briefings.

NOTES

1. W. Dale Nelson, *Who Speaks for the President? The White House Press Secretary from Cleveland to Clinton* (Syracuse: Syracuse University Press, 1998), 3.
2. Jeremy D. Mayer, "The Presidency and Image Management: Discipline in Pursuit of Illusion," *Presidential Studies Quarterly* (September 2004).

3. Dan Froomkin, "Ft. Polk Troops Practiced Their Hoo-ahs," *Washington Post,* February 18, 2004.
4. Jim Shella, "Some Audience Members Told Not to Wear Ties for Bush Speech." WISH TV (Indianapolis). June 2, 2003. http://www.wishtv.com/Global/story.asp?s=%20%201278487
5. Elizabeth Bushmiller, "'Top Gun' and His Image-Makers," *New York Times,* May 16, 2003: A1.
6. David McCullough, *1776* (New York: Simon & Schuster, 2005).
7. Geraldine Sealey, "Look Who Couldn't Come to Dinner," *Salon,* March 10, 2004.
8. Dave Lindorff, "Keeping Dissent Invisible," *Salon,* October 16, 2003.
9. Howard Kurtz, *Spin Cycle* (New York: Free Press, 1998), 204–6.
10. John Anthony Maltese, *Spin Control,* 2nd ed. (Chapel Hill: University of North Carolina Press, 1994), 186.
11. Harry Jaffe, "Correspondents Call White House Press Briefings 'Useless,'" *Washingtonian Online,* September 26, 2003. http://www.washingtonian.com/inwashington/buzz/briefings.html
12. Michael Waldman, *POTUS Speaks* (New York: Simon & Schuster, 2000).
13. Jim Rutenberg, "White House Keeps a Grip on Its News," *New York Times,* October 14, 2002.
14. Ibid.
15. Rick Shenkman, "What George W. Bush and William Howard Taft Have in Common," History News Network, August 27, 2001. http://historynewsnetwork.org/articles/article.html?id=221
16. Helen Thomas, "Thirty Nine Times Before the Mast: Introduction." In *The Nixon Presidential Press Conferences* (New York: Coleman Enterprises, 1978), iv.
17. William Safire, "Question Time," *New York Times,* February 15, 2001.
18. Shenkman, "What George W. Bush and William Howard Taft Have in Common."
19. Kurtz, *Spin Cycle,* 9–10.
20. Ibid., 92.
21. Jan Uebelherr, "Medicare Video News Release Raises Media Hackles," *Journal Sentinel Online,* March 18, 2004. http://www.jsonline.com/enter/tvradio/mar.4/215698.asp
22. Greg Toppo, "Education Dept. Paid Commentator to Promote Law," *USA Today,* January 7, 2005.
23. Kurtz, *Spin Cycle,* 30–31.
24. Ibid., 96–98.

25. Maltese, *Spin Control*.
26. Martha Joynt Kumar, "Communications Operations in the White House of President George W. Bush: Making News On His Terms," *Presidential Studies Quarterly* 33: 2(June 2003): 384.
27. Kurtz, *Spin Cycle*, 42–43.
28. List compiled in Mike Allen, "White House Marks Invasion Anniversary," *Washington Post*, March 14, 2004: A21.
29. Ron Susskind, *The Price of Loyalty* (New York: Simon & Schuster, 2004).
30. Samuel Kernell, *Going Public: New Strategies of Presidential Leadership* (Washington, DC: CQ Press, 1997); Jeffrey Tulis, *The Rhetorical Presidency* (Princeton: Princeton University Press, 1987).
31. George C. Edwards, *Falling on Deaf Ears: The Limits of the Bully Pulpit* (New Haven: Yale University Press, 2003).
32. This doesn't include Nixon, who left office before completing his term. James Pfiffner, *The Modern Presidency* (New York: St. Martin's Press, 1994), 221.

CHAPTER 8

Institutions in Conflict: The Media and the Military

If the people really knew, the war would be stopped tomorrow. But of course they don't know and can't know. The correspondents don't write and the censor would not pass the truth.

—British Prime Minister Lloyd George, in the midst of World War I[1]

*T*here is no more serious political issue than war. It is in war that the nation can call upon its citizens to make the ultimate sacrifice for the state. It is in war that mistaken policies can lead to the immediate end of the nation itself. All but the most absolute defenders of the rights of the press realize that in wartime the government must sometimes infringe on free speech and the free press. Yet it is when war is debated that accurate information and critical analysis by the media are most necessary. The media's gravest responsibility is to expose governments that deceive the public into fighting unnecessary wars or that delude the public into failing to prepare for just and probable ones. For all of these reasons, the balance between the rights of the press and the needs of a wartime government is the most delicate issue in political journalism.

Perhaps no area of journalism has been as altered by the birth of electronic media as has war coverage. The immediacy and vivid nature of video brings the sights and sounds of war home in a way that print simply cannot. Does video make war more appealing and oddly beautiful, as Walter Benjamin anticipated, because of its drama and the seductive flash of fire and metal machines in conflict? For all its horror, war "radiates a deceptively beautiful light," as famed Vietnam reporter Malcolm Browne put it.[2] Or does video make war less palatable, as bloody corpses pile up on the screen, bringing home the cost of war? Does this make wars less frequent, because democratic publics will revolt against such images, no matter how their leaders try to justify them? Or, as Neil Postman would argue, has video made war easier for leaders to sell because the complexity and truth of an international crisis cannot be conveyed over the medium? Are journalists more likely to simply rubber-stamp the government's war policies because questioning them would require thought and difficult analysis on the part of viewers?

This chapter briefly explores the history of military journalism, outlines why journalists and soldiers are almost destined to clash, discusses the question of nationalism in war journalism, and examines operational security, humanitarian sensitivity, and government tactics of media management in war. It also examines three case studies of the military and media interacting: the Vietnam conflict (1959–1975), the Persian Gulf War (1991), and the Iraq War (2003–?).

WAR JOURNALISM EMERGES: SENSATIONALISM, PROPAGANDA, AND COURAGE

Reports from the battlefield are as old as conflict itself. War's centrality to the security and maintenance of any society contributes to a keen interest in the outcome of conflict. The first true military correspondent was Henry Crabb Robinson, who covered Napoleon's 1807 campaign.[3] The first war correspondent to become a celebrity for his coverage, however, was William Howard Russell, who covered the bloody Crimean War (1854–1856) among Britain, France, and Russia. Russell's early dispatches set the standard for all later war journalists in that he tried to capture the vivid horror of war for his readers back in England:

> The dead laid out as they died, were laying (sic) side by side with the living and the latter presented a spectacle beyond all imagination. The commonest accessory of a hospital were wanting, there was not the least attention paid to decency or cleanliness— the stench was appalling . . . the sick appeared to be tended by the sick and the dying by the dying.[4]

Russell's horrific reports of unnecessary death and maiming led to major reforms in the military hospital system. Like many subsequent war journalists, however, Russell's own government accused him of lying and helping the enemy with his reports.

The Civil War broke out as American journalism was just entering the mass media era, forever changing print journalism if for no other reason than the invention of the byline. Union General Joseph Hooker, disgusted by inaccurate reporting about his activities, ordered that reporters affix their names to their stories so they could be held individually accountable for errors.[5] It was also the first war in which journalists' accounts sent via telegraph often arrived in the hands of political leaders before the military's own reports. Journalism in both North and South was extraordinarily biased, and both governments sought to suppress newspapers that were viewed as hostile. Russell, a British reporter attempting to provide objective coverage, was eventually banned by both sides. Mob violence against newspapers also occurred during the Civil War.[6]

During the Spanish American War (1898), many noticed that war was good for mass media's bottom line. Citizens pay much more attention to politics during wartime and spend more cash to get the best information possible. But was it the most accurate information they wanted, or the most lurid, sensationalistic, and jingoistic?

As the media became more aware of their monetary interest in conflict, the government also became far more aware of its political interest in war journalism. World War I represented the first large-scale organized efforts by governments to shape the news about war to serve government ends. This conflict put the word "propaganda" into wide circulation. The U.S. military deployed "public affairs officers" to put the war effort in the best possible light. As one World War I public affairs officer put it, his job was to be "a public liar to keep up the spirit of the armies and peoples of our sides."[7] The governments in both Great Britain and the United States propagated false or exaggerated stories about German atrocities through heavy-handed propaganda efforts.[8] This led to a backlash of cynicism and mistrust toward government press management in wartime.

By World War II, the government's efforts at media control focused on several principles. First, unlike their opponents in Nazi Germany, the propaganda in the democratic countries would be "subtle, indirect, and . . . invisible" because "people are more likely to accept a propaganda message if they are unaware that they are being propagandized."[9] Reporters were allowed access to the frontlines in many cases, but they were subjected to heavy censorship. The government hoped that by censoring at the source of the news, it would not need to intrude into the media's editing room. The goal of government was to maintain the support of the populace at home. As morale at home seemed to be flagging, the government began to give the media more stories about Japanese atrocities and inhumanity to whip up hatred against the Japanese.*

One constant throughout the history of military journalism has been the great danger in which war correspondents do their work. Since the invasion of Iraq in 2003, ninety-nine media employees have died covering the war. Not only is this the highest number of media casualties since World War II, but it may also be a higher fatality rate than that experienced by American troops in Iraq.[10] In getting close to war, journalists take many of the same risks as soldiers. The Geneva Convention, the international legal code governing war, explicitly grants journalists protections as civilians.† However, journalists may endanger their protection by taking up arms or fighting on behalf of their nation while covering wars. Journalists as diverse as Ernest Hemingway and Geraldo Rivera have been accused of violating their professional obligations in this way.

CULTURE CLASH: SOLDIERS AND REPORTERS

Particularly since the Vietnam era, the American military has perceived the media to be hostile. There are several reasons for this. First, whether accurate or not (see Case Study I on page 219), the perception that the media were largely responsible for the loss of Vietnam is a widespread belief among military leaders. As General Bernard Trainor put it, "the credo of the military seems to have become 'duty, honor,

---

*One of the key targets of U.S. propaganda during WW II was African Americans. Suffering terrible oppression at the hands of white Americans, many black Americans could not understand why they should risk death for a country that denied them freedom. Increasing that support was a crucial task for America's military propagandists.

†Several U.S. laws seek to protect journalists as well. One with particular relevance to conflict is the law forbidding the CIA to use as agents or assets persons accredited as journalists with American media outlets. The intention of the law is to convince foreign governments that American journalists are not CIA spies. Unfortunately, the law has not been successful; in addition to all the combat risks, American journalists captured during wars are frequently accused of spying.

country, and hate the media.'" Trainor contends that the media are seen by many in the military as "unpatriotic, left-wing, anti-military."[11]

The clash between the media and the military goes deeper than any hostility that lingers from Vietnam, however. A cultural divide between the two professions may be a much larger source of conflict. The values of the military are patriotism, obedience, loyalty, and hierarchy. No military runs democratically, and outside interference in military matters is resented.[12] These values are necessary to the success of military missions and are inculcated through careful and rigorous training. As conservative David Horowitz put it, "to create the perfect killing machine, the military works hard to drain recruits of their individuality and their self-interested desires in order to make them think like cogs in a machine."[13] Only through such rigorous training can the military convince citizens to sacrifice themselves for their fellow soldiers and to kill others they do not know. By contrast, the media attract nonconformists, iconoclasts, and those prone to questioning all authority. Particularly since the massive media mergers of the last decade, journalists are not unfamiliar with hierarchies, but discipline within large media corporations does not approach the rigidity of the military's chain of command.

In part, the conflict may also be due to issues of class. If there was a halcyon day during which the military and the media saw their interests as largely coinciding, it was the World War II era. Journalists like Ernie Pyle (see Box) saw little difference between themselves and the "grunts" in the common soldiery. As we have seen, during the twentieth century, journalism became far more of an elite profession, often requiring a graduate degree. Journalists, particularly journalists working for national media outlets, tend to come from the upper income strata of society. By contrast, the enlisted ranks of the all-volunteer military tend to come from the working and lower middle classes.[14] In the past, when military service was mandatory or at least quite common, a substantial portion of journalists had served in the military or had close family members who did. Today it is rare for a journalist to have a military background,* and even those assigned to cover the military full

---

*One key exception is the *Washington Post*'s Bob Woodward, who had a career as a naval intelligence officer before he entered journalism. It may be that this experience gave Woodward insight into military and intelligence affairs, as well as the ability to get military sources to open up because he understands the military in a way that non-vet journalists seldom do.

ERNIE PYLE
The GI's Reporter

Ernie Pyle was the most famous American journalist of World War II. His simple eyewitness accounts of Americans in battle made him extremely popular with readers back home. But his willingness to endure the hardships of the soldiers' lives and to share their real feelings of unhappiness, frustration, and anger at officers made him a hero to the common soldiers most of all. They embraced Pyle as one of their own and read him enthusiastically. Pyle, who had served in the military before becoming a reporter, was always on the side of the troops, whether they were grousing about poor food or bravely fighting their way off the beach at Normandy. Unlike many modern reporters, Pyle wore the uniform of the United States, and he took pride in his emotional bonds with the soldiers. There was no question of objectivity in Pyle's coverage of the war against fascism. Pyle's death by a Japanese sniper in the waning weeks of World War II struck many soldiers as one of the cruelest losses of a cruel war.

In this column, Pyle wrote of the terrible human costs of victory as the Allies stormed the beaches of France to defeat the Germans:

> The strong, swirling tides of the Normandy coastline shift the contours of the sandy beach as they move in and out. They carry soldiers' bodies out to sea, and later they return them. They cover the corpses of heroes with sand, and then in their whims they uncover them. . . . As I plowed out over the wet sand of the beach on that first day ashore, I walked around what seemed to be a couple of pieces of driftwood sticking out of the sand. But they weren't driftwood. They were a soldier's two feet. He was completely covered by the shifting sands except for his feet. The toes of his GI shoes pointed toward the land he had come so far to see, and which he saw so briefly.[15]

As World War II veteran and war historian Paul Fussell has noted, one of the frustrations of serving for many GI's was the conviction that the public at home were being given a false and misleading impression of what the war was actually like.[16] Pyle, by contrast, tried to convey the horror of World War II as well as its grim necessity.

time often lack basic knowledge about war and the armed forces.[17] Many media organizations, particularly broadcast networks, hire generalists as reporters rather than correspondents with an expertise in a particular beat. Instead of hiring full-time reporters with military knowledge or experience, it is much cheaper to bring in retired military officers as experts whenever conflict breaks out.

One key cause of the post-Vietnam clash between journalists and the military is that prior to Vietnam, American journalists looked at war through the prism of nationalism. They often wore the same uniforms as regular troops and did not aspire to be objective about America and its enemies. In Vietnam, reporters began to be far more distinguishable from the troops, not only in uniform but also in outlook. Even so, very few journalists traveled to North Vietnam, and those who did so faced accusations of inappropriate conduct and even treason. After all, no American journalists had covered World War II from Tokyo or Berlin. There were no interviews with Hitler by top American journalists once war was declared between the two nations. Just as war cut off trade among nations at war, reporters from nations in conflict were typically deported immediately at the onset of hostilities if they weren't imprisoned as spies.

Vietnam, America's least popular war before the Iraq conflict, was difficult for the media to cover. Among the difficulties was that many of the claims made by the U.S. government turned out to be false. This was also true in earlier wars, but it did not lead to the type of breakdown that occurred in Vietnam (see Box). One new factor contributing to the gulf between journalists and soldiers is the conflict between patriotism or nationalism and the professional obligations of journalism, a conflict that is even more intense today than in Vietnam. The modern media corporation can be seen as a transnational actor without allegiance to any one nation. Journalists are also becoming more global in their outlook. During the 1990s, CNN became very popular in many nations around the world. Similarly, the British Broadcasting Corporation (BBC) has become less provincial and more global in its coverage. The militaries of the world, however, remain almost entirely nationalistic in their outlook. There is no doubt about where their allegiances lie. As the media become less tied to a specific nation, their loyalty may be more questioned by the military.

**SHOULD THE FIRST AMENDMENT
APPLY TO THE MILITARY?**

Imagine you are a commissioned officer in the United States military, famed for his heroism and his visionary intellect, who believes that the government is making a tragic error in its grand strategy, an error that will lead to unnecessary deaths in the next war. You have tried to get your superiors, including the president, to see the wisdom of your views, but you have failed. Should you talk to the press in the hopes that you can convince the public to pressure Congress and the president? Or should you remain silent and wait for disaster?

This was the situation of General Billy Mitchell in the 1920s. Mitchell had pioneered the use of air power in World War I and believed that future wars would be decided in the air. He was the first to demonstrate, in a secret test, that planes could destroy even the most armored warship, a fact that the Navy in particular wanted to hide. Mitchell believed that if the United States did not fully fund an air force, it would lose the next war. He began leaking the results of his studies to the press as well as authoring prescient articles about the future of war in the air. The military hierarchy warned Mitchell to stop these activities and eventually punished him for insubordination and disobeying direct orders in a high-profile court martial. Years later, after Mitchell died, and after his predictions about air power had all come true, the military still refused to revoke his convictions.[18] Widely acknowledged as the father of the Air Force, Mitchell remained a troubling figure for the military, which prizes obedience to authority above all.

Sometimes the military code of obedience prevents press coverage of terrible acts. What should a soldier do if he believes the military is covering up the mass rape and murder of civilians? Early on March 16, 1968, approximately seventy-five American soldiers attacked the village of **My Lai** in Vietnam. Over the next four hours, an estimated four hundred unarmed civilians were executed by the troops. One lieutenant, William Calley, directed his men to throw a frightened group of elderly men, women, and children into a drainage ditch and shoot them all. When a two-year-old Vietnamese child crawled out of the ditch, Calley threw him back in and continued firing. Although many of the troops refused the orders, not a single soldier resigned or contacted the media about the officially sanctioned killings, which were clearly in violation of the Geneva Convention, U.S. law, and the rules of military procedure. On the contrary, the military engaged in a successful cover-up of the My Lai massacre for months. Those who had not participated but were present were ordered not to talk. Only much later, when one ex-GI wrote to Congress and the story was picked up by intrepid journalist Seymour Hersh, did the public learn of these horrible actions.[19] Those in the military who speak outside the chain of command to the media face such severe punishments that it often prevents them from leaking even the most heinous acts to the press.

Punishing those who talk to the press in ways unapproved by the Pentagon is entirely constitutional. All members of the military voluntarily surrender many constitutional rights when they enlist. Among those surrendered privileges are the First Amendment right to speak out. Military officers, in addition to facing severe penalties for speaking to the press about military operations, also may not be critical of the president or any of their superiors without violating the Uniform Code of Military Justice, which bans "contemptuous words" about top officials.[20] During the Clinton presidency, a uniformed officer gave a public speech in which he mocked the president's sexual conduct and personal history. Although many expected that he would be prosecuted, the Clinton White House chose not to pursue a case that might have further exacerbated the existing tensions between the administration and the military. Still, a clear warning was sent down the military chain of command, reminding officers that such criticism could end careers.

It is not clear how far the military can go in regulating the speech of its members on matters less directly related to their jobs. In 2003 the anti-Muslim comments of a top Pentagon officer, William Boykin, attracted massive media attention. Among several inflammatory statements, perhaps the most controversial was when Boykin alleged that during a battle against Somali forces he realized that his troops would win because they were fighting for a real God, the Christian God, against an enemy whose Islamic god was false. The Pentagon, stung by the criticism and embarrassed by the damage the comments had done to America's image in the Muslim world, launched an investigation of Boykin.[21] Eventually Boykin's comments, made in speeches to religious groups during his off-duty time, were considered within the zone of protected freedom, although he was severely cautioned. But the message remains consistent; those who wear the nation's uniform may not speak as freely to the press or the public about their views as other Americans do. Those who defend our nation's cherished freedoms not only risk their lives on behalf of the rest of us, they also agree to give up certain freedoms at the same time.

PATRIOTISM AND THE MEDIA: DOES JOURNALISM "FOLLOW THE FLAG" OR THE TRUTH?

In a 1996 speech, Dan Rather of CBS News conceded that media coverage of the 1991 Persian Gulf War had been terribly biased and often was inaccurate. He concluded that in wartime "journalism tends to **follow the flag.**"[22] Rather is one of many journalists who have felt torn between their profession and their patriotism. The media in the post-9/11 environment were very worried that they would be perceived as unpatriotic, and major news networks labored to show their support for the president, the military, and the nation. The three major cable networks competed to put more American flags on the screen at any given time, with Fox the clear winner, occasionally showing the red, white, and blue in its set, its backdrop, the lapels of its hosts, and two video intercuts. Fox News, according to CNN reporter Christiane Amanpour, forced other networks to adopt a far more pro-American and pro-administration tone than they would have otherwise, particularly during the post-9/11 wars in Afghanistan and Iraq. These pressures led to the networks failing to investigate more intensely the weakness of the rationales for the Iraq war. According to Amanpour,

> I think the press was muzzled, and I think the press self-muzzled. I'm sorry to say, but certainly television and, perhaps . . . my station was intimidated by the administration and its foot soldiers at Fox news. And it did . . . put a climate of fear and self-censorship . . . in terms of the kind of broadcast work we did.[23]

The danger of appearing less patriotic was the loss of millions of viewers, a price too high to pay. Tellingly, Fox News responded to Amanpour's criticism by linking her to terrorism, calling her a "spokeswoman for al Qaeda." Fox has long sought ways in which to distinguish its coverage from the networks that it accused of having an anti-American, anti-Bush, or antimilitary bias. Fox made it a policy to refer to suicide bombers as "homicide bombers," as a way of highlighting Fox's strong antiterrorism stance.*

The tension between the tenets of journalism and the pull of patriotism was higher during the Iraq War than during any American conflict since the Civil War (see Case Study III on page 224). When the lead singer of the country group the Dixie Chicks criticized President Bush just before the war, Clear Channel, the largest network of radio stations in the country, banned their records. The same corporation promoted prowar rallies sponsored by several of its stations around the country, acts that critics tied to the corporate leaders' links to the Bush administration. Accusations of liberal bias were not uncommon either. As the occupation of Iraq dragged on and the number of casualties rose, Ted Koppel of *Nightline* decided to devote an entire show to the simple act of reading the names of American troops killed in Iraq while showing their photos. Some saw this as an attempt to remind Americans of the sacrifices made in their names, but others accused Koppel of seeking to damage morale at home and hurt support for the war and for President Bush. One conservative network of stations refused to broadcast the show for this reason.

Some antiwar activists, however, felt that the war's popularity was a product of the media's prowar bias. They alleged that the media's coverage of the antiwar movement had been deeply hostile. Moreover, the antiwar movement against invading Iraq was far larger than the antiwar movement against Vietnam in the early years of that conflict, yet it got much less coverage. The low level of coverage for antiwar messages was exactly what the military had desired since Vietnam, but it seemed that the media were self-censoring these messages. In fact, several marketing consultants to the industry were explicitly telling radio and television networks that covering antiwar demonstrations would hurt their ratings. Focus

---

*The emptiness of the tactic is aptly exposed by the fact that the neologism "homicide bomber" actually contains less information than "suicide bomber": after all, every deadly bomber, even those who don't stick around for the blast, commit homicide. Often, Fox's own anchors would forget the policy and call self-immolating killers "suicide bombers" or even "suicide homicide bombers."

groups and surveys suggested that American media consumers didn't want to hear about antiwar demonstrations, and covering them too intensively could lead to a station being branded liberal or unpatriotic. Instead, stations were advised to promote themselves as patriotic, incorporating the flag and the pledge of allegiance in their daily coverage.[24]

MEDIA AND OPERATIONAL SECURITY: DO LOOSE REPORTER LIPS SINK AMERICAN SHIPS?

Of all the justifications for government monitoring and control of the media in wartime, the most defensible one is **operational security.** If the media report that a particular military action by the United States is imminent, the loss of surprise may mean many more casualties. The need for secrecy in certain aspects of war is self-evident. Specific information, such as the sailing times of troop ships or the disposition of U.S. forces in a conflict zone, can be very useful to America's enemies. As discussed in Chapter 6, in the two major cases on prior restraint of the media, *Near v. Minnesota* (1931) and the Pentagon Papers case (1971), the Supreme Court explicitly recognized a right of the government to protect this type of information from press exposure.

During World War II, the military demanded that reporters submit to pervasive censorship. All reports had to be carefully analyzed for potential damage to the war effort. This level of censorship contributed to much more confidential information being passed to reporters on a daily basis. Top commanders such as General Patton could openly discuss tactics and strategies with reporters, secure in the knowledge that all their stories would be carefully vetted.[25] Today, with instantaneous satellite telephone reports on major cable television networks, there isn't time for the military to make certain that vital information is not accidentally disclosed, even assuming that the media would submit to broad censorship.

Can the media be trusted with military plans? The record is certainly mixed. During the invasion of Panama in 1989, a leak by a member of the pool of reporters set up to cover the invasion could have alerted Panamanian forces of the impending invasion.[26] During the Persian Gulf War, the media reported about an artillery duel between Iraqi forces and the 82nd Airborne. Commanding General Norman Schwartzkopf would later complain that if Iraq had been a more formidable opponent, that one indiscretion could have caused the loss of thousands of soldiers' lives because knowing the location of specific units can be a vital clue to figuring out the overall pattern of deployment of your enemy.[27] By contrast, the media kept secret the identity of a hostage held by Hezbollah in Lebanon for several months in the 1980s.[28] Although it would have been a huge scoop for any news agency to report that the CIA station chief had been captured by a leading terrorist group, reporters were convinced that revealing his identity would result in his torture and death.*

Deciding what information can be passed along to the public, and when, is extraordinarily difficult. Some advocates of censorship have argued that the government should ensure that information about the specific capacities of weapons systems not be published even in peacetime because once hostilities begin the information will put troops in danger. Others have argued that secrecy is foreign to democratic government and that governments will claim operational security as a method of keeping the public in the dark about its unpleasant or unpopular activities. What is clear is that the method of government censorship in the name of operational security has undergone a radical shift. Today the censorship of information takes place at the intersection of the media and the military, before a story is written or taped. Given how rapidly information is transmitted once the media have it, a system such as the one in place during World War II could never be implemented again. When a journalist is punished today for violating operational security, as happened to broadcaster Geraldo Rivera during the Afghanistan war, the punishment must come after the fact: banishment from the war zone, which was Rivera's experience.

VIDEO AND THE HORROR OF WAR:
TOO PAINFUL TO SHOW?

In 2004 Nick Berg, a young American trying to get work in Iraq during the American occupation, was kidnapped by al Qaeda and beheaded. The terrorists released a video of his killing on the Web, but no American network showed the actual decapitation, which was

---

*Ultimately, the terrorists discovered who he was via other means, and he was tortured and executed.

prolonged and ended with his bloody head being held like a trophy for the camera. Some criticized the media for sheltering the public from the true evil of our enemies; others applauded the rare restraint shown by the networks.

During the invasion of Iraq in 2003, several U.S. troops were captured by Iraqi forces. Videotapes and photos of these captives as well as American casualties were released by Iraq to Al Jazeera, an Arab cable news network. The American media wrestled with the question of whether to run such images on their front pages and in their news broadcasts. Many major newspapers, such as the *Washington Post*, the *New York Times*, and *USA Today*, refused to use the photos; other important papers such as the *Chicago Tribune* and the *Los Angeles Times* ran the photos. The *New York Post* even put a photo of a smirking Iraqi standing over slain Americans with a giant headline screaming "SAVAGES!"[29] The editor of the conservative *Washington Times* defended his decision to use the graphic photos of American captives: "It shows the American public the true face of the enemy, who we're dealing with, that they would take these prisoners and treat them like that."[30]

Images of the wounded, dying, and dead are certainly powerful. Some conservatives have accused liberals in the media of showing U.S. casualties and the civilian casualties resulting from American actions in order to convince the American public that a specific conflict is ill-advised. According to ABC's Ted Koppel, who showed such images on his program, his motivation was professional: "I feel we (the media) do have an obligation to remind people in the most graphic way that war is a dreadful thing."[31] There is certainly a perception among many in the military in the post-Vietnam era that such images damage the reputation of the armed forces and the public's support for a specific conflict. In 1993, when the networks broadcast the image of a dead American soldier being dragged through the streets of Mogadishu, Somalia, pressure for an American withdrawal grew.

Prior to recent conflicts, one of the iconic images of the cost of war was the arrival at Dover Air Force base of caskets of the deceased. A laxly enforced rule against such images, put in place in the 1990s, became strictly observed during the George W. Bush administration. Many analysts suspected that the rule was intended to prevent the media from regularly reminding the public of the mounting casualties in Iraq. Similarly, the military, which rapidly releases photos of troops and sailors involved in heroic actions, refuses to release photos of the deceased in Iraq, forcing media outlets to rely on the families of the deceased.

It isn't clear that broadcasting ghastly images of Americans suffering or somber images of American families grieving over their dead soldiers actually weakens the nation's support for a conflict. These images may serve to strengthen the belief that a harsh military response is necessary. This was certainly the belief of American and British propaganda officers during World War I, who released information on German atrocities to whip up domestic fervor. In 2001 the sight of bleeding and burning Americans in New York and Arlington, Virginia, following the 9/11 attacks certainly caused the nation to rally for a military response, and the people's affection for and trust in the military rose appreciably.

One key to establishing whether media organizations are attempting to affect policy makers with the atrocities they cover is whether a specific media outlet has a consistent and universal policy about what type of images it will or will not broadcast. Fox News vice president John Moody argued that it was wrong for networks to show the video of American troops captured by Iraqis because "I don't think it furthers the story . . . it's a little bit like watching a snuff movie, it's so awful."[32] Yet the same network, along with many others, broadcast images of captured and dead Iraqis.

There are also far more personal concerns. The dead and wounded soldiers captured on video or in a photograph are individuals with families and friends. The global satellite media can put a dead man's face on the screen of his family's television long before the government has informed his wife that her husband has been killed. Even after notification has taken place, to what extent is death and suffering private? Again, the question of disparate treatment arises. Many American media organizations do not show the faces of American casualties in ways that can be identified, particularly before their families have been notified. Yet during the coverage of the prison abuse scandals at Abu Ghraib prison in Iraq, naked Iraqis were shown being abused and tortured by American soldiers, with their genitals blurred but their faces clearly identifiable. Do the American media owe considerations of sensitivity and privacy only to Americans? Given that some of the prisoners were sodomized with objects by their American captors, they were victims of sexual assault, and such victims, when American, routinely have their identities shielded by the American press.

On top of all the political and personal concerns, there are marketing considerations. News organizations must deal with the fact that "there is both an eager appetite for, and a sincere disgust with, graphic images."[33] War is good for the circulation of newspapers and for the ratings of broadcast networks. The first Gulf War made celebrities of many journalists, including Wolf Blitzer and Peter Arnett, and brought home CNN's dominance of breaking news. The wars in Iraq and Afghanistan made Fox News's sudden defeat of CNN evident. Networks compete by getting as close as possible to the bloodshed of war. Yet while the public flocks to watch the violent imagery of conflict, outlets that appear to be ghoulishly exploiting the suffering of our troops could pay a high price in canceled subscriptions and lost viewers. *Washington Post* editor Leonard Downie believes a daily newspaper should "behave like a good houseguest."[34] Does a good houseguest show pictures of Iraqi children decapitated by an American bombing raid?

These commercial concerns may partially explain the different treatment of civil casualties between American and Arab networks. American movies feature extraordinarily graphic violence, and American television features bullet-ridden bodies that would be much more difficult to show in some Western European nations. Yet in covering real wars, American media executives show far fewer images of war casualties, particularly when the casualties were caused by American weapons. By contrast, Arab viewers are very familiar with graphic pictures of Palestinian corpses and wounded children, victims of the Arab–Israeli conflict. The United States—the source of the most violent (and profitable) movies on the globe, the home of such blood orgies as *Kill Bill* and *Natural Born Killers*—is simply far more squeamish about its news coverage of real death and dying.

Consequently, the war that viewers of Arab television saw was starkly different from the war on American television screens. Not only did al Jazeera broadcast video of Iraqis interrogating American captives and images of dead Americans far more frequently, it also covered civilian casualties with great fervor. As media analyst Michael Massing noted:

> Al Jazeera took us to hospital wards to show us screaming children, women in pain, men without limbs. The camera lingered on stumps, head wounds, and tubes inserted in nostrils and chests. On gurneys in hallways lay bodies bandaged, bloodied, and burned. Doctors and nurses described how they were being overwhelmed by casualties and how they lacked the supplies needed to treat them. On al Jazeera, then, the war was seen mainly through

> the plight of its victims, while the brutality of the Baathists and their horrifying methods were hardly mentioned. . . . Yet Western television programs seemed to tilt in the opposite direction, showing a war of liberation without victims. . . . In the case of Iraq, the conflict Americans saw was highly sanitized, with laser-guided weapons slamming into their intended targets with great precision. . . . Spared exposure to the victims of war, Americans had little idea of its human costs.[35]

Of course, one could counter that viewers of al Jazeera might have had an exaggerated sense of the human costs of the war in Iraq. Although civilian casualties certainly occurred, the precision weaponry used by the Americans was far superior to the blunt and devastating weapons used in past wars. As President Bush correctly observed later, the skill and technological sophistication of U.S. forces allowed for the removal of the Hussein regime without major civilian casualties, whereas removal of the Hitler regime had required that the Allies in World War II flatten entire cities, leaving Germany a shattered wreck.

In the midst of the Iraq War, viewers of al Jazeera might have fallen victim to two misapprehensions: America was losing the war (look at the number of captive Americans), and the war was taking a disproportionately heavy toll on Iraqi civilians. When America was scant days from a triumphant entry in Baghdad, the powerful images of American bodies convinced one American viewer of al Jazeera that the war effort was "so badly derailed that our forces can't even collect their own casualties," creating the picture "of an American war effort going disastrously wrong." Viewers of American news had a far more accurate picture of the progress of the war and its likely outcome, but viewers of Arab networks had a much sharper sense of the human costs of the war.*

When it comes to war, images of suffering are unquestionably powerful, but their very power may go a long way to creating inaccurate perceptions in their viewers. Unaccompanied by analysis and uninterpreted by knowledgeable journalists, a graphic and bloody image may be worth far less than a thousand words if the goal of war journalism is to explain conflict to the public.

---

*The Arab media has a history of deceiving its people with boisterous reports of the progress of war, and when the wars end with Arab defeats, as in 1967, 1973, and 2003, the Arab populace often feels not only humiliated but stunned because their media had been telling them of great battlefield successes.

GOVERNMENT TACTICS: MANAGING
THE MEDIA IN WAR

Governments in democratic societies have come up with different strategies for managing the media in times of war. These tactics range from complete control and censorship to comparative freedom. In the United States restrictions on the press in war have been largely accepted as legal. As Supreme Court Justice Oliver Wendell Holmes observed in *Schenck v. U.S.* (1919):

> When a nation is at war, many things that might be said in time of peace are such a hindrance to its effort that their utterance will not be endured so long as men fight, and that no Court could regard them as protected by any constitutional right.[36]

In the more distant past, the executive branch has not waited for, or even tolerated, judicial oversight of its regulation of the media. During the Civil War, our nation's greatest military crisis, Abraham Lincoln authorized the federal government to close opposition newspapers despite the First Amendment.

More recently, however, the rights of the press to cover war have been both broadened and more widely observed by the military and the entire government. The government, however, retains the power to censor when the need is great enough. Whether any particular Supreme Court will uphold a specific action by the executive branch is difficult to anticipate. In reviewing the tactics used by the military to manage the media, however, it is important to recognize that not all of these would be considered legal in a specific circumstance. The degree of control must be proportionate to the threat to the military and to the nation.

Classifying the News: Keeping Secrets Safe by Statute

Unlike Great Britain and many other democracies, the United States has no explicit Official Secrets Act, which would punish officials for disclosing classified information except as it relates directly to national security.[37] Several U.S. government officials have faced prosecution for theft of government property for unauthorized leaks, but these prosecutions usually don't succeed. The Espionage Act of 1917 has also been used against government employees who give classified information to the press.[38] Government officials who sign nondisclosure agreements as part of their employment (as all intelligence operatives do) may also face severe civil penalties for leaking secrets, even years after their retirement.[39] The broadest statute applicable to classified military information could conceivably be used against journalists; it demands up to ten years in prison for those who disclose important military secrets if they "have reason to believe that the information is to be used to the injury of the United States, or to the advantage of any foreign nation."[40] Even so, the government has not used that statute successfully against any journalist in peace or war.

Some believe that the government classifies far too many things as secret, a criticism heard particularly during the George W. Bush administration, which has tried very hard to expand the zone of secrecy around executive decision making.[41] When everything is top secret, the distinction between truly dangerous secrets and merely embarrassing facts is lost. The point of classification, however, may be that it allows the government to punish those who go to the media with a loss of security clearance. Someone who has made a career in the national security area, whether in or out of government, can have a very difficult time continuing without access to classified information.

Following Orders: Stopping the Media by Command

The greatest limit on the ability of journalists to acquire information about military operations is the military's tradition of obedience and loyalty. Unlike average citizens or even other government employees, members of the military face immediate and substantial penalties for the unauthorized disclosure of information to the media. This is true at all ranks of the military. As the nation prepared for the Gulf War in 1990, Air Force Chief of Staff Michael J. Dugan gave an interview to two reporters in which he described aspects of the air war being planned against Iraq. Secretary of Defense Richard Cheney fired Dugan immediately; one media indiscretion ended a decorated military career.[42] Cheney sent a clear message to all the top brass: if you talk out of turn to reporters, there will be no second chances.

In Vietnam, reporters roamed relatively freely among the troops, and some of the interviews with soldiers who disagreed with the war greatly angered the Pentagon. Scarred by this, recent military leaders have acted swiftly against enlisted men who speak out. The summer of 2003 was a dispirited time for some enlisted soldiers in Iraq, who were surprised to find out that they were not heading home after their swift victory over Saddam Hussein but rather were spending the summer in the desert heat as an increasingly unpopular army of occupation. Soldiers of the Army's Second Brigade stationed in Fallujah aired their complaints about the occupation during live national television on *Good Morning America*. The disciplinary response from the Pentagon was rapid, and some officers who had not acted to shield their troops from the media privately told reporters that "at least six of us here will lose our careers."[43] After this incident, it was much more difficult for the media to get members of the military to speak on camera and be identified, unless they were giving positive, preapproved messages about the war. The ability of the military to swiftly punish those who speak to the media is one of the great challenges to reporters seeking to report the truth about a conflict.

Appealing to the Media's Conscience and Patriotism

The Pentagon confronted a media crisis in the spring of 2004. Military guards at Abu Ghraib prison in Iraq had tortured and abused prisoners the previous year. The military had been investigating the incidents for months, but it had managed to prevent extensive press coverage. *Sixty Minutes II*, a CBS news program, acquired graphic photos of the abuse and was planning to broadcast them. Given the dicey situation in Iraq, in which American troops were coming under daily attack by enraged Iraqis, the Chairman of the Joint Chiefs made a personal appeal to CBS to delay broadcast because the pictures of Iraqis being tortured and sexually humiliated would further inflame Iraqis against the occupying troops. In deference to the safety of American troops, CBS put off the story until other news outlets began to acquire the photos. Faced with competitive pressures, CBS ran the story, and the military reluctantly cooperated.

Should CBS have agreed to the delay? There are many occasions in the history of media–military relations in which a simple appeal to the conscience and patriotism of journalists and editors has prevented or delayed coverage of military secrets or operations. Typically, the request needs to be made by a top official, and it has to be a convincing claim that airing the story will directly threaten U.S. lives or the security of ongoing military operations. It is not an appeal that the government can make with great frequency, however, because the media will honor it only in extreme cases. The more that the military or the White House falsely claims a threat to American lives, as the Nixon administration did in the Pentagon Papers case, the less respect future requests will have. Among the motivations for the media to agree to the request are the potential negative side effects of being held responsible by the American public for running a story that gravely damaged national security or cost military lives.

Balancing the need to inform the public with the need to ensure the safety of troops engaged in a specific operation is a difficult task. The very best reporters are the ones who smoke out a story weeks or months ahead of others and somehow get the ungettable story. These journalists view security classifications and the military code of silence as challenges to be overcome, not as barriers to be honored. Yet, when they get that story, they may face a crisis of conscience before running it, particularly if the top military authority in the nation is on the phone, assuring them that running the story will lead directly to the deaths of eighteen-year-old soldiers.

The CBS delay of Abu Ghraib ended in a fairly typical fashion. Holding a story that is an exclusive scoop is one thing. But honoring the military's request when other organizations may not, and losing the exclusive and highly profitable story, is another.

Pool Reporting: Managing the Media in Groups

When individual journalists are present in a war zone such as Vietnam, several negative outcomes are likely in the eyes of the military. First, the competitive pressure of the media market will encourage journalists to take risks as they compete to get closer to the story. Military lives can be lost in rescue missions to save reporters or their escorts. Second, the presence of reporters in a war zone is inherently disruptive for our military: it adds one more type of noncombatant that troops must avoid shooting and one more guise for guerrilla fighters to adopt to deceive and kill soldiers. Third, it is tough for the military to keep track of dozens of journalists in a war zone, and this makes censorship or even public relations much more difficult. **Pool reporting** by a preselected group of journalists traveling together under the protection and guidance of the military appeared to be a solution to these problems.

After Vietnam, the military's hostility to the press led to a total media blackout during the quick invasion of Grenada in 1983. No reporters were allowed anywhere near the war zone because the military commander of the invasion objected, and President Reagan (and the public, according to polls[44]) supported the media's exclusion, made in the name of operational security.[45] However, media criticism of the military's action was severe. By the time of the invasion of Panama in 1989, a new system of pool reporting had been put in place. Anticipating that hostilities against Panama could be launched on short notice, the military put together a list of reporters from a diverse set of media outlets and put them "on-call" for rapid and secret deployment to Panama. The intent of the pool system was to provide operational security for the military and battlefield access for the media.

Unfortunately, it didn't quite work out that way for either party. First, the secrecy of the pool was violated by a journalist who leaked that hostilities were imminent prior to his deployment. Although the leak was not published, and did no real damage, the military was understandably displeased.[46] Moreover, once the pool of reporters arrived in Panama, they were kept away from the battlefield, denied permission to photograph caskets or talk to the wounded, and were even subjected to a stale lecture on Panamanian history while the sounds of conflict raged outside. Even more frustrating, the rest of the military forces had not been informed of the pool's presence and often refused to cooperate with the pool until they received authorization from higher command authorities.[47] Pool reporting did little to make either side in the military–media divide happy. But it still remains on option for the military, which the media has a difficult time refusing.

Pentagon Public Relations: Playing the Media's Game

When the Union Army of General Tecumseh Sherman entered Atlanta in 1865 and burned it to the ground in the midst of the Civil War, there were no public relations experts on hand to advise Sherman on how to handle media inquiries about his actions. Perhaps there should have been; Sherman's methods of total warfare have remained controversial, at least in the American South. One of the great shifts in the relationship between the media and the military is the tens of millions of dollars the military now spend persuading the press and the public that it is a benevolent institution. The post-Vietnam military may be convinced, culturally, that the media are against them, but that has only encouraged them to take the battle to the media in a way the media understand: public relations. Successful modern generals must be prepared to "do media" just as ably as they craft battle plans for war, and the Pentagon has responded by promoting polished, telegenic men to high positions, such as generals Colin Powell, Norman Schwartzkopf, Richard Myers, and Thomas W. Kelly.[48] The Pentagon's chief spokesperson has occupied an increasingly prominent role in the American media, and the Pentagon's overall skill at media management has improved immensely.

Working through the media or speaking directly to the public, the military now engages in a vast and sophisticated attempt to shape their image. This became controversial during Vietnam, as Senator William Fulbright pointed out in a book that attacked the military's propaganda machine:

> Besides the millions spent by the separate services on publicity, other millions are spent by the office of the Secretary of Defense itself in its role as coordinator of military information and as a purveyor, too. . . . There is little doubt that the Department of Defense and the separate services are hard at work providing positive information to the American public and initiating and supporting activities to build up good public relations, but these efforts, in my view, are more designed to persuade the American people that the military is "good for you" than genuinely to inform.[49]

The military views the media as a battleground in which to wage war for resources and public support. When a military project's budget is threatened, the military, like any public bureaucracy, lobbies Congress to protect the funding, often utilizing media outlets. This competition intensified in the last decades of the twentieth century during times when the federal government experienced record deficits.[50] The military's public relations staff is often assisted by direct marketing by large military contractors. You may have wondered why manufacturers of military jets like the F-16 bother to advertise in glossy magazines. No private citizen would be allowed to own such lethal aircraft, and only a handful could afford the multimillion-dollar price tag. The purpose is to burnish the company's image with the public and to enhance the political viability of the plane and related projects. Often the target of such advertising is Congress.

The military also uses the media to boost morale within the ranks. With hundreds of bases around the world, the military provides radio and television, vitally important to troops serving in isolated areas. Armed Forces Radio has more than 1,000 outlets in 174 countries and is also heard on naval vessels, with an estimated audience of more than a million listeners. It faces a tough task to remain fair and balanced because it is often the only station in English that a service member can receive. Controversy arose in the 1990s when the network provided conservative talk radio host Rush Limbaugh with the only uninterrupted hour of talk on its radio network. The military insisted that it was providing Limbaugh because he was the most popular talk show in America rather than because he was a prominent conservative and pointed out that no liberal of comparative popularity was available. However, critics pointed out that Limbaugh frequently claims that Democrats and liberals hate America and that he passes along unsubstantiated allegations about the sex lives of Democratic leaders.[51] Should the military media, which are taxpayer financed, support this without a counterbalance? Or would it be government censorship to remove Limbaugh's program because of its political content? Further, should the military's network broadcast shows that negatively depict the military? Separating the duty to inform and entertain the troops from the military's own public relations efforts is quite difficult.

The military sponsors numerous newspapers and magazines for its fighting forces, and these occasionally raise even more difficult questions about government censorship. The largest of the sponsored journals, *Stars and Stripes,* bills itself as the "authorized, independent daily newspaper of the Defense Department for the U.S. military community." The Pentagon supplies about a third of its budget, but it is supposed to have editorial independence. In 2003 *Stars and Stripes* began receiving many letters from service members in Iraq complaining about various aspects of the occupation. Determined to investigate the morale among troops, the paper sent teams of reporters across Iraq, ultimately surveying some two thousand service members. The findings contradicted what military spokespersons were telling reporters: nearly one-third of the troops rated their unit's morale as "very low" or "low," and many felt that their mission was not clearly defined. The editors of the paper were pressured to tone down the stories, and Secretary of Defense Rumsfeld ridiculed the survey in a press conference the next day. Rumsfeld later attempted to cut the paper's budget, an act perceived by editors and reporters as punishment for dissent.[52] What is the job of reporters who work for media outlets funded by the Pentagon? Should they be reporters or boosters of morale?

One final method in which the military practices public relations is perhaps the most subtle: movie cooperation. Each year Hollywood produces several movies with military themes, particularly action flicks. To increase the realism of these movies, producers occasionally seek direct cooperation with the military. A movie that portrays the military in a positive light, such as Tom Cruise's *Top Gun*, is far more likely to get the assistance of the military than *Full Metal Jacket*, Stanley Kubrick's dark portrayal of brutality in Vietnam. *Top Gun*, a heroic and dramatic portrait of military aviation, was credited with a spike in enlistments. Given that the nation's leading soldier, retired General Colin Powell, credits movies with spurring his own childhood interest in the Army,[53] it is no surprise that the modern military sees cooperation with Hollywood as a useful recruiting device and a way to ensure a positive public image for the armed services.

CASE STUDY I: DID THE PRESS LOSE VIETNAM?

It would not be an exaggeration to say that Vietnam was the great turning point in relations between the military and the American media. Vietnam was the first war in which television news played a vital role. During Korea, evening news broadcasts were only fifteen minutes in length, and the networks were often dependent on the government for footage of the conflict. Pictures that would convey a negative message about the war seldom appeared, and the rightness of the conflict was rarely questioned by journalists in any sustained fashion. Many journalists and pundits criticized specific tactics used in Korea, but few argued that the fight against communism was not worth the sacrifices.[54] By contrast, the fundamental question of whether the Vietnam conflict was winnable or worth the effort was asked by many journalists by 1968. Another key difference between Korea and Vietnam was that Korea was not covered nearly as extensively by the media. After initially failing to put much emphasis on the Vietnam War, by 1968 the American press had approximately one thousand credentialed journalists covering the war at any given time.[55] Vietnam, the first war to take place after television had become the dominant form of political communication, was unlike anything that had come before.

Some believe Vietnam was a war lost in the American press, which inaccurately conveyed the impression to the American public that the war was hopeless. Such critics point most particularly to the **Tet Offensive** of January 1968, in which the forces of North Vietnam and their guerrilla allies, the Viet Cong, launched a broad series of strikes against American and South Vietnamese targets all across

South Vietnam. Confronted by graphic evidence of massive resistance to American policy, despite the optimistic claims of our leaders, the media promptly portrayed the Tet Offensive as evidence of the failure of President Johnson's Vietnam policy. Legendary broadcast journalist Walter Cronkite concluded on the air in February of 1968: "it is increasingly clear to this reporter that the only rational way out then will be to negotiate, not as victors, but as honorable people who lived up to their pledge to defend democracy, and did the best they could." Cronkite's analysis included the observation that the best the nation could hope for in Vietnam was not victory but stalemate.[56] Hearing the most trusted journalist in the nation give such blunt conclusions reportedly led President Johnson to mourn that if he'd lost Cronkite's confidence, he'd lost the nation's.

According to many in the military, while Tet provided dramatic images of American power being challenged, the media missed the true story of Tet; it was a crushing military defeat for the North Vietnamese, in which no strategic objective was achieved, and indeed, the enemy suffered very disproportionate casualties. Among the strongest critics of the media's role in Vietnam was General William Westmoreland, who led U.S. forces in the conflict. He complained of television reporting that was

> almost exclusively violent, miserable or controversial; guns firing, men falling, helicopters crashing, buildings toppling, huts burning, refugees fleeing, women wailing. A shot of a single building in ruins could give the impression of an entire town destroyed. The propensity of the cameramen . . . to pose their commentators before a wrecked C-130 and deliver reports in a tone of voice suggesting doomsday was all too common. Only scant attention was paid to pacification, civic action, medical assistance, the way life went on in a generally normal way for most of the people most of the time.[57]

Westmoreland spoke for many frustrated Vietnam veterans, who felt that key battles, particularly Tet, were decisive American victories that became crushing defeats when refracted through the jaded lens of the media.

Regardless of whether Tet was inaccurately depicted, the media clearly changed after Tet. Before Tet, the media censored extremely graphic footage, and only a fourth of network footage included actual combat. After Tet, the censors at the major networks allowed much more blunt images of combat to be televised, and with greater frequency.[58] According to some military critics, the media turned Tet into a victory for the Vietcong even though the communists won no territory and did not directly defeat the American military. They won instead the war of the airwaves, demonstrating to the media and the American public that the conflict would not end any time soon, nor would victory be achieved without even greater sacrifices in lives and treasure. The public, convinced by the inaccurate pictures of the media, lost its stomach for Vietnam, according to those who blame journalists for the defeat.

This was a conventional view on Vietnam and the media for a number of years, and it remains the opinion of many in the active military. However, counterarguments eventually emerged. For media analyst William V. Kennedy, "television reporting in Vietnam was utterly irrelevant to the outcome of the war."[59] The media didn't convince the public to lose faith in its military leadership; the media simply reflected the public's growing unease with a conflict that seemed to be endless and of dubious worth. As Table 8.1 shows, public support had been declining long before Tet. Moreover, since the public's level of support for the wars in both Vietnam and Korea roughly tracked the number of casualties, how could the media be blamed for a decline in support for Vietnam but not Korea?[60] Perhaps the key difference between Korea and Vietnam was that the newly elected Eisenhower in 1953 saw the decline in public support during Korea as a reason to negotiate a difficult peace, whereas President Nixon in 1969 chose to continue an increasingly unpopular war. If this is true, then the media cannot be blamed for the Vietnam defeat. Some studies even suggested that those who watched television news were more likely to support the military than were those who read newspapers.[61]

The truth about whether the media were decisive in "losing" Vietnam may never be fully known. What remained in the anguished

TABLE 8.1   Percentage of Americans who believed it was a mistake for America to send troops to South Vietnam

Date	Not a Mistake	Mistake
August 1965	61%	24%
November 1967	46%	45%
March 1968 (after Tet Offensive)	41%	49%
August 1968	35%	56%

Source: Young, P., & Jesser, P. *The Media and the Military: From the Crimea to Desert Strike* (New York: St. Martin's Press, 1997), p. 85.

aftermath of America's greatest military defeat, however, was a great divide between the military and journalists. Some reporters were bitter that they had been used in the early years of the war as a conduit for a number of false stories, such as the initial engagement with North Vietnamese naval forces in the Gulf of Tonkin. From that initial deception in 1964, which gave the Johnson administration the excuse to escalate the U.S. commitment, to the final humiliation of the fall of Saigon in 1975, many in the media felt that the military and the executive branch as a whole were not being honest about Vietnam. Whether it was inaccurate and inflated body counts of killed Vietcong, deception about the costs of the war, or cover-ups of massacres by U.S. troops, some journalists felt used and lied to. The Pentagon did not even admit that Marines were involved in extensive combat operations until June 1965 when the spike in Marine deaths forced it to reveal the truth.[62] Such casual deceptions of the press, for no conceivable reason of operational security or privacy, eventually led to reflexive distrust of the Pentagon among the press.

On the other side of the divide, many veterans of Vietnam, who lost years, friends, and limbs in a painful and difficult war, believed strongly that the press had been instrumental in prolonging their suffering and defeating their heroic efforts. Some even believed that specific journalists had behaved as traitors to their nation, aiding and abetting the enemy's war effort through their biased reporting. Among the many casualties of America's longest war can be numbered the trust between these two vital institutions of American public life, the military and the media.

CASE STUDY II: THE PERSIAN GULF WAR AS MILITARY VIDEO GAME

In 1991 the United States engaged in its largest military conflict since Vietnam when it sent half a million troops against the forces of Saddam Hussein in an effort to dislodge the Iraqi dictator from the nation of Kuwait. The military conflicts involving U.S. forces between Vietnam and the Persian Gulf War, such as the invasions of Panama and Grenada, had been relatively small in scale and brief in duration. The Gulf War was the first true test of the post-Vietnam relationship between the media and the military, and by most accounts the military was dominant and unyielding in the way it treated the press.

The months leading up to the Gulf War saw the reappearance on a grand scale of propaganda intended to demonize the nation's enemy. To increase domestic support for the war, the government of Kuwait paid a Washington lobbying firm, Hill and Knowlton, $11.8 million to promote a war against Saddam Hussein through press conferences on Iraqi torture, T-shirts, bumper stickers, and even an alliance of churches praying for Kuwait's liberation. Hill and Knowlton also targeted business groups and environmentalists. In the most infamous example, the firm ensured national media coverage of a false story about Iraqi troops wantonly killing Kuwaiti babies. Only after the war did the press discover that the story was a lie, long after the public had been convinced to support the conflict.[63]

Once the conflict began, the press was kept away from the front to a great degree. Even the few members of the media who were put into press pools intended to give them a closer look at the conflict saw very little actual combat. As John Fialka of the *Wall Street Journal* observed,

> We were escorted away from most of the violence because bodies of the dead chopped up by artillery, pulverized by B-52 raids, or lacerated by friendly fire don't play well, politically.[64]

During the forty-two days of the Gulf War, the media were not allowed to roam freely in the combat zone. Every journalist had to have an escort, and copy was subject to review. A few brave journalists rode out the war in the capital of Iraq and reported on the aerial assault on Baghdad, but most of the war coverage featured military press conferences,[65] which showcased high-tech video footage of flawless precision weaponry eliminating Iraqi targets. This was a war depicted almost without blood or mistakes. Even the contrast between the informed, confident senior military officers and the unkempt journalists worked in favor of the military.[66] The press, dependent on the armed forces for footage, information, and permission to cover the war, was largely reduced "to the status of a court jester," unable to challenge the veracity of the military's upbeat account of the war's progress.[67]

So great was the manipulation of the media that following the war, seventeen major news organizations complained about the level of censorship and control, which they felt was unprecedented in American history.[68] The American Society of Newspaper Editors labeled the media's treatment in the Gulf War "the international humiliation of the profession of journalism."[69] Yet there was very little public support for the media's position, and the war remained a popular one with the citizenry. From the perspective of the Pentagon, there was little to dislike about the media–military relationship in the Persian Gulf War. Amid tight control of the press, public support for the war never wavered, operational security was preserved, and the conflict ended in a rapid triumph for America and its allies. Why change a winning strategy?

CASE STUDY III: IRAQ AS REALITY TV?

Long before a shot was fired in the brief war fought against Iraq in the spring of 2003, the Bush administration had carefully planned a multifaceted media campaign to disseminate facts and American views about the conflict. On the eve of war, media staffers from the White House, the National Security Council, and the Defense and State Departments, met to coordinate their efforts.[70] The Iraq war also represented the first test of the new Office of Global Communications (OGC) within the White House, set up to portray America's actions in a positive light. Staffed by a number of political veterans, the OGC aimed to convince Americans and foreigners that the war was both justified and being conducted in a moral and ethical fashion.[71]

This type of elaborate media planning was unprecedented for any war, but what attracted the most attention during the Iraq war was the return of a relatively old tactic, **embedded reporting.** Embedding is the association of a specific reporter or broadcast team with a particular military unit. It was practiced somewhat informally by reporters in World War II and in other conflicts. However, following the Persian Gulf War, the media's complaints about being controlled and even humiliated by the military reached a crescendo. One particular complaint was that the press had been kept far from the action. The military responded by creating a new type of embedding. It involved journalists being trained and regulated by the military prior to arrival in the war zone. They were warned about what sort of operational information they were forbidden to report and also warned about showing identifiable American troops in agony or death. Hundreds of American and foreign journalists were eventually embedded with military units throughout the Iraqi conflict.[72] The only major exception was that Special Operations forces and CIA units were not generally paired with reporters. As with World

War II, some journalists even witnessed secret planning for military operations, although they were warned of criminal prosecution if they disclosed the information without authorization.[73]

The key change, however, was that journalists, not military censors, were largely responsible for policing what was or was not acceptable. Why did the military take this risk? First, embedding fit the mood of the nation in 2003. If the first war against Iraq was a "video game" in which precision munitions antiseptically and surgically eliminated buildings, the second war was sold by the media to the public as reality television. Second, there was little operational danger in showing what life was like for an infantry unit on the road to Baghdad, so long as the exact location and destination was not broadcast. This was particularly true against a weak and dispirited foe like Saddam's military. Finally, the embedding brought journalists into daily contact with individuals in the military. Embedding did a great deal to heal the cultural divide between journalists and soldiers. In sharing the risks and understanding the sacrifices and dangers that every soldier and sailor undertook, reporters grew to sympathize with their subjects to such an extent that some worried they had lost their objectivity.[74] In a hostile environment, in which the military was directly protecting journalists from Iraqi bullets and grenades, it was only natural for journalists to portray the warriors of America far more positively than they might otherwise have. And the American public, taken "live" to war as no nation has ever been before, responded with surges in patriotism and support for the troops. Although such surges occur almost reflexively whenever American troops are in combat, it seems likely that the positive and exciting coverage increased support for the conflict.

Just as the rapid victory in the Iraq war was produced by a technological revolution in warfare, embedding was made possible by a revolution in media technologies. In Vietnam, news footage was shot on film, flown back to the United States for development, and then broadcast. This process often took dozens of hours to complete, even in the most urgent circumstances. By contrast, in the Iraq War digital footage was available instantaneously through satellite links and the Internet.

But were those pictures, however immediate and unprecedented, "accurate"? Some critics felt that the more than five hundred embedded reporters provided unforgettable images of conflict but left out many of the inevitable costs of war. The embedded reporters seldom showed dead Iraqis, although thousands of civilians died and many more were wounded. Similarly, it was a rare embedded report that contained dead, dying, or wounded Americans. The pictures of war that Americans saw may have been accurate, but they were very incomplete.[75]

The interaction of the military and the media in the initial stages of the Iraq War was highly successful in two ways. First, the military got extremely positive coverage, perhaps even more so than in the Gulf War. The public enjoyed the "reality TV" aspects of embedded journalism, although sophisticated viewers realized that some war coverage bore as much resemblance to reality as an episode of *Survivor* did. Second, the media reaped money in higher income due to increased viewers and readers. The true media winner may have been Fox News, which saw its ratings rise much faster than those of its main competitors. Both the military and the media had reasons to be satisfied with their improved relationship. However, after the war ended and a bloody prolonged occupation began, some members of the media began to wonder if they had failed in their key responsibility of informing the public. A bitter debate erupted about whether the media had too easily accepted Bush administration claims about Iraqi weapons of mass destruction and Iraq's alleged operational links to al Qaeda. Did the media perform their watchdog duties effectively in the months leading up to the conflict, given that little evidence for either assertion was ever shown? Did they sacrifice analysis and oversight in return for broadcasting dramatic, patriotic, and highly profitable footage of U.S. troops in battle?

Another effect of the Iraq War on journalism was a partial "renationalization" of the media. Consider CNN. Knowing that its major competitor was Fox News, and that Fox would be unabashedly promoting the war in Iraq, CNN could not afford to be portrayed as less supportive. At the same time, CNN's international competitors, such as the BBC, al Jazeera, and a host of smaller regional and national networks, would gain market share in foreign countries if CNN were jingoistic or overly pro-American in its coverage. The solution was to have two separate CNNs, one for the United States and one for the rest of the world.

> Six months before the war began . . . executives at CNN headquarters in Atlanta met regularly to plan separate broadcasts for America and the world. Those executives knew that (Paula) Zahn's girl-next-door manner and (Aaron) Brown's spacey monologues would not go down well with the British, French, or Germans, much less the Egyptians or Turks, and so the network,

at huge expense, fielded two parallel but separate teams to cover the war. . . . The international edition was refreshingly free of the self-congratulatory talk of its domestic one. . . . CNN International bore more resemblance to the BBC than to its domestic edition—a difference that showed just how market-driven were the tone and content of the broadcasts. For the most part, US news organizations gave Americans the war they thought Americans wanted to see.[76]

Apparently, Americans wanted war journalism that was upbeat, optimistic, and relentlessly pro-American, and that is what they were shown. The foreign audiences wanted something different, and CNN was willing to meet them halfway.

As the Iraq conflict entered a third year, familiar tensions between the media and the military emerged. One incident occurred in a mosque during the Marine attack on the restive central Iraqi city of Fallujah. A Marine shot and killed a wounded, unarmed Iraqi who was waiting for medical attention. The killing was captured on video by NBC reporter Kevin Sites, and clips of the execution of an unarmed Iraqi by an American Marine were shown on Arab and European television all around the world. Characteristically, most American networks decided not to show the actual killing. The damage to American prestige and reputation was substantial. Defenders of the Marine noted that a member of his unit had recently been killed by a booby-trapped Iraqi corpse, and that the Marine had not only just come from fighting in a bitter guerrilla conflict but had been wounded just the day before.[77]

The NBC reporter received multiple death threats from angry Americans, who felt that by broadcasting the incident he had damaged the war effort and the safety of America's military. Conservative columnist and blogger Hugh Hewitt asked whether Sites and NBC should face legal penalties for reporting facts that hurt the war effort:

Now we have to ask some hard questions about the media's complicity in the death of American soldiers and Marines and possibly civilians. . . . Is it aiding and abetting the enemy to release video footage that is certain to inflame anti-American sentiment in the region? If so, what should the penalty for NBC be? If not, are there any circumstances under which the release of video by a news organization leading to the death of Americans would or should be punishable, at least by the loss of licenses granted with the understanding that the broadcaster would serve "the public interest?"[78]

This was exactly the type of incident that opponents of embedded journalism had feared. The camera, with its all-seeing eye, captured the raw brutality of war in ways that the viewer at home had never seen before. All wars have moments of such cruelty and fear-driven brutality. But a military that permits journalists to travel in close quarters with combat troops risks being made to look uniquely inhumane. Surely before America's next major conflict the military will reexamine whether the costs of such exposure are worth the benefits that the military received from embedding reporters.

CONCLUSION: CHANGES AND TRENDS

There has been tremendous change in the relationship between the military and the media in the United States, changes caused by technology, politics, and history. At the same time, fundamental concerns remain similar, such as operational security, the difficulty of unbiased reporting in wartime, and concerns over home front morale. Where is this relationship going next?

First, it seems clear that technology will continue to alter the relationship. One key example of the potential for new technology to provide independent sources of information to the media came in 1991. Following the invasion of Kuwait by Saddam Hussein in August of 1990, the Pentagon had claimed that satellite photos showed Iraqi troops massing for an invasion of Saudi Arabia. This claim helped convince Congress and the public that Saddam Hussein was a menace who threatened vital U.S. interests, which led them to support Bush's rapid injection of troops into Saudi Arabia. A few months later, the *St. Petersburg Times* published a report that Iraqi troops had not been poised to attack Saudi Arabia. Its source? Russian satellite photos, which it had independently analyzed. The U.S. government promised it would produce evidence supporting its original claim, but it never did. It remains unclear whether Iraqi troops were ever in the threatening posture alleged by military officials.[79] The Pentagon used to have a monopoly on a lot of information, but the revolution in electronic technology is reducing the amount of information that is exclusive to the government. This should make the media stronger in their battles with the military over coverage, although it has seldom done so as yet.

Second, technology will also continue to bring the battlefield closer to the viewer at home. If a war is ever fought between two industrialized, modern countries, the Internet will likely provide embedded reports from both sides to citizens of both countries. If one side chooses not to show certain grisly aspects of war, the other may well do so. In any case, more of the actual brutality of war is inevitably going to be accessible in future wars given the ubiquitous nature of digital technology. American soldiers working as prison guards captured many abusive incidents perpetrated against Iraqi detainees using their own cell phone cameras. Although the government acted quickly to ban cell phone cameras to prevent further embarrassing exposures, in the future troops from many nations will surely carry tinier digital cameras into battle so that real-time battlefield information can be broadcast to their commanders. When such footage inevitably gets into the media and captures the true, horrible face of war in all its brutality, will this make waging wars more difficult? Or will the public become desensitized to violence through repetitive exposure?

Third, the relationship between the military and the media provides one counterpoint to the globalizing trend of the international media. As described in Chapter 7, modern media empires are often transnational. The first wars of the twenty-first century suggest that conflict can reignite nationalistic views, which make it difficult for citizens of one country to watch news coverage from another national perspective. Many viewers in Europe and the Arab world rejected the American cable media's pro-American slant, yet to maintain market share in the United States, U.S. networks had to be seen as supportive of the war. Whether this effect is peculiar to Americans or whether reversal of the globalizing trend will appear in other countries is unclear. The "**renationalization**" of transnational media networks would be a major change in the global media environment.

Fourth, questions about the nature of war will continue to change the media-military relationship. The invasion of Iraq was done with such technological sophistication that fewer than two hundred thousand American and allied troops were able to defeat a larger Iraqi military and subjugate a nation of twenty-five million people, although it should be noted that the invasion force was too small to ensure domestic security. The twenty-first century saw the first widespread use of robotic weapons, including the fearsome new Predator, which hovers above battlefields waiting for targets for its deadly missiles. The number of casualties in the defeat and occupation of Iraq is still a tiny fraction of those involved in previous wars and occupations, such as in the Philippines or when the British occupied Iraq in the 1920s. Will the media continue to care as much about war if the trend of fewer and fewer casualties continues? The media have not focused much attention on American military engagements that do not put American lives at risk, such as the Clinton administration's bombing of

Sudan in 1998 or the U.S. military presence in Kosovo. If the U.S. military continues its evolution into an all-volunteer force of soldiers who wage war from a safe distance, will the media continue to make war the biggest story of any given moment?

Finally, the second war against Iraq has reinvigorated the debate about the appropriate role of the media in war. Should the media more directly challenge claims by the administration and the Pentagon? It was clear to many observers that the foreign press was much more aggressive in questioning false American claims of Iraqi WMD than were American journalists. Will we go through another period in which trust between the media and the military breaks down, as happened after the Vietnam War? Or will the euphoria over the ratings success of embedded reporters help preserve the newly strengthened relationship? Much will depend, in the end, on history's judgment of the Iraq War itself. Vietnam damaged trust between these two vital institutions not only because the military lied to reporters but also because it was a great catastrophe for the nation. If Iraq, by contrast, becomes a functioning and secure democracy, doubts about the military's actions and the media's reactions will ease.

Regardless of how history views Iraq, though, one constant will remain. In democratic societies where the media possess liberty to question government actions, the military's desire for secrecy and positive press will continue to clash with the media's demand for information and honesty.

KEY TERMS AND PEOPLE

embedded reporting	pool reporting
follow the flag	Ernie Pyle
My Lai	renationalization
operational security	Tet Offensive

DISCUSSION QUESTIONS

1. Should the U.S. media strive to be neutral between the United States and its opponent in a war? Would a media outlet lose financially if it tried to do this?
2. Do you worry that the media might endanger American lives in its coverage of war and national security? Should the government do more to protect secrets, or does it do too much already?

3. In your opinion, did the embedded reporting of the Iraq War improve the quality of the war coverage?
4. As you look at the coverage of the U.S. military by different media outlets, do you notice a systematic difference in the treatment of the military?
5. Suppose you were the journalist in Iraq who videotaped the execution of a wounded Iraqi. If you were convinced that the broadcast of your video would hurt the U.S. war effort and eventually lead to more American casualties, would you still give your video to your supervisor for transmission? Are the duties of a journalist and the duties of a patriot inevitably in conflict?

ADDITIONAL RESOURCES

The Military and the Media, by William Kennedy, is a comprehensive treatment of the topic.

Newsmen and National Defense: Is Conflict Inevitable? edited by Lloyd J. Matthews, is a somewhat dated but insightful collection of essays on the topic from military leaders, journalists, politicians, and academics.

Ernie's War: The Best of Ernie Pyle's World War II Dispatches, edited by David Nichols, is a collection of some of the most famous military journalism in U.S. history.

ONLINE RESOURCES

www.defenselink.mil is the Department of Defense's official Web site, showing how sophisticated the military has become at presenting its case to the country.

www.estripes.com/index.asp is the home page for *Stars and Stripes,* the quasi-independent newspaper of the armed forces.

www.afrts.osd.mil is the home page for the Armed Forces Radio and Television Service, which provides electronic information and entertainment to the military.

The Mudville Gazette (www.mudvillegazette.com) tracks "milblogs," or military themed blogs. Many are written by active duty service members (sometimes called "sblogs" for blogs by soldiers), others by veterans and military spouses. Its motto, "Good people sleep peaceably in their beds at night only because rough men stand ready to do violence on their behalf," conveys its promilitary stance, but it includes both pro–Iraq War and anti–Iraq War blogs in its roster.

NOTES

1. Peter Young and Peter Jesser, *The Media and the Military: From the Crimea to Desert Strike* (New York: St. Martin's Press, 1997), 34–35.
2. David Plotz, "War Correspondents: Their Dirty Little Secret," *Slate*, November 2, 2001.
3. Young and Jesser, *The Media*, 22.
4. Ibid., 23.
5. Ed Offley, "The Military–Media Relationship in the Digital Age." In *Digital War: A View from the Front Lines*, Robert L. Bateman, ed. (Novato, CA: Presidio Press, 1997), 263.
6. *Cambridge History of English and American Literature*, Vol. XVII (New York: G. P. Putnam's Sons, 1907–1921), 5.
7. William M. Hammond, "The Army and Public Affairs: A Glance Back." In *Newsmen and National Defense: Is Conflict Inevitable?* Lloyd J. Matthews, ed. (Washington: Brasseys, 1991), 8.
8. Lyn Gorman and David McLean, *Media and Society in the Twentieth Century* (Malden, MA: Blackwell, 2003), 98–99.
9. Ibid., 93–98.
10. http://www.rsf.org/special_iraq_en.php3
11. Bernard E. Trainor, "The Military and the Media: A Troubled Embrace." In *Newsmen and National Defense: Is Conflict Inevitable?* Lloyd J. Matthews, ed. (Washington: Brasseys, 1991), 122.
12. Ibid., 122–23.
13. Chris Bray, "The Media and GI Joe: How the Press Gets the Military Wrong—and Why It Matters," *Reason* (February 2002).
14. Philip Weiss, "Here's New Face of U.S. Military: Lynndie England," *New York Observer*, May 31, 2004: 1.
15. Ernie Pyle, *Ernie's War: The Best of Ernie Pyle's World War II Dispatches,* David Nichols, ed. (New York: Random House, 1986), 282–84.
16. Bray, "The Media and GI Joe."
17. Ibid.
18. Colonel Lloyd J. Matthews, "The Speech Rights of Air Professionals," *Aerospace Power Journal* (Fall 1998).

19. Michael Bilton and Kevin Sim, *Four Hours in My Lai* (New York: Viking, 1992).
20. Uniform Code of Military Justice, Section 888, Article 88.
21. Shaun Waterman, "Top Saudi Adviser Outraged by Boykin's Words on Islam," *Washington Times,* October 23, 2003: A1.
22. Robert Jensen, "Dan Rather and the Problem with Patriotism: Steps Toward the Redemption of American Journalism and Democracy," *Global Media Journal* 2 (Fall 2003): 1.
23. Peter Johnson, "Amanpour: CNN Practiced Self-Censorship," *USA Today,* September 15, 2003.
24. Paul Farhi, "For Broadcast Media, Patriotism Pays: Consultants Tell Radio, TV Clients That Protest Coverage Drives Off Viewers," *Washington Post,* March 28, 2003: C01.
25. Steven Livingston, "Clarifying the CNN Effect: An Examination of Media Effects According to Type of Military Intervention." Shorenstein Center Research Paper R-18, 1997: 5.
26. David R. Gergen, "Diplomacy in a Television Age." In *The Media and Foreign Policy,* Simon Serfaty, ed. (New York: St. Martin's Press, 1990), 59.
27. Livingston, "Clarifying the CNN Effect," 5.
28. Gergen, "Diplomacy," 57.
29. Howard Kurtz, "Too Painful to Publish? Media Grapple with Showing POW Pictures," *Washington Post,* March 25, 2003: C1.
30. Ibid.
31. Ibid.
32. Ibid.
33. Philip Kennicott, "The Illustrated Horror of Conflict: Images Convey Facts That Are Hard to Face," *Washington Post,* March 25, 2003: C1.
34. Kurtz, "Too Painful."
35. Michael Massing, "The Unseen War." New York Review of Books. May 29, 2003.
36. *Schenck v. United States* 249 US 47 (1919).
37. US Code, Title 18, Part I, Chapter 37, Sec 798.
38. John W. Dean, "President Bush's Unofficial Official Secrets Act," Findlaw. September 23, 2003. http://writ.news.findlaw.com/dean/20030926.html
39. *Snepp v. United States* 444 US 507 (1980).
40. Title 18, Part I, Chapter 37, Sec 793.
41. Adam Clymer, "Government Openness at Issue as Bush Holds onto Records," *New York Times,* January 3, 2003: A1.

42. Matthews, "The Speech Rights of Air Professionals."
43. Robert Collier, "Pentagon Retaliates Against GIs Who Spoke Out on TV," *San Francisco Chronicle,* July 18, 2003: A1.
44. William V. Kennedy, *The Military and the Media* (Westport, CT: Praeger, 1993), 114.
45. Gergen, "Diplomacy," 56–57.
46. Ibid., 60.
47. Fred S. Hoffmann, "The Panama Press Pool Deployment: A Critique." In *Newsmen & National Defense: Is Conflict Inevitable?* Lloyd J. Matthews, ed. (Washington: Brasseys, 1991), 93, 102.
48. Kennedy, *The Military,* x–xi.
49. J. William Fulbright, *The Pentagon Propaganda Machine* (New York: Vintage, 1971), 32–33.
50. Offley, "The Military–Media Relationship," 259.
51. Eric Boehlert, "Rush's Forced Conscripts," *Salon,* May 26, 2004.
52. Robert Schlesinger, "Spars and Stripes," *Washington Monthly,* May 2004: 9.
53. Colin Powell, *My American Journey* (New York: Random House, 1995), 26.
54. Gorman and McLean, *Media and Society,* 171.
55. Young and Jesser, *The Media,* 87.
56. Matthew Robert Kerbel, *Remote & Controlled: Media Politics in a Cynical Age* (Boulder, CO: Westview, 1995), 47.
57. Young and Jesser, *The Media,* 88.
58. Kerbel, *Remote & Controlled,* 45–46.
59. Kennedy, *The Military,* 112.
60. Gorman and McLean, *Media and Society,* 172–74.
61. Young and Jesser, *The Media,* 86.
62. Ibid., 84–86.
63. Ibid., 169–72.
64. Livingston, "Clarifying the CNN Effect," 4.
65. Gorman and McLean, *Media and Society,* 176–79.
66. Kennedy, *The Military,* 120.
67. Ibid., 117.
68. Ibid., 11.
69. Young and Jesser, *The Media,* 1.
70. Karen DeYoung, "Bush Message Machine Is Set to Roll with Its Own War Plans," *Washington Post,* March 19, 2003: A1.
71. Ibid.
72. Ibid.

73. Rick Atkinson, "Embedded in Iraq: Was It Worth It?" *Washington Post*, May 4, 2003: B3.
74. Lyndsey Layton, "Embedded in Iraq: Was It Worth It?" *Washington Post*, May 4, 2003: B3.
75. Massing, "The Unseen War."
76. Ibid.
77. Dan Murphy, "Setback to US Image in War," *Christian Science Monitor*, November 17, 2004.
78. Hugh Hewitt, "Media Complicity in the Deaths of American Soldiers." Hughhewitt.com, November 17, 2004.
79. Offley, *The Military–Media Relationship*, 267–70.

CHAPTER 9

Congress and the Media: Covering the Sausage Factory of Legislation

O n March 19, 1979, television came to Capitol Hill, or more precisely to the floor of the House of Representatives. Prior to that moment, the televised images of congressional debates were limited to the occasional committee hearing. The floor debates of both branches of Congress, which constituted the climax of lawmaking, had been off limits to the televised media. Americans who could not travel to Washington had been forced to rely on the accounts of reporters in the galleries, or the versions of the speeches printed in the *Congressional Record*. Now America would see Congress live from the comfort of their living rooms.

The debate over whether to open Congress up to cameras had been long and bitter. Many feared that television would negatively affect congressional operations and reduce public respect for Congress. Proponents, however, argued that Congress was in a competitive struggle with the institution of the presidency, which was acquiring more and more power over public opinion through daily television coverage. Although the side favoring television was eventually victorious, it would be another seven years before the Senate reluctantly followed the House's lead. Not surprisingly, one of the key reasons the Senate agreed to broadcast its debates was the growing perception among senators that they were losing prestige and publicity to the House because of the House's openness to video.[1]

This split between a secretive Senate and a "let-it-all-hang-out" House has a long history in American media politics. Shortly after the first Congress was brought into session, the House made a space for reporters to watch and record floor debate for the newspapers, whereas the Senate tried to preserve private debate.[2] Even after the Senate relented and allowed reporters to witness some floor debates, Senate deliberations on treaties and nominations were not regularly open to reporters until the twentieth century. Many senators believed that letting the media into their deliberations would damage the ability of an educated elite to make the correct decisions for the country. The tensions between media access and effective congressional government continue today, but today they are typically resolved in favor of the media.

This chapter examines how Congress and the media have interacted, before and after the moment when the cameras were turned on. What role do the media play in congressional deliberation and leadership? How do interest groups lobbying Congress use the media? Has television forever altered the way Congress behaves?

THE PUBLIC IMAGE OF CONGRESS

Throughout American history, Congress has suffered from negative portrayals of its actions and occupants. Humorist Mark Twain once observed that America has no native criminal class, except Congress. The unpopularity of the national legislature is hardly an American phenomenon. Bismarck, the great German statesman of the late nineteenth century, observed that "anyone who likes sausage or legislation should watch neither being made" because finding out the ingredients of sausage or legislation would surprise and dismay the average citizen. Bismarck was suggesting that the reality of the legislative process was almost inherently unpalatable. Compromises on fundamental issues, vote trading and vote shifting, delay, inequality in power and influence, stubborn entrenched interests, pork barrel bills, lobbying, gridlock, and confusion all characterize the legislative process in every country from time to time. Most critics of democratic government, from Hitler on the right to Lenin on the left, have emphasized these negative aspects of legislatures, often using the media to rally the public for more efficient and effective government. In the United States, presidential candidates often exploit the negative image of Congress to "run against Washington" as a corrupt and gridlocked city presided over by an ineffective Congress. Their success in doing so has relied on the media's portrait of Congress as just such a place.

STATE AND LOCAL POLITICS AND THE MEDIA

Thanks to the nature of American federalism, a great deal of political power is not exercised by Congress, the president, or the federal judiciary but by state and local governments. The evolution of media power at these levels has not been as rapid as at the national level, but it is clearly following the same model. Television became dominant at the national level first, then began to dominate at the state level, and now even local elections and policy debates are sometimes most influenced by local television coverage. Sometimes, though, a political jurisdiction is not covered by local television news because there are so many municipal and county governments in the station's range. In those areas, the newspaper remains the dominant medium.

While the media's role in national politics is heavily studied, the lower the level of government, the less research one finds.[3] What we do know suggests that the media are less powerful at the lower levels because party loyalties are stronger and voters may be less willing to shift.[4] There is also simply less coverage of these campaigns by the media, which also limits their influence.

Other research suggests that the media are more influential on politics at the local level because state and local politics

Yet the public perception of Congress is paradoxical: while disapproving of Congress, most Americans also have a high opinion of their own member, as confirmed in numerous studies. This paradox may be explained in part by the nature of media coverage of Congress. A particular representative in Congress is covered by local media, and the coverage tends to be positive. The typical hometown newspaper of a member of Congress prints about fifteen articles a month that mention the representative, and most cover events that have local benefits rather than aspects of national politics that involve the member.[5] Thus coverage depicts the local legislator as bringing resources to the area, which few oppose, rather than highlighting his or her role in controversial congressional votes involving difficult issues such as abortion and free trade. Sometimes the local media take their news stories straight from members of Congress. One operate in a low information environment. When Americans have a lower existing level of knowledge about a candidate or a campaign, each new piece of information broadcast by the media may have a greater impact. All but the most disconnected voters will have heard something about the presidential candidates by the last week before an election, and they will have made at least a few preliminary evaluations about the issues or the candidates. The same is not as true for candidates further down the ballot; many voters may truly be blank slates about these races.

Another subject for further research in this area is the increasing concentration of local media power and its possible effect on local and state campaign coverage. In the classic machine model of politics in the late nineteenth and early twentieth century, the local political machines controlled not just the political infrastructure but typically the local media as well. Sometimes the leader of the political machine was a newspaper publisher. In Frank Capra's famous political film, *Mr. Smith Goes to Washington*, the machine that Smith fights against uses its control of local media to deceive the public. With the rise of electronic media, the government attempted to reduce the possibility of local dominance through licensing rules. The recent weakening of these rules makes the danger of biased local coverage much greater.

study suggests that the average incumbent member of Congress could expect to have a story appear in the local newspapers every other week, based almost entirely on press releases from his or her office, often without including opposing views.[6] For decades, small local newspapers have run columns by members of Congress. The relationship benefited both newspaper and representative. The column was free, and the member got a chance to advertise his or her activities and beliefs.

Coverage of Congress on local television is also more positive than national television news. As newscaster Cokie Roberts (and daughter of two members of Congress) observed, local television makes some representatives "media stars in their home towns."[7] Members take advantage of free studios provided to them by the Congress and the two parties to record radio and television shows for local networks back home. It is also easy for local television news anchors to do satellite interviews with members from Washington using these studios. Most local television networks cannot afford to have a full-time Washington correspondent, but the free studios give their viewers the false impression that they have a presence in Washington.[8] Some members now produce Video News Releases in place of print press releases, and sometimes they are broadcast by local news stations. Just as presidents get softer coverage from local reporters than from national correspondents, members of Congress get far easier coverage from their hometown media.

By contrast, the national network news does not even mention the average member of Congress once in a given year, even in passing.[9] They focus on Congress as an institution and often in a negative manner, such as "Congress failed again today to pass a budget on time." At the national level, the typical member is lucky to get a single positive mention. National media also make a greater attempt at balance; it is rare for a major story to be covered without insight from figures from both parties. The image of Congress in the national press is harsh and far from what the public wants. In their book, *Congress as Public Enemy*, political scientists John Hibbing and Elizabeth Theiss-Morse discuss how what the public wants and what it sees from Congress are radically different:

> People do not wish to see uncertainty, conflicting opinions, long debate, competing interests, confusion, bargaining and compromised, imperfect solutions. They want government to do its job quietly and efficiently, sans conflict and sans fuss.[10]

Other branches of government may frequently disappoint the public, but Congress, the most open and accessible branch, seems to do so most frequently. It is the branch least likely to deliver quiet and efficient decisions without conflict. It may be that many of the public's negative views about Congress are a product of the media accurately depicting aspects of congressional behavior; the public is merely responding with predictable disdain. It could also be that the portrait of Congress painted by the media is incomplete and emphasizes these negative aspects. When Congress acts swiftly and without too much conflict to address an emerging problem before it becomes a crisis, journalists may ignore this action because it doesn't give them the drama they desire.

The effects of the media may be far greater than the public's approval or disapproval of Congress; the media also serve to weaken Congress. As noted in Chapter 7, the modern press has a bias toward the simple clear narrative of the presidency. The complex story of legislation, with its multiplicity of actors, power centers, and interests, does not lend itself to easy explanation. Again, this typifies all legislatures, even premodern ones. In Robert Graves's marvelous account of the early Roman empire, *Claudius the God*, the Emperor Claudius reluctantly agrees to be worshipped, since, as he explains to the Roman Senate, it is easier for the provincial Romans to worship one Emperor as a God than to erect hundreds of statues of Roman Senators. In the same way, the modern media erect a video God, the president, because it would be far too difficult for the media to "worship" the 535 members of Congress.

In part, by putting the president ahead of Congress as a priority, the media are responding to changes in the relative power of Congress and the presidency. When Congress was dominant in the nineteenth century, journalists did focus at least as much attention on the national legislature as on the presidency. The rise of strong, media-savvy presidents like Theodore Roosevelt helped bring more coverage to the presidency. Yet the enhanced media focus on the president is both cause and effect of the lessening of congressional power. Members of Congress are covered less because they have lost power to the president, and they lose more power because they are covered less.

The rise of television, in particular, has made Congress weaker than the president. The complexity of Congress becomes even less understandable through the prism of televised news. As a result, the media depict Congress as the "junior member of the federal partnership," far below the president in power and importance.[11] The depiction can become a self-fulfilling prophecy if a president is skillful in using his media-created power.

The most basic truth about the public image of Congress is that the public knows less and cares less about Congress than it does about the presidency. Most Americans cannot name the leaders of Congress at any given time; in 1995, after a year of the most intense publicity given to a House Speaker in modern times, only 49 percent of Americans could correctly identify Newt Gingrich as the speaker. Only 41 percent of Americans say they follow news about Congress closely or somewhat closely, compared to 66 percent for the president.[12] Even with the local media blaring their names, only a third of Americans know the name of their member in the House of Representatives, and only 50 percent can name their senators.[13] The media may be partially responsible for this comparative lack of knowledge and interest in Congress among the public, if only by contributing to the overall negative impression of Congress. After all, House Speaker Tip O'Neill, described at the time as "the most televised speaker in history," appeared on less than 7 percent of newscasts on any given night, whereas President Reagan, his institutional and partisan opponent, appeared in approximately 97 percent of newscasts, usually two or three times.[14]

HOW MEMBERS OF CONGRESS USE THE MEDIA

Congressional scholar David Mayhew argued in his seminal book, *Congress: The Electoral Connection,* that almost all congressional activity is motivated by the desire for reelection. Mayhew then analyzed how members engaged in three key behaviors in pursuit of reelection: **advertising** (simply getting their name out to the constituents), **credit claiming** (attaching their name to popular projects, particularly those that have local benefits), and **position taking** (broadcasting their popular issue stances regardless of whether legislation passes). What was shocking to many readers at the time was that Mayhew did not include "passing legislation" as one of the core functions of members of Congress. Instead, members put crafting good public policy as a distant fourth to the three activities that could directly guarantee reelection. Perhaps Congress had always been the institution that Mayhew described, but it is also possible that to the extent that this picture of Congress was accurate, it was because the new media environment was changing congressional priorities. Congressional scholar Norman Ornstein believes that Mayhew's analysis came just at the point when Congress was moving from a "closed system" into one that was much more open to public scrutiny, in large part by the media.[15]

Obviously the media are vital to the success of any of the endeavors that Mayhew sees members focusing on. Of course, members can advertise their names, take positions, and claim credit for local projects using paid media such as television advertising or newspaper ads or by sending out free mailings to constituents (called "franking"). But news media, or free media, is the preferred method, both because it is free and because it is likely that the voters perceive it to be far more objective and credible than something directly from a politician. The foremost goal of the use of the media for every member must be positive press, particularly from the local media. A survey of forty press secretaries found that almost all felt that their main job was to make their boss look good in the home-town media rather than in the national press.[16]

For most members of Congress, the key liaison to the media is their **congressional press secretary.** The rise of the press secretary is one of the stunning developments in the last fifty years of congressional life. In 1963, only six senators had full-time press secretaries. Today everyone does, and some have deputies and assistants. Within the small fiefdom that is the modern congressional office, press secretaries are increasingly powerful, ranking third or sometimes second in the office hierarchy.[17]

What can members do that will get them free media time? One popular technique is to **sponsor** major legislation or a government program. Generations of college students have received Pell Grants, tuition assistance named for a then-sitting senator, Claiborne Pell. More recently the media have extensively covered the McCain-Feingold law on campaign finance. Rather than using the much longer formal name of the law (Bipartisan Campaign Reform Act of 2002), it is known in the media by the names of its two Senate sponsors. McCain-Feingold has been worth millions of dollars in free publicity for John McCain (R–AZ) and Russ Feingold (D–WI). Unfortunately for new members, it is rare for a junior senator or representative to get his or her name on any legislation, let alone on one of the few featured prominently in the national media. Although this strategy is very effective, it is too much of a long shot to be reliable for most members.

A member can also hope that floor speeches and committee statements will be covered by the press. This is a faint hope, however, absent extraordinary circumstances such as an appearance at a hearing by a celebrity or aggressive questioning of a Cabinet official at the height of a scandal. So many speeches and committee statements are given each day on Capitol Hill that to gain coverage one must be unique, powerful, and often risky. When Senator Joe Lieberman (D–CT) during the Lewinsky scandal went to the floor of the Senate to harshly criticize President Clinton, the speech was widely covered because Lieberman was the first major Democrat to harshly judge Clinton's sexual conduct. Although the press was almost uniformly positive toward Lieberman's speech, if the rest of the party had not followed Lieberman and begun to openly criticize aspects of Clinton's conduct, Lieberman might well have paid a heavy political price. Many times a speech intended to gain press attention succeeds all too well in getting attention, but of the negative variety.

When a new project in a member's state or district is announced by the executive branch, most members issue a press release or hold a press conference claiming credit. Sometimes, as a special favor to an important member, the executive branch will allow the member the privilege of making the first announcement in the hope of garnering more publicity. Unfortunately, press releases announcing actions and votes taken by members are widely ignored except by some local news organizations. Congressional reporters are faced with a daily blizzard of press releases, and they quickly learn to separate the important ones from the weekly puffery released by almost every office. Press conferences that do not feature the leadership or an already high-profile issue are likely to be poorly attended.

There are, of course, less traditional means. Members can take part in demonstrations and rallies. Some members of Congress have even been arrested, and this usually gets press coverage. In July 2004, Congressman Charles Rangel (D–NY) protested outside the Sudanese Embassy against the Darfur genocide, and his arrest was widely reported in the media. As with bold speeches, however, these nontraditional tactics run the risk of backfiring as an incumbent can sacrifice the dignity of his or her office. One of the best ways to get coverage as a member of Congress is to run for president, which illustrates quite well the media's unbalanced coverage of the two branches. In 1996 Bob Dornan (R–CA) ran a quixotic campaign for the Republican presidential nomination. In 2004 Dennis Kucinich (D–OH) ran a similar campaign for the Democratic nomination. Although both men were on the ideological extremes of their parties, and both had served in Congress for several terms, none of their previous activities equaled the press attention they received for running for president, even though their chances for victory were nearly zero. Even minor figures in the presidential race get more coverage than major congressional leaders.

Media attention can be a double-edged sword. Members who become too prominent in the national media may appear aloof or disconnected from their districts, a charge that many challengers have used successfully against powerful members of Congress.[18] The perception that Dornan had lost touch with his district in a grandiose leap for the presidency contributed to the loss of his seat in the next election, for example.

One way Congress uses the media is to float **trial balloons** or to answer trial balloons floated by the president and his staff. A trial balloon is an idea that is not formally proposed and that often comes forth anonymously in the media, as in "Sources on the Finance Committee say that a national sales tax is under consideration." If the sales tax meets with universal disapproval, the member (or staffer) who talked to the media about it has left no paper trail to give ammunition to opponents in future campaigns. If, however, the response is positive or at least neutral, the trial balloon might become an actual proposal. In this way, the media can be used as a means of communication between the White House and the Congress.

DISTORTING THE LEGISLATIVE PROCESS: HOW THE MEDIA MISSES THE STORY

During a brief period in the 1990s, Jim Traficant (D–OH) became the second-most quoted member of the House of Representatives. What major legislative accomplishment had Traficant done to merit this? What government malfeasance had he exposed? What issue had he brought to national attention? None. Traficant was widely known as a kook, a faux populist with a propensity for bombastic speeches featuring rather disgusting gastrointestinal references. What made him so widely quoted were his late night speeches that had no legislative impact but were full of memorable one-liners. In announcing his opposition to President Clinton's tax plan, Traficant said, "I am not for this damn plan. And I say . . . shove this big tax increase up your compromise!"[19]

One chronic problem with the way the media cover Congress is that the picture of the legislative process they present is terribly distorted, as illustrated by their elevation of Traficant to high prominence. The Congress that Americans watch on the network news often bears only a passing resemblance to the actual Congress. The legislative process, in particular, is poorly transmitted to the television news viewer.

Every American child learns how a bill becomes a law in civics class. A simple version of the process includes writing the bill, its referral to one or more committees, markup in subcommittees, floor votes in the two chambers, if necessary a conference committee to iron out differences between the House and the Senate, and on to the president. Much of this process, however, is omitted in media coverage of Congress. The decision to refer a bill to a particular committee, or to a set of committees, can shape its fate as much as any amendment.

Actions taken by the usually low-profile Rules Committee in the House can determine whether a bill survives or is killed. The complexity of the legislative process is absent in the mainstream media, particularly in television. And the media have a strong bias toward conflict. A close vote in the Senate Judiciary Committee on a Supreme Court nominee with troubling ethics will get much more attention than a unanimous vote behind a universally admired judicial expert. Media critics have focused on the "negativity bias" journalists bring to coverage of the presidential campaign, but it may be an even bigger problem with depictions of the legislative process. A nail-biter of a floor vote on free trade with allegations of influence peddling by corporate lobbyists will get more coverage than a vote on the same issue that is expected to be a landslide. The media simply prefer to cover a fight, not a resolved issue.

The process of coming to a peaceful agreement prior to a vote is perhaps the most important aspect of legislative procedure, and the most hidden.[20] Building a successful coalition through meetings with party and regional caucuses, negotiations among party leaders and presidential aides, and interactions with major interest groups and lobbyists can take months and years. It occurs out of the public view and involves compromises and trades the public may never hear about. Thus the media distort the process in two ways; they miss the vital importance of negotiations to avoid conflict and they overemphasize those moments when cooperation breaks down, particularly if there is a negative aspect of scandal or corruption.

The media also distort Congress by focusing too much attention on final debates and votes on the floors of the two chambers. In 1885 political scientist and later President of the United States Woodrow Wilson wrote, "Congress in Committee is Congress at work. Congress in session is Congress on display." If it is still true today that what Congress does in floor debates is often for display, then the media largely miss the important aspects of Congress. Votes on the floor of the House and Senate are the final steps in a long and convoluted path. Committees tend to be far more important arenas for shaping legislation, particularly in the House. The vast majority of bills die in committee without ever receiving a floor vote. Yet the national media fail to cover committee hearings unless the issue is already at a very high level of public interest or a celebrity is going to testify.

Why do the media ignore most committee hearings? At one level, this is understandable. At any given moment during the legislative session, there may be a dozen committees or subcommittees meeting on Capitol Hill. The media have no way of knowing which bill will ultimately survive to get a floor vote. Should they put scarce resources to work covering a bill that may end up dying long before it reaches the president's desk? Committee votes tend to be much less dramatic than floor votes, further lessening the media's interest in covering them.

Consider the challenge facing a television news director deciding whether to cover an important action by a conference committee. Conference committees are vital to the legislative process because they work out differences between similar bills passed by the Senate and the House. Many times, the conference committee is more important than the preceding floor votes or the actions in the regular Senate and House committees. Yet because most conference committees meet away from cameras, there is no compelling image of debate or conflict associated with the story. If a media outlet does decide to cover it, the outlet might put the reporter in front of Capitol Hill and, while the reporter describes the action, shift the image to file footage relating to the issue at hand. Still, it is hardly riveting television, which helps explain why so many aspects of Congress that are central to the legislative process are simply left out of the media picture.

Even when the media do cover committee proceedings, the coverage may be skewed toward committees handling sexier and flashier topics rather than the most powerful committees in Congress. In a study of which Senate committees attracted more television news coverage of their proceedings over a five-year period, the top five were Foreign Relations, Judiciary, Budget, Governmental Affairs, and Appropriations. The least covered were Intelligence, Rules and Administration, Small Business, Veterans Affairs, and Indian Affairs.[21] Although the bottom five seem to accurately reflect low-power status, the attention at the top seems out of balance. In any list of the most powerful Senate committees, Appropriations is usually at the top because it controls all discretionary spending bills, but two key power committees are missing, Defense and Finance (the committee dealing with taxes). The committees on Foreign Relations and the Judiciary are known for their involvement in high-profile political issues such as aid to Israel and school prayer. The Governmental Affairs Committee often focuses on scandalous exposés of executive branch malfeasance, featuring moments of dramatic testimony. These committees get on television more often not because they are more important but because the topics they cover are more suitable to broadcast media coverage.

C-SPAN

Congress Comes to Your Living Room

C-SPAN, the Cable-Satellite Public Affairs Network, was made possible by the increased popularity of local cable stations and the increasing accessibility and affordability of video and satellite technology. Launched at the same time that the House of Representatives agreed to be broadcast, this innovative news channel initially focused on floor debates in the House. Today it operates twenty-four hours a day, seven days a week, on two separate channels, C-SPAN 1 and C-SPAN-2, and covers diverse events from committee hearings to author talks to call-in shows to presidential debates and even political comedy roasts. One poll found that 12 percent of Americans are regular viewers of C-SPAN, with another 31 percent saying they sometimes watch it.[22]

C-SPAN's tiny budget comes not from tax dollars but from fees paid by the cable and satellite industry. C-SPAN is able to cover so much for so little because it does not attempt to do what the rest of the media does: filter and analyze the news. The only filtering that C-SPAN does is deciding what event to cover; once an event is chosen, it is usually carried without interruption or commentary by a small camera crew. It truly is a case of "C-SPAN reports, you decide." Unlike traditional public television, which offers analysis and encapsulation of the news on programs such as the *News Hour with Jim Lehrer,* C-SPAN lets the raw feed speak for itself.

Does C-SPAN actually influence the political world? Politicians stereotypically refer to "C-SPAN junkies" as those who watch hours of Senate and House debate long after even most members of Congress would admit to utter boredom. At any given moment of the broadcast day, the viewership of C-SPAN is much smaller than almost any other news outlet. It is difficult, therefore, to argue that C-SPAN has the kind of direct impact of CBS or Fox News, particularly considering that many of the political junkies are committed partisans unlikely to be persuaded by what they watch. But that doesn't mean that C-SPAN is without influence. Consider the fate of former Majority Leader Trent Lott (R–MS). C-SPAN broadcast Lott's tribute to retiring Senator Strom Thurmond (R–SC) at

Thurmond's one hundredth birthday party in December of 2002. During his speech, Lott said this:

> I want to say this about my state: When Strom Thurmond ran for president, we voted for him. We're proud of it. And if the rest of the country had followed our lead, we wouldn't have had all these problems over all these years either.

Because Thurmond's 1948 run for the presidency was largely based on his opposition to black progress, integration, and civil rights, Lott's comments could be seen as an endorsement of those racist views. But the mainstream journalists in the room didn't really notice anything problematic about Lott's remark (nor did anyone else present). Only when C-SPAN viewers began to chatter about the quote on the Internet, particularly on political blogs, did the mainstream media erupt in a firestorm of controversy. Ultimately, Lott was forced to step down as Majority Leader. Had there been no C-SPAN bringing a relatively obscure political event into millions of homes, it is likely that Lott would never have been held accountable for his comments. Not only did C-SPAN start the issue rolling, it also provided the rest of the media with the devastating video clip of the comment. If the words had only been in print, it would have been far easier for Lott to duck responsibility, and the mainstream media would have covered it far less because they would have lacked the crucial visual element.

In the broadest sense, C-SPAN represents the resilient sensibility that electronic media have some public responsibility, even cable television. Broadcast media are much more heavily regulated because it was understood that the airwaves, with their limited bandwidth, must serve the public interest. Broadcast television from its earliest days has included political news by government mandate. Cable has much less regulation, and some channels are entirely devoid of any coverage of politics. C-SPAN provides the cable television viewer with easy access to raw political coverage.

C-SPAN's influence may be greater than that of any other media on one key set of viewers: the 535 members of Congress and their thousands of staffers. Ninety percent of Congress says it consults C-SPAN on a daily basis, and it is constantly on the air in most congressional offices.[23]

The media also tend to overemphasize the impact of floor speeches. In the House of Representatives, a rule permits **one minutes** at the close of the legislative day. These brief speeches were intended to give back bench representatives a chance to vent their views on diverse subjects, views often not tied to any viable piece of legislation. The House, in which the majority party dominates the legislative process, is often a frustrating place for the minority party. When television came to the House in 1979, Republicans had been in the minority since 1955, and there was no end to Democratic dominance in sight. Republicans began to use the one minutes to deliver anti-Democratic messages, taking advantage of the national telecast of these remarks on **C-SPAN,** the national cable channel devoted to covering Congress and politics generally (see Box).

Although these speeches were almost irrelevant to the legislative process, they began to attract a small, dedicated viewership, and they started to irritate the Democratic leadership, in part because of strident criticism of the ethics of individual Democratic legislators and the competence and integrity of the Democratic majority as a whole. The cameras seemed to show bold legislators addressing a rapt congressional session with their conservative speeches. Some one minutes were such good theater, often involving props, that they were covered in the mainstream media, which liked the humor and drama. In one memorable speech by Jim Nussle (R–IA) in 1991, Nussle appeared wearing a paper bag over his head to indicate his shame at being part of Congress amidst the House banking scandal. The bizarre image of a bagged head addressing Congress produced massive media attention for the Republicans' demands and gave an often-ignored legislative minority a national voice, although it also subjected Nussle to some ridicule for his theatrics.

Earlier, a speech by Robert Walker (R–PA) intensely angered the House Democratic leadership. In his speech, Walker challenged any Democrat to come forward and contest his claims. The audience at home had no way of knowing that the chamber was, as it usually is, almost entirely empty. Instead, it looked like Walker was cowing Democrats, who were either too cowardly or too inept to respond to his eloquent challenge. In retaliation, Speaker Tip O'Neill commanded that the cameras be forced to pan the chamber and reveal that Walker's bold challenge had been issued to an empty chamber.[24] O'Neill was trying to show that one-minute speeches had as much impact on the legislative process as letters to the editor do on the running of the *New York Times*. Over time leaders of Congress have learned that what happens in the media eventually matters in Congress, even if the media's depiction is gravely misleading. The after-debate speeches by Republicans may have played a key role in inciting public anger against Congress, leading to the Republican revolution of 1994. Even when the media distort the truth about congressional procedures, the manner of the distortion may be of great importance.

There are also moments when the media effectively and accurately convey the human dramas that sometimes occur in Congress. One such moment was the resignation of Senator Bob Packwood (R–OR) in 1995. Packwood, a leading moderate Republican, was brought down by allegations of sexual misconduct, detailed in his personal diary. For days the question of whether Packwood would resign, or attempt to fight expulsion, convulsed the Senate. It takes two-thirds of the Senate to expel a member, and Packwood took to the floor to fight for his political life. The speeches for and against him were passionate and personal. When Packwood ultimately decided to resign in a tearful speech to a packed Senate, the American people had the chance to see every agonized moment. Television news, which fails to capture the complexity of legislation or of the legislative process, did convey the sadness and gravity of a powerful man's fall from power.

Yet even in this moment of success for television coverage of Congress distortion exists. For months coverage of the lurid allegations of harassment of young interns and lobbyists by a lecherous Packwood had received top billing in the media, whereas the welfare reform bill that Packwood was shepherding through the Senate was comparatively ignored. Welfare reform eventually altered the lives of millions of impoverished Americans and represented one of the most radical and popular changes in American entitlement programs in history. A viewer of the media might have been forgiven for assuming that Packwood's disgrace was more important than the little-discussed welfare bill.

There is little chance of the modern media presenting a fuller picture of Congress anytime soon. Even the elite, highbrow media, such as the *New York Times*, do not. A study of one hundred *Times* stories about Congress revealed that only five were **process oriented.** By "process oriented" the researchers meant stories that focused on the substance of the legislative issues, as well as the complexity of Congress's operation, as opposed to which political party would benefit or be hurt by the legislation. A separate study found that over the period 1972 through 1992 coverage of Congress throughout the media became scandal centered.[25] As usual, it is too simplistic to blame the media for this; there are sober, serious, detailed analyses of congressional procedure and legislative issues in such publications as *National Journal* and *Congressional Quarterly*. The public could choose to read those, or watch C-SPAN, instead of more popular media outlets. Judging by numbers of readers and viewers, the public prefers the simplified, distorted view of Congress.

THE MEDIA AS A CENTRIFUGAL FORCE IN CONGRESS: WEAKENING AND CHANGING LEADERSHIP

As the power of the media in American politics has grown, it has changed Congress in fundamental ways. One key alteration is that the media have helped decentralize Congress by weakening the leadership of Congress. One scholar described the entirety of congressional history and process as a conflict between forces that centralize Congress and forces that split it apart, the centripetal and centrifugal tendencies that have characterized the branch at various times.[26] Modern televised media can act as a force against the single greatest centralizing agent in Congress, the party leadership. This may be the most subtle and important effect of electronic media upon Congress.

Prior to the advent of the television era, Congress was a far more hierarchical and elite-driven institution. Junior members were expected to serve long apprenticeships to more senior members, deferring to their party's leaders and to committee chairs in voting and speeches. There were always mavericks and rebels against the seniority system in both the House and the Senate, but the main path to power and success lay in careful and slow attention to legislative work that was approved by the party leadership. Those with long records of service in Congress held the power through the seniority and committee systems. There was a distinction between the **show horses,** who catered to the media, and the **work horses,** who paid attention to the committee leaders and did the slow grunt work on complex legislation. Work horses became committee chairs and party leaders, gaining institutional power within Congress. Show horses saw congressional service as a stepping stone to a governorship or even the presidency, often had shorter careers, and failed to achieve leadership posts in Congress. Legislative veterans spoke with disdain of most show horse members of Congress.

Television fundamentally changed these ideal types. First, it added media savvy and sound bite skill to the list of qualifications for leadership. In the past, congressional leaders had often been untelegenic and sometimes inept or undistinguished public speakers. When they appeared on television in the 1950s, they often seemed unfamiliar with the rules of the medium. Work horses like Lyndon Johnson, who tried to move from the powerful position of Senate Majority Leader into the presidency, were very much outclassed by show horses like John Kennedy, who sparkled on television. Johnson's complaint about the 1960 race for the Democratic nomination was that his unmatched record of legislative achievement should have given him more coverage and credibility when he was running against a junior senator from Massachusetts who had accomplished very little in the Senate. But television was already beginning to dominate the race for the White House, and Kennedy was much more adept at it than Johnson, despite Johnson's glittering résumé of legislative accomplishments. As television took hold in Congress in the 1970s, party leaders in Congress were expected to be skilled at presenting their party's views on television.[27] This was particularly vital when the presidency was controlled by the opposition party.

Today the leaders of Congress make appearances almost every month on Sunday talk shows, articulating the views of the party caucus. Such events were rare in the past and of far less importance. Even the strong norm of seniority has given way to the need for the party in the Senate or House to be represented well on television. When Senator George Mitchell (D–ME) became Majority Leader over a dozen more senior colleagues, the cause of his rapid rise was widely attributed to his talent on television. In 2002, when Senate Republicans had to find a new leader in a hurry, they chose a man who had been in elected politics for less than a decade, Bill Frist of Tennessee, in large part because he was thought to be a capable public spokesperson for the party. Many conservatives also attribute the failures of the Republican Revolution of 1994 not to policy mistakes or errors on the substance of the issues but to House Speaker Newt Gingrich's inability to project a positive image on television. Congressional leadership today is intimately related to success on television.

These dramatic claims about the effects of television media on congressional leadership have not gone unchallenged. Leading political scholar Stephen Hess, in his 1986 book on the Senate, *The Ultimate Insiders,* challenged the emerging conventional wisdom that television had altered the nature of congressional leadership and power within Congress. Hess found that the media in 1983 did not spend more time focusing on those without seniority than had the media in 1953. Hess showed that the Sunday talk shows, network news, and print reporters still focused disproportionate attention on those in leadership positions within the party and on committees. He asked whether the conventional wisdom about the media rising to power in Congress was merely a product of most members and staffers being news junkies. They perceive the media to be an important influence on leadership and legislation, even if media actually is not.[28] Hess's work is a good example of the value of rethinking established truths, but the problem with this analysis is that the people chosen to lead Congress, and to a lesser extent the committees, are much more attuned to television politics than in the past. Majority leaders are today chosen in part because they will command media attention, and they are chosen with much less regard to seniority.

Television has not just altered how one becomes a leader in Congress. It has also altered the balance of power between leaders and followers. In the old congressional system, junior members had to "pay their dues" and respect their elders before they took on central roles in important debates. Today even the newest member feels safe in staking out new policy turf and taking a leading role in legislative action and debate. There were, of course, meteoric rises to power in the era before television, particularly among gifted orators such as Henry Clay, or those who had famous names, such as Bobby Kennedy. But the norm held that most members should not be too prominent too soon. Television has forever changed that, giving all members incentives to get on the news as soon and as often as possible. The old joke on Capitol Hill that "the most dangerous place in Washington is between Senator X and a television camera!"—implying that this particular show horse would knock you over in the rush to get media coverage—has lost its power to amuse. Today members of Congress understand that seeking positive media attention whenever possible is simply part of the job description.

CONGRESS VERSUS THE MEDIA

If the media have played a role in depicting Congress negatively, Congress surely has not shrunk from negatively characterizing the press. In a 1995 random poll of 155 members of Congress, members complained about the media focusing far too much attention on their personal lives and failing to educate the public about the legislative process. Most of the members (89 percent) said they had been "burned" by a false or misleading press story. The hostility of members of Congress toward the media extends back to the earliest days of the republic; consider the opinions expressed on the floor of the Senate by a Connecticut Democrat in 1839:

> [Congressional reporters are] miserable slanderers, hirelings hanging on to the skirts of literature, earning a miserable subsistence from their vile and dirty misrepresentations of the proceedings here . . . venal and profligate scribblers, who were sent here to earn a disreputable living by catering to the depraved appetite of the papers they work for.[29]

Congress used to regulate the reporters who covered it by restricting those who could be credentialed. A few journalists were even held in contempt of Congress and imprisoned. There was arguably a need for oversight; some lobbyists were pretending to be journalists, and some journalists would make money on the side as lobbyists. Some reporters were taking money from corporations or politicians to spin stories about legislation a certain way.[30]

In the last century the congressional press became self-regulating. Credentials are in the hands of the Standing Committee of Correspondents, a group elected by the members of the congressional media. At one point, the committee passed legislation requiring members to disclose outside sources of income in response to congressional complaints that just as members of Congress had to be aware of conflicts of interest so, too, should the journalists covering these issues. After all, if a top journalist is paid thousands of dollars to address the insurance industry, will he or she more favorably cover insurance issues that arise on Capitol Hill? However, the congressional press revolted and voted out the committee members who had supported this rule.[31] In 1995 the Senate passed a nonbinding resolution suggesting that congressional reporters be required to file financial disclosure forms similar to those filed by Senators.[32] Although the proposal had no effect, it signaled the continuing frustration felt by politicians who believe that the media, which demands absolute integrity and avoidance of even the appearance of impropriety from them, are far less open about their own activities.

As with the rest of the media, relations between Congress and the reporters who cover it changed as the media went from the access era to the watchdog and junkyard dog eras of journalism. According to Jim Cannon, who had been both a reporter and chief of staff to the Senate Majority Leader, the access era on Capitol Hill was starkly different:

> Capitol reporters looked out for their friends in Congress: they followed an unwritten code. You did not write that House Republican Leader Charles Halleck of Indiana was drunk on the House floor last night. You did not quote the racist slurs that Representative Tad Walters, a notorious bigot from Pennsylvania, used in normal conversation. You did not report that Tennessee Senator Estes Kefauver chased women almost as assiduously as he pursued headlines. It was not that reporters were conspiring in a cover-up; they tolerated the few aberrations in a Congressional club where most members were responsible, hard-working public servants dedicated to the public interest. . . . They respected Congress as an institution.[33]

It is almost inconceivable that the congressional press corps would not report such things in the current climate. Today members of Congress may have more hostile feelings toward the press simply because the press are trolling through their private lives, looking for sexual, financial, or political scandals.

CONGRESS ON THE WEB: AN UNFILTERED LEGISLATURE?

Among the many changes House Speaker Newt Gingrich advocated as part of his Republican Revolution was bringing the new technology of the Internet to Congress as a democratizing force. In January of 1995 the newly sworn-in leader of Congress promised that the Republicans would make every bill, every amendment, and every conference report available online to all Americans.[34] Today Gingrich's vision has been fully realized as Thomas, a searchable database of the *Congressional Record* and nearly every proposal before Congress. The *Congressional Record* is the daily account of every speech made as well as a lot of material that is "admitted to the record" without being spoken. Considering that floor debates alone generate an average of two hundred pages of text a day, hardbound volumes of the *Congressional Record* used to take up entire shelves in many libraries. Today the Web site, as well as CD-ROM versions, make the *Record* more accessible and cheaper.[35] Using Thomas, the average citizen can follow a particular piece of legislation from proposal to adoption.

Since 1995 it has become the norm for every member of Congress to have an official Web site. Some Web sites feature regular updates on member activities as well as methods for contacting staff with concerns and opinions. Others take interactivity to the next step, providing bulletin boards and online surveys so constituents can get the sense that the member is listening to their concerns. Members vary greatly in how much support they give to their Web sites, with some making it a priority as a way to talk around the "filter" of the media. One key limitation is that the Web site cannot directly aid the reelection campaign because it represents an expenditure of official government funds. Therefore, most members also set up a reelection Web site that handles campaign information, online versions of television commercials, and campaign organization materials.

Given all the ways for Congress to directly inform members of the public about its activities, one might believe that the Web has weakened the mainstream media by empowering citizens to inform themselves. For some, this has certainly been the case. However, the reaction of most Americans surfing Thomas or their representative's Web site may well be that there is simply too much unfiltered information available to absorb. Without the experienced guidance of veteran congressional journalists, the average citizen may be unable to distinguish important floor debates from symbolic or ephemeral speeches. Also, interest in Congress may be so low among the general population that they may seldom, if ever, visit congressional Web sites, depending on the media to tell them when Congress is doing something very important. The public may unconsciously appreciate the agenda-setting function of the media.

Perhaps because of the key role played by Republicans in launching Congress into the Internet age in 1995, the quality of Web sites run by congressional Republicans is significantly higher than those sponsored by congressional Democrats, according to a nonpartisan think tank analysis.[36] The same report shows rapid increases in the quality of congressional Web sites and greater allocation of staff resources to their maintenance. If these wily politicians are putting scarce staff time into Web sites, they clearly believe these Internet windows into Congress are an effective way to improve reelection prospects.

Whatever the future of Congress online, the Internet revolution has made partially false the claim by political scientist Herb Asher that "everything that people learn about Congress is mediated."[37] Thanks to the Web and C-SPAN, the public can, if it wishes, get a largely unfiltered picture of Congress.

INTEREST GROUPS AND THE MEDIA:
TALKING TO CONGRESS THROUGH THE PRESS

Interest groups are central to the American political system. As the media have grown in power, interest groups have had to learn how to play the game of media politics just as other political actors have. Today many interest groups use the media to persuade Congress. Scholars of interest groups tend to divide the strategies of these organizations into "inside" and "outside" tactics. Inside tactics interact directly on political institutions such as Congress, far from the public eye. Lobbying a member, donating to his or her campaign, or initiating a lawsuit are inside tactics that don't rely on public opinion or the media for success. Outside tactics, by contrast, often rely on the media for maximum effect.

Consider the Center for Science in the Public Interest (CSPI). This small nutritional advocacy group with a fifteen-million-dollar annual budget relies on the media for most of its impact. CSPI seeks tighter regulations on the food and restaurant industries, often in the form of enhanced labeling (you can learn more at www.cspinet.org). These industries and their allies in Congress resist CSPI's efforts. The main tactic CSPI uses to win battles over food regulations is to release scientific studies to the media in the hope of increasing pressure on Congress and regulatory agencies to act. CSPI cannot afford to make significant donations to political campaigns, hire teams of lobbyists to persuade legislators to vote their way, or employ teams of lawyers to litigate rulings of regulatory agencies. Instead, CSPI contracts for scientific studies and hopes for free media coverage. Because the key to success is media attention, CSPI often focuses on alarming topics such as the dangerous hidden fat content in foods served in Chinese restaurants.

CSPI releases reports that seem to be designed for frightening headlines and short, scary news clips, but they have to be wary. To gain coverage, CSPI has to maintain a reputation as a purveyor of reliable scientific information. The restaurant and food industry has created a counter group, CSPI Scam (Cspiscam.com), which attacks the data presented by CSPI. The two groups both want to influence Congress and the Food and Drug Administration but clearly aim to do so primarily through the media and the public. This puts the media in the position of adjudicating the validity of the claims of two small interest groups long before Congress gets involved.

In the modern media politics environment, interest groups have had to rapidly increase their "outside" tactics to get into the media. According to former White House Chief of Staff James Baker, the best way to convince Congress on a given issue is to implement a media-friendly message that would persuade the public. Many interest groups have adopted this grand strategy.[38] Companies can purchase advertising, not to sell products but to whip up the appearance of support for legislation that benefits their bottom line. One of the best examples of this occurred during the 1996 telecommunications reform debate. An arcane bill to most Americans, it was vital to the profitability of telephone and cable companies. Both sides advertised on national television, encouraging viewers to call their representatives, and even facilitating the phone calls through a central switchboard. This mimicry of grassroots activism (also called **Astroturf activism** because it is artificial grassroots) used paid media to influence Congress. Another way interest groups use the media is to take out ads in the Washington, D.C., area to try to speak to members of Congress and their staffers directly.[39]

Like members of Congress, interest groups prefer free news coverage to paid media, and largely for the same reasons. Groups without a great deal of money are particularly dependent on free media.[40] Strategies such as sit-ins, marches, and rallies can produce the dramatic footage the media loves. Other groups use press conferences to announce official reports in the hope that the media will trumpet their findings to the public, and thereby to Congress.

In all of these ways, we see interest groups using the media to relay their messages to Congress. Of the many signs of the rise of media power in American politics, the media's role as a main avenue of communication between interest groups and Congress is among the most conclusive. The press, which originally was a mediating institution between the people and their government, now intrudes between Congress and interest groups, another crucial mediating institution.

CONCLUSION: A DISTORTION BECOMING REAL?

If Walter Benjamin's great hope for video was that it would remove elite filters and take viewers to previously hidden places, he would be disappointed with the media's coverage of Congress. It is heavily filtered through a distorting lens. Modern technology has brought

Congress into our living rooms and shown us what the public never saw before, but most of the true power moments in Congress still take place behind closed doors. The deals and negotiations that precede most floor debates and the consulting and bickering among lobbyists and staffers that precede committee hearings on legislation are still off-limits to cameras.

Moreover, the worry of Neil Postman, that video technology inevitably removes complexity, seems more applicable to the media's coverage of Congress than to any other aspect of our politics. Indeed, because the media find it so hard to simplify Congress, they often ignore it. When Congress is featured in the media, it is often so simplified that it would be better off ignored.

In a paradoxical way, the distorted picture of Congress that the media present has significant real-world effects. Beyond making the president more powerful, reducing trust in Congress, and changing how leadership is practiced or achieved in Congress, the media's greatest actual effect on Congress may be to induce greater gridlock. For most of American history, Congress has successfully achieved its primary function: approving a budget for the government. Raising and spending money is the core legislative function and perhaps the most important task of Congress other than deciding whether to take the nation to war. Indeed, until 1920, presidents did not even submit budgets as they were entirely written on Capitol Hill. In the last thirty years, Congress has repeatedly failed to meet its deadlines for completing the new budget. More often than not Congress has to pass continuing resolutions to keep the government open. These resolutions have a deleterious effect on the government's ability to effectively enact coherent new policies because they simply maintain existing spending indefinitely. Sometimes a government agency will receive its new fiscal budget with only seven months remaining to implement new policies.

Worse, on several occasions the government, or significant parts of it, had to shut down entirely due to budgetary impasses within Congress or between Congress and the president. Both shutdowns and continuing resolutions can have grave implications for the effectiveness and fiscal health of government. There are many competing explanations for these recent failures: an unprecedented propensity for divided government, runaway entitlement spending, or a polarized Congress. But one explanation for the budgetary gridlock may well be the introduction of video media to Capitol Hill.

What does the media have to do with gridlock? Before the modern media revolution, the leaders of Congress had much more power over the junior members of their party caucuses, whether the leadership was with the party or the committee chairs. Many major issues were solved by negotiations among a very small group of people, who were empowered to make ironclad deals on behalf of their followers. It was a much less egalitarian Congress, perhaps, but it seldom resulted in government shutdowns and continuing resolutions. What those leaders had that modern congressional leaders lack is more than just raw power; they also had flexibility. Instead of negotiations and discussions among small groups from both parties, today we have posturing on television. Video technology may have contributed to a Congress in which compromise is far more difficult to reach. As former Congressman Mickey Edwards (R–OK) put it,

> The problem is, when you are forced to say things in front of the cameras, you get yourself locked into a position that becomes very, very hard to back off of.[41]

Before cameras were allowed into committee hearings and floor debates, positions could shift much more easily. A "video rigidity" that hardens stances before negotiations even begin may be partially responsible for the recent string of budgetary failures in Congress.

Moreover, the media have played a fundamental role in the bitter personal attacks that are a prominent part of recent congressional politics. The leaders of the two parties often developed real friendships throughout much of congressional history. Democrat Tip O'Neill and Republican Bob Michels, two leaders of the House for much of the 1970s and 1980s, could fight each other all day on the floor and share a warm friendly evening afterward. In an era in which allegations of personal impropriety and scandal are one of the few guaranteed ways to get media attention, the personal relationships among partisans on Capitol Hill have frayed. In the 1990s Newt Gingrich led the Republicans to majority status in part by launching bitter ethical attacks against two successive House Speakers. Once Gingrich was Speaker, Democrats quickly raised ethical accusations against Gingrich and contributed to harsh depictions of his personal life in the media. The "politics of personal destruction" is not limited to the executive branch. It may be even more prevalent in Congress because of the greater challenge of getting media attention and the looser controls over the 535 members. When politics means not just defeating the other side's ideas but convincing the public, through the media, that the opposition is led by scoundrels, compromise becomes far more difficult to reach.

Thus a media that shows America a bitter, bickering, gridlocked Congress also plays a role in worsening the very ills it derides. Some have proposed that Congress take steps to reduce the media's power, or at least to promote Congress's image with the public. Because of its division into so many separate offices and committees, Congress puts very little effort into improving its public image in the press.[42] Unlike the president, who works to enhance or preserve public respect for the presidency for reasons of ambition if not institutional patriotism, members of Congress see their personal ambition and Congress's public standing as often in conflict and certainly not as directly linked as is the president to the presidency. Many members of Congress present themselves to the public as being opposed to the tone, style, and ethos of Congress—they win elections by running Congress down. Some have suggested creating a centralized office in Congress that would work to improve the general image of Congress, but the proposal seems highly unlikely in the current climate.

Despite the media's distortions and the presence of unfiltered access to Congress via C-SPAN and the Internet, the media remain the dominant influence on the public's impressions of and approval for Congress. Consequently, the "sausage factory" process responsible for passing national laws is unlikely to become more popular with the average American.

KEY TERMS

advertising	position taking
Astroturf activism	process oriented
congressional press secretary	show horses
credit claiming	sponsor
C-SPAN	trial balloons
one minutes	work horses

DISCUSSION QUESTIONS

1. What impressions of Congress have you gained from the media? Are your impressions generally positive or negative? Are they accurate?
2. Have you ever been asked by an interest group to pressure Congress in a way that would be covered by the media? Have you ever attended a demonstration that was for or against

legislation? Do you think the media coverage affected the outcome of the congressional legislation?
3. Do you ever watch C-SPAN? If not, why not?
4. Do you believe that the press generally provides better coverage, or at least more coverage, for the president than it does for Congress?
5. What do you think Congress could do to improve the coverage it gets from the media?

ADDITIONAL RESOURCES

Congress as Public Enemy, by John Hibbing and Elizabeth Theiss-Morse, is an excellent examination of why Congress is so unpopular with the public.

Making Laws and Making News: Media Strategies in the U.S. House of Representatives, by Timothy Cook, is one of the best academic studies of how changes in the media have affected how Congress works.

The Ultimate Insiders, by Stephen Hess, argues that the media have not changed Congress as much as many other scholars believe.

ONLINE RESOURCES

Thomas is the Web site run by the Library of Congress that tracks every piece of legislation in each congressional session. You can get the text to all bills, laws, and committee reports here: thomas.loc.congress

All members of Congress have official Web sites of varying quality. A complete listing of House members' Web sites, along with committee Web sites, can be found at www.house.gov/house/MemberWWW.shtml. Senators are listed at www.senate.gov/general/contact_information/senators_cfm.cfm. These Web sites are legally distinct from the Web sites that the members' campaigns run.

NOTES

1. Stephen Hess, *Live from Capitol Hill! Studies of Congress and the Media* (Washington DC: Brookings, 1991), 35.

2. Donald A. Ritchie, *Press Gallery: Congress and the Rise of the Washington Correspondent* (Cambridge: Harvard University Press, 1992), 7–9.
3. Doris Graber, *Mass Media and American Politics,* 6th ed. (Washington, DC: Congressional Quarterly, 2002), 236.
4. Ibid., 238.
5. R. Douglas Arnold, *Congress, the Press, and Political Accountability* (New York: Russell Sage, 2004), 61.
6. Study by Michael Robinson, cited in *Congress and Its Members,* 8th ed., Roger H. Davidson and Walter J. Oleszek (Washington, DC: Congressional Quarterly), 155.
7. Quoted in Davidson and Oleszek, *Congress and Its Members,* 156.
8. Ibid., 154–55.
9. Arnold, *Congress,* 2.
10. John R. Hibbing and Elizabeth Theiss-Morse, *Congress as Public Enemy* (Cambridge, UK: Cambridge University Press, 1995), 147.
11. Matthew R. Kerbel, *Remote and Controlled: Media Politics in a Cynical Age* (Boulder, CO: Westview Press, 1999), 117.
12. Elaine S. Povich, *Partners and Adversaries* (Washington, DC: Freedom Forum, 1996), 147.
13. Ibid., 152. Other studies have shown that although members of the public often cannot recall the name of their representative when asked, many more can recognize it on a list of names.
14. Hess, *Live from Capitol Hill!,* 103.
15. Quoted in Kerbel, *Remote and Controlled,* 115.
16. Stephen Hess, *The Ultimate Insiders: U.S. Senators in the National Media* (Washington, DC: Brookings, 1986), 104.
17. Povich, *Partners,* 42.
18. Hess, *The Ultimate Insiders,* 83.
19. Povich, *Partners,* 82.
20. Daniel Callahan, William Green, Bruce Jennings, and Martin Linsky, *Congress and the Media: The Ethical Connection* (Hastings-on-Hudson, NY: Hastings Center, 1985), 14.
21. Hess, *The Ultimate Insiders,* 32.
22. Pew Research Center for the People & the Press, "The C-SPAN Audience After 25 Years . . ." Press Release, March 2, 2004.
23. Povich, *Partners,* 160.
24. Ibid., 82
25. Mark Rozell, *In Contempt of Congress: Postwar Press Coverage on Capitol Hill* (Westport, CT: Praeger, 1996), 129–30.

26. Burdett A. Loomis, *The Contemporary Congress* (New York: Bedford/St. Martin's, 1999).
27. Steven S. Smith, "Forces of Change in Senate Party Leadership and Organization." In *Congress Reconsidered*, Lawrence C. Dodd and Bruce I. Oppenheimer, eds. (Washington, DC: Congressional Quarterly Press, 1993), 280–81.
28. Hess, *The Ultimate Insiders*, 100–101.
29. Hess, *Live from Capitol Hill!*, 20.
30. Ibid., 20–21.
31. Ibid., 31.
32. Rozell, *In Contempt of Congress*, 129.
33. Jim Cannon, "Congress and the Media: The Loss of Trust." In *Partners and Adversaries* (Washington, DC: Freedom Forum, 1996), 69.
34. Richard Davis and Diana Owen, *New Media and American Politics* (New York: Oxford, 1998), 117–18.
35. Mildred Amer, "Congressional Record: Its Production, Distribution, and Accessibility." Congressional Research Service Report, 2003.
36. "Congress On-Line: Turning the Corner on the Information Age." A report by the Congressional Management Foundation, 2003.
37. Quoted in Rozell, *In Contempt of Congress*, 130.
38. Timothy E. Cook, "Outsider and Insider Strategies: Can Complementarity Work?" In *Politics and the Media*, Richard Davis, ed. (Englewood Cliffs, NJ: Prentice Hall, 1994), 254.
39. Jarol B. Manheim, "What's Good for Mobil Oil." In *Politics and the Media*, Richard Davis, ed. (Englewood Cliffs, NJ: Prentice Hall, 1994), 279–80.
40. Edie Goldenberg, "Resource Poor Groups." In *Politics and the Media*, Richard Davis, ed. (Englewood Cliffs, NJ: Prentice Hall, 1994), 290–93.
41. Ibid., 84.
42. Rozell, *In Contempt of Congress*, 133.

CHAPTER 10

Mediated Elections: Campaigns and Modern Journalism

Today's presidential campaign is essentially a mass media campaign.

—Political Scientist Tom Patterson[1]

[T]he knowledge revolution raises the prospect of dominant media influence— of mediacracy instead of aristocracy or democracy.

—Pundit Kevin Phillips[2]

*I*n a democratic republic such as the United States, the authority of government ultimately rests upon the people's approval as measured in periodic elections. The media's role in this process is to serve as conduits of information upon which voters may base their decisions and to officiate in the electoral boxing match, deciding which tactics and strategies are legitimate and effective. In recent decades television has risen to dominate the coverage of elections, and the raw power possessed by the media during a campaign has grown. This is not only because television media may be more powerful at shaping perceptions but also because electronic media, except the Internet, are increasingly concentrated in fewer and fewer corporations. In addition, as parties and party loyalties have grown weaker, the ability of journalists to affect the outcome of elections has become greater.

At the same time, traditional campaign journalism faces the challenge of newer media outlets, such as television talk shows, modern talk radio, Web sites, and blogs, which have arisen in part because candidates wanted other ways to get their campaign messages out to the public.

Despite these new media, television remains dominant in the process, both in terms of news coverage and in advertising, or paid media. In recent elections, as many as 83 percent of voters cited television as their source of information on presidential candidates, far outpacing all other types of media.[3] So how has this modern cacophony of electronic media shaped political campaigns in the United States?

This chapter reviews how television journalism works in campaigns, primarily focusing on the highest profile elections, those for president. It then examines paid media in campaigns, polls in campaigns, and the new media's role in modern campaigns. It concludes by considering several reforms that have been proposed to improve the coverage of U.S. political campaigns.

PRESIDENTIAL CAMPAIGNS

In U.S. elections the presidential campaign sets the standard of innovation, which all other levels of politics follow. Tactics that emerge at the presidential level quickly find their way into congressional and gubernatorial elections in the larger states. Television strategies that were innovative at the presidential level in the 1960s are now appearing at the state legislative level.

Presidential campaigns can be divided into five periods: the pre-primary stage, the primaries, the conventions, the general election, and the presidential debates. The media play a different role in each of these.

Pre-Primary Media: The Great Mentioner

The pre-primary period of presidential election has no formal beginning and ends only when the first votes in the Iowa caucus are tabulated, usually in January of the election year. It could be said that the pre-primary begins as soon as the last election ends because pundits begin speculating about what the election results will mean for various potential nominees four years ahead. One senator pursuing the White House spoke of the **great mentioner** to describe how simply by word of mouth among reporters and politicians a governor or senator could become viewed as qualified for the nomination race. In other political systems, party leaders choose the next nominee; in the United States the media have acquired, largely by accident, a large say in who is seen as capable of launching a two- or three-year campaign for the White House. Perhaps because the disorganized media play such a central role, the process of selecting a nominee takes longer and is less predictable in the United States than in any other democracy.

Even though the "mentioning" of various presidential and vice presidential candidates can begin years before the election, widespread media coverage of possible nominees begins two years before the election. During this period, candidates vie for media attention and funds as they travel the country. Perhaps the most important function the media perform in this period is to establish who the "frontrunner" is in each party. If the incumbent president is eligible for reelection, he is automatically the frontrunner in his party, but the situation is usually highly fluid in the challenging party. The party out of power surrenders to the media a great deal of the power to determine the putative frontrunner for the presidential nomination.

The media can do this through several means. First, and perhaps most important, the media sponsor **pre-primary polls.** In the spring of 2005, more than three years before the 2008 presidential election, a Gallup–USA Today poll made national headlines because for the first time a majority of Americans said they would vote for New York Senator Hillary Clinton for president.[4] What is the value of such polls in any real predictive sense? As an accurate assessment of how voters will behave three years later, there are many reasons to doubt that this poll has much merit. Those who responded to the survey have no way of knowing what the issues in 2008 will be, what situation the nation will be in, what opponent Clinton might face, who the running mates will be, and whether any attractive third party or independent candidates will run. The Clinton poll was quite odd; it asked if a respondent would vote for Clinton as a stand-alone question rather than asking if the voter would prefer Clinton over a specific or generic Republican, or in comparison with a number of other possible Democratic nominees. Pre-primary polls that ask voters to choose among a list of candidates are also flawed; they are often better measures of name recognition long before lesser known candidates have begun to advertise. Voters may simply be giving positive reactions to names they've heard before. They certainly aren't making any complex decisions based on the issue positions of the candidates because most candidates take few such positions far ahead of the election year.

There are many reasons to doubt the worth of such polls in terms of actually measuring voter intent, but no one should doubt their impact. In the vast majority of recent nomination contests, the candidate who was ahead in polls of his party's voters prior to the first presidential primary won the nomination.[5] The media's selection of the frontrunner can become a self-fulfilling prophecy before the first voter casts a ballot: media coverage can lead directly to successful fund-raising, which leads to advertising, which leads to higher name recognition and better poll performance and, eventually, to votes.[6] The media establish the political viability of a candidate for the White House months before the first contests in Iowa. Consider the Republican nomination fight of 1999–2000. Texas Governor George W. Bush received a third more media coverage than all of his many competitors combined.[7] Was this serious imbalance caused by the media correctly judging that Bush had the best chance to win the nomination? Or were the media influencing the process so that Bush had a nearly insurmountable lead in fund-raising and name recognition? It is likely that there is a degree of truth to both answers, but in either case, the media are central to the pre-primary period of the presidential contest. And remember that power of the great mentioner? It's still around. After all, someone in the media has to decide which names to list as possible candidates in the poll, often long before any of them have announced that they are running. Just being listed boosts name recognition and political viability.

Primary Period: The Expectations Game

Although state primaries between presidential candidates for party nominations have been around for more than a hundred years in one form or another, they were not decisive in selecting nominees until 1972. In primaries, candidates for a party nomination compete for support from voters who identify with a particular party. In some states voters must be registered as party supporters—state laws differ about who can vote in a party primary. This system was designed to be more democratic than the convention system of selection, which persisted from 1832 to 1968. The convention system was dominated by party elites and their political machines; the primary system was supposed to put the average voter first. From January to April of a presidential election year, voters in each state go to the polls to choose among a list of party candidates. Based on the statewide outcome, candidates win a number of delegates to their party's convention, which is held in the summer before the election. The candidate who wins an outright majority of delegates to the convention automatically gets his or her party's nomination. The primary reform may have succeeded in weakening the party leaders, but arguably it has strengthened not the people but the media. At least, that is the argument political scientist Tom Patterson made in his influential book on campaigns and the media, *Out of Order*. The media may be at the height of their power during the primary period due to absence of the dominant influence on voting—party loyalty. In the general election, many, if not most, voters are deeply affected by the party labels on the candidates, but in a primary every candidate is of the same party. Moreover, primary voters are often choosing among five or more candidates. Only those considered "viable" or "newsworthy" get much attention from the national media. If citizens don't hear about a candidate before they enter a polling station, their support is highly unlikely.

There are two additional reasons the media's power during the primary period is considerable: the focus on the first two contests and the overall **frontloading** of the primaries. Two states have come to dominate the party primaries among both Democrats and Republicans: the **New Hampshire primary** (since 1952) and the **Iowa caucus** (since 1972). Both states are remarkably unrepresentative of the nation, being overwhelmingly white and lacking urban centers. The number of delegates selected in these contests is less than 2 percent of the total required to win the nomination. Yet any candidate for the presidency offered a choice between getting the support of party activists in Iowa or California will choose Iowa every time, even though California's primary awards more than twenty times the delegates decided in Iowa.

Why take tiny Iowa over gigantic California, which controls more delegates than any other state? The Iowa caucus takes place months before the California contest, and a candidate declared by the media to be the winner of Iowa or New Hampshire is immediately awarded political viability and massive media attention, which helps the candidate fund-raise and win later contests. In some years, the two early primaries receive more coverage than all the other primaries combined.[8] So much media attention is focused on New Hampshire and Iowa that it actually has an economic impact on these small states. With all the major U.S. news companies sending teams of reporters and all the campaigns sending hundreds of volunteers and paid staffers, the payoff to state coffers is in the tens of millions of dollars starting months before the balloting begins. Candidates must pay attention to these tiny primaries because the media set expectations that campaigns ignore at their grave peril. It is a rare nominee indeed who didn't win at least one of these two contests because they provide such solid momentum going into the next round of primaries.

Momentum is crucial to success because of the frontloading in primaries that has taken place since 1976. In the early days, primaries were spread out from late February to June. Even though large states often voted months after the New Hampshire primary, there would still be important choices for their voters. Since 1972, however, most nomination fights are over within a few days or weeks following the New Hampshire primary. In response, many states began to hold their primaries earlier in the hope of remaining influential upon the choice. As more and more states did this, the importance of New Hampshire and Iowa only increased. A candidate who loses in those contests now has almost no time to recover momentum.

Of course, in primaries it is possible to lose while winning and win while losing. Running the **expectations game** may be the most mysterious power the media possess in the primary period: they define what victory and defeat are for each primary. If two candidates in an early primary divide the electorate 51 percent to 49 percent, the media might call that a tie or decide that it is a victory for one candidate or the other, depending on how each was expected to do. In 1972 the media decided that one candidate, Senator Edmund Muskie of Maine, had to win the Democratic primary in New Hampshire by more than 50 percent in a multicandidate field. When he didn't, they declared him the loser, a defeat from which his campaign never recovered.[9] In the weeks before the 1992 New Hampshire Democratic primary, by contrast, Arkansas Governor Bill Clinton's campaign was rocked by scandals involving his draft record and an extramarital affair. When he nevertheless finished a strong third, significantly above the most recent polls, the media declared him still viable and even the "comeback kid."*

Beyond establishing who won or lost, the media sometimes ignore the results and declare a candidate unelectable. In 1996 conservative pundit Pat Buchanan won the New Hampshire primary, usually a key achievement in gaining the nomination. However, instead of granting Buchanan legitimacy and momentum, the media declared that there was a crisis in the Republican Party. The cause of the crisis? According to the media, Buchanan was unelectable—he lacked "political viability." Buchanan's past as an alleged anti-Semite and far right conservative, as well as the unsavory extremist and racist affiliations of several key supporters,[10] would prevent him from winning the general election even if he could follow up New Hampshire with more primary victories.[11] Whether this was true when it was said, the media played a role in making it true.

It is inevitable that the media will make judgments about the potential of various campaigns. The media separate out the legitimate candidates from those who are running quixotic or hopeless campaigns. Given how little attention most Americans pay to politics generally, and to primary campaigns in particular, the media are performing a necessary function by giving the most airtime to the top two or three candidates. Some primary seasons begin with as many as ten candidates in a single party; there's no way the media could or should give equal time to all ten.

Paradoxically, while the media pick the front-runner, they also have an interest in making the nomination race a true fight. If you are a national reporter covering the leading candidate in the primaries, the lack of a close contest will mean less attention to your reporting. If every primary from January to May is won by the same front-runner as expected, the primaries will seldom be at the top of the media agenda because there will be very little news. This helps explain why some studies find that the media give favorable coverage to trailing candidates and tend to give less favorable coverage to the front-running candidate in primary contests.[12]

There is one sense in which the media's power in primaries may be limited. Turnout in presidential primaries can be surprisingly

---

*Clinton became one of the rare nominees to win neither New Hampshire nor Iowa. In 1992 the media declared the contest in Iowa irrelevant, because Tom Harkin, an Iowa senator, was running for the nomination and was expected to win handily. No other candidate had any incentive to compete in Iowa, and the only question was whether Harkin would manage to meet expectations.

low. As few as 5 percent of the electorate may turn out, and 20 percent is considered successful in many states. Voters in primaries tend to be wealthier, better-educated, more partisan, and more informed about politics—qualities that tend to make voters less affected by media bias and media power. Primaries are low information environments even for these elite voters, so the media's impact remains substantial.

The Conventions: Made for the Media

For more than a hundred years, political parties used conventions to select the nominee for president. Party leaders and delegates gathered in a large hall in the summer before an election and chose the nominee, his running mate, and the party's platform of issue positions. Sometimes lasting two weeks, conventions were often great political dramas, with backroom deals, electrifying speeches, and impromptu political rallies on the convention floor. A few conventions were deadlocked for more than one hundred separate votes over several days, resulting in great tension and uncertainty over the nomination.

Today conventions are sad echoes of these decisive political meetings of the past. Many political scientists believe the upheaval of the 1968 convention and the ensuing reforms ultimately removed power from the conventions and gave it to the primaries, but the rise of television was central to the decline of the convention. When the first televised convention appeared on America's screens in 1952, the young networks gave more than seventy hours of time to each party's convention. However, even then news directors realized that conventions featured hours and hours of activities that were boring for viewers. Television crews were forced to look for human interest stories among the delegates to enliven the procedural parliamentary maneuvering and repetitive speeches that made up the bulk of political conventions.[13]

When conventions had power, it was often exercised in a very visually unattractive and contentious way. When conventions were actually making decisions and affecting outcomes, viewers who were not already committed to that party might be turned off by the turmoil on their televisions. In 1968, when the mayor of Chicago and his supporters at the Democratic convention screamed anti-Semitic slurs and obscenities at a Jewish senator who was criticizing the mayor's police response to demonstrations outside the hall, every

American with an elementary grasp of lip-reading knew exactly what was happening. Such impassioned and ugly confrontations were far from unknown in earlier conventions, but now they were brought to the nation's living rooms. Similarly, when conservative Republican delegates at the 1964 convention responded with outrage and mob anger at the speech of a moderate Republican, it made them seem extreme to many viewers. Television, as many have observed, is a "cool" medium in which hot passion and rage seldom look appealing.

At the 1972 Democratic convention, a different disconnect between convention practices and television norms emerged: scheduling. Traditionally, conventions were only quasi-scheduled. Much like the U.S. Senate, one side at a political convention could use delaying tactics to prolong debate in hopes of shifting votes or wearing out the opposition, or at least forcing a compromise. It was often impossible to predict which political issues or votes would erupt in lengthy debate, noisy rallies, and multiple votes. The 1972 convention was quite contentious, with racial, sexual, and political minorities taking up large amounts of the floor time. The schedule was thrown off by so much debate that the nominee, George McGovern, gave his acceptance speech after midnight when much of the nation was already asleep. The acceptance speech is when the nominee claims victory, tries to unite his party, and introduces himself to the nation; it is usually the most important moment of any convention. McGovern and the Democrats looked disorganized, extremist, and amateurish on television, all of which would have been less important in the pretelevision era. Before television, when floor fights pushed the nominee's acceptance speech into the wee hours of the morning, the voters would still read the speech in the newspapers as if it had happened in prime time.

After the debacles of the 1964 Republican and 1968 and 1972 Democratic conventions, the party leadership began to craft conventions that would make "better" television. They reduced the number of votes and cut back on the length of speeches. They began to design prime time hours with an eye toward television coverage. To avoid looking divided and disorganized, party leaders sought with increasing success to solve all contentious issues prior to the convention. Year after year conventions became more scripted and scheduled. They began to resemble a Hollywood award show more than a political convention of the 1950s, complete with celebrity guest speakers and major musical acts.

The paradox of conventions in the age of television dominance is that all of these changes worked all too well at making conventions placid and peaceful, but simultaneously made them supremely boring. Many Americans used to follow conventions avidly to find out who would be nominated for president and vice president and what issues the parties would take a stand on. Many Americans who were not delegates would travel to conventions just to witness the spectacle. The drama and passion of conventions that made them newsworthy and exciting were produced by the same uncertainty and tension that made them such potential television disasters for parties. Parties faced a choice: make conventions safe and boring and slowly lose viewers or allow conventions to continue to make some decisions (such as selecting the running mate or stances on important hot-button issues) and risk a televised meltdown and clash of party factions. Parties have chosen safe boredom every four years since 1972. On those rare occasions when unscripted or off-message events intrude into the conventions, or when factions begin to clash on the floor, the media quickly brand the moment a disaster for the party because it shows disunity and a failure of control. The media say they want controversy and conflict but punish the party that allows it to happen on the floor of a convention.

Today convention coverage is seen as a burden by the mainstream media, and networks compete to show less and less. In 1996, when NBC opted to show an episode of the sitcom *Seinfeld* instead of the acceptance speech of the Republican vice presidential nominee, it had double the number of viewers of the other two networks combined.[14] Bereft of almost all power to affect the nomination or the platform, delegates at the convention have been transformed into live backdrops, mainly for the keynote and acceptance speeches. The major speeches by the nominees, their spouses, former presidents, and the keynote introduction of the nominees are usually the only things covered on the major media. Even these speeches are now focused on providing one or two popular sound bites that will capture the campaign theme in brief. The emphasis of the modern convention is on entertainment in a desperate attempt to keep viewers tuned in.

It could be argued that the three broadcast networks shouldn't show as much of the conventions as they have in the past. Not only are conventions less powerful and interesting, but cable news channels and political Web sites can now cover them from opening to closing each day. Thus, only prime time highlights need to be shown on the major broadcast networks. The problem with this solution is that it may convey the attitude that politics is not for everyone but should concern only those who make a career or a hobby of it. Also, it ignores the fact that millions of Americans do not have cable television or Internet access. For those voters, whatever is not shown on broadcast television will not be seen or heard.

The changes television has brought about in conventions go deeper than simply failing to give as much airtime as in the past. In 1956 in one of the first academic studies of televised conventions, Charles Thomson of the Brookings Institution wrote that television might produce some positive changes, such as diminishing the importance of regional concerns, forcing parties to remain focused on national questions, and removing procedural shenanigans and parliamentary maneuvers. But Thomson prophetically warned about one substantial drawback to televised conventions:

> In view of the well-established emphasis of television on entertainment, the possibility exists that it will stress entertainment values to an inordinate degree, presenting the conventions as entertainment rather than a serious event that is covered for the instruction of the politically curious.[15]

Thomson's fear, which anticipates the critiques of Neil Postman on television politics generally, was certainly justified. Conventions today have become inordinately focused on attracting viewers by satisfying their need for entertainment. Television cameras may have made conventions accessible to multitudes and helped remove an elitist element in our politics by reducing the power of political bosses, but also largely thanks to television journalism, conventions are merely shadows of the powerful events they once were.

The General Election: Issues Diminished, Character Emphasized

Most Americans don't pay much attention to the race for the presidency until after the conventions, and many do not until the last month before election day. Those who are least interested in and least informed about politics are likely to be most influenced by late campaign messages.[16] Of course, it should be noted that they are also the least likely to vote.

The media's greatest influence on the general election comes in two broad categories: issues and personalities. Studies of voters suggest that four major concerns are paramount in a voter's decision on which presidential candidate to support: party loyalty, an assessment of the general state of the nation (usually its economic condition), a response to the issues raised in the campaign, and an evaluation of the personal character and conduct of the candidate. The general election campaign coverage will probably not affect whether voters consider themselves Democrats or Republicans, so party loyalty is comparatively immune from short-term media influence. Similarly, the media could not, even if they wished to, convince large numbers of voters that the economy was doing poorly if it were not, or vice versa. Some allege that the media play up economic troubles when candidates they dislike are in office and ignore economic problems when they favor an incumbent president, but it is doubtful that this would have a great deal of influence even if the media are making this effort. On the latter two criteria, however, the media have a tremendous impact. Using their agenda-setting power, media can promote an issue in the campaign. Using their power over a candidate's image, the media can decisively shape public perceptions of a candidate's character and personality.

In an idealized vision of democracy, the electorate should be making their choices solely on the issue positions put forward by the candidates and the parties. Yet finding an "issue voter" in any study of elections is challenging. To determine that a particular voter voted in a certain way because of a particular issue or set of issues, other possible motives, such as other issues, party loyalty, or the charisma of the candidates, must be eliminated. Moreover, studies have long shown that many, if not most, voters have remarkably little information on issues and where candidates stand on them.[17]

One final barrier to issue voting in presidential elections is that the media do a remarkably bad job conveying the complexity of the issues facing the nation. Consider the question of what should be done with the government surplus in 2000, which was a major issue in the presidential campaign. For the first time in decades the federal government was collecting more in tax revenue than it was spending on programs and interest on the national debt. Should the money be spent on new federal programs? Should it be used to reduce taxes? Should it be used to pay down the debt and eventually reduce both interest rates and the interest paid on the national debt? The implications for the nation's future fiscal health, economic prosperity, and social policy were vast and complex. Republican George W. Bush argued that the surpluses would last for years and that the nation could afford large tax cuts because "after all, it's your money, not Washington's." Democrat Al Gore argued that the money should be put aside "in a lock box" until a solution to the looming Social Security crisis was found. It would only be exaggerating a little to say that the media reduced these differing issue positions to the battle between "tax cuts" and "lock box."

We should not be surprised that television campaign coverage fails to convey the complexity of issues such as federal surpluses or deficits. On television the average campaign story runs ninety seconds.[18] Often, the report begins with a discussion of what the candidate did on a particular day, and where, and only then addresses the content of the speech that was given, even for a major policy announcement. In response to the brevity and rareness of issue coverage, campaigns have responded by devising sound bites, short phrases to capture their most important and attractive issue positions. These dramatic or humorous phrases are repeated endlessly in the hope that the media will be forced to cover them.

Even when the media do cover issues, they frequently do it poorly. They tend to focus on minor factual errors in the presentation of issue positions or tiny misstatements rather than engaging in broad assessments of the value of policy proposals. In part this is because journalists can be accused of bias if they make any judgments about a candidate's position on an issue. If they stick to easily investigated black and white facts, such accusations are more difficult to make.[19] As Tom Patterson points out, the media will cover a candidate's position on an issue if they suspect he is ill-informed on it or doesn't have a position at all. "Candidate X has no Social Security proposal" is an easy, factual headline. Journalists are less likely to cover an issue such as Social Security if both candidates have detailed policy positions on it. Covering issues in detail not only exposes journalists to charges of bias but also is comparatively expensive for reporters. Understanding how the federal budget works and how future policies will affect it, and comparing the policies and projections of the two campaigns, could take weeks or months of sustained study. Reporters can and often do rely on "impartial" experts to assess these proposals, but gathering and interviewing a balanced panel of experts is much harder than simply having the reporter make a political assessment about the issue: Is it helping the candidate win the election? This is called **horse race coverage:** it gives the appearance of issue coverage without the reality.

In horse race coverage, campaign reporters consider every aspect of the campaign as a strategic or tactical effort to gain votes or as blunders or mistakes that have lost votes. Just like announcers at a horse race, journalists tell the voters over and over again who is in the lead, who is falling behind, and who is likely to win the race. Horse race coverage is present throughout the presidential campaign but is perhaps most egregious in the general election. Horse race coverage teaches citizens to be cynical and skeptical about everything a politician says because every move by a candidate is seen as a short-sighted grab at particular constituencies in the electorate. Instead of going into detail about the competing merits of the two campaigns' proposals for the federal surplus in 2000, many reporters talked about whether the two proposals were moving votes, as measured by polls or based on their assessment of the voters' responses. The horse race "frame" appears in both print and television journalism but seems to be more prominent on television. A study of the coverage of the 2000 election by media scholar Robert Lichter found that 71 percent of network television stories on the campaign had a horse race emphasis.[20]

Ironically, the one presidential election in recent times when horse race coverage declined was the 1996 contest between Dole and Clinton. Dole was so consistently behind Clinton throughout the general election campaign that for once the horse race topic was more boring than the issues. A static, relatively fixed lead for Clinton did not make for an exciting storyline, so journalists were almost forced to cover the issues. However, the overall amount of airtime that the campaign received was significantly less than in close elections, so issues got a bigger slice of a much smaller pie.[21]

Clearly, television journalism and its weaknesses only exacerbate the scarcity of detailed issue discussions in presidential campaigns. From its earliest appearance, television was expected to reduce both the number of issues addressed and the level of sophistication in their discussion.[22] The recent history of television campaign coverage confirms this expectation. Roger Ailes, one of the geniuses behind several Republican presidential media campaigns (and now head of Fox News, the conservative cable network), pointed out how irrelevant issues are to most campaign reporters:

> Let's face it, there are three things that the media are interested in: pictures, mistakes, and attacks. That's the one sure way of getting coverage. You try to avoid as many mistakes as you can. You try to

give them as many pictures as you can. And if you need coverage, you attack, and you will get coverage. It's my orchestra pit theory of politics. If you have two guys on stage and one says "I have a solution to the Middle East problem" and the other guy falls in the orchestra pit, who do you think is going to be on the evening news?"[23]

The message from Ailes for candidates today is to avoid complex issue positions, which seldom pay off and frequently lead to mistakes, and seek out safe simple positions, which can easily be packaged for those few seconds of airtime the media give to issues. And don't fall off the stage as Republican candidate Bob Dole did in 1996, generating massive media coverage and drawing attention to his advanced age.

There is one "issue," however, that television journalism has emphasized: the character issue. Assessing the character of candidates has many aspects, including their personality, their past private conduct, and even their looks and their family. Certainly, the integrity of a leader in terms of his or her tolerance of corruption and lawbreaking has direct political implications. However, to the extent that the character issue is about private conduct, emotion, image, and charisma, it is hardly a political issue at all in the deeper sense of the word. Why does television pay attention to such aspects? In part it is a bias of the medium: television does a poor job of conveying the complexity of issues and a much better job of projecting personalities. The quality of a candidate's ideas is difficult to assess and project through television journalism, but his or her attractiveness and charisma (or lack of these qualities) can be shown in a single video clip.

The job of the modern campaign staff is as much media manipulation through image adjustment as it is media management. The media focus relentlessly on the president as a person, reducing the campaign to the perceived character of the two opponents. What is candidate image? It is both truth and lie, both accurate perception and the gap between reality and perception. It is not policy, record, or substance, even if it can be connected to these facts. Image is built up day by day, slowly accreting sediment at the bottom of the lake of public opinion. Images can be startlingly resilient, in part because of the media's tendency to reinforce whatever the public image has become. As one of the great presidential image managers Reagan aide Michael Deaver observed, "in the television age, image sometimes is as useful as substance."[24]

The public image of a candidate is produced in a complex inter-action among four elements: the "reality" of the nominee's charac-ter, actions, and positions; the image projected by the candidate's staff; the attempted redefinitions of the candidate's image by political opponents; and the cacophony of media assessments. Together they create the inchoate and shifting image of one candidate within the collective minds of Americans.

To understand how crucial television is in personalizing the campaign for the White House, consider how the rules of image politics limit who can become president. Although the American populace is among the most obese in the world, the last president to be truly overweight was William Howard Taft in 1912. The last bald man elected president was Dwight Eisenhower. Given that estimates of the number of bald or mostly bald men above age thirty-five in the general population range from 40 to 70 percent, it is astounding that the sixteen men who ran for the major party nom-inations in 2000 and 2004 were all follicularly gifted. Not one of them was significantly overweight, and the eventual winner was re-markably svelte. Washington may be, as one quip has it, Hollywood for ugly people, but at the top it is now run by people who are quite attractive, or at least not unattractive. If we consider Kennedy the first president of the television age, the trend toward physical attractiveness becomes clear. The last four presidents (Reagan, Bush I, Clinton, Bush II) are far more attractive than the preceding four (Johnson, Nixon, Ford, Carter). The increased importance of per-sonal appearance may be the clearest example of the triumph of personal characteristics and image over matters of substance in American presidential campaigns.

The media's attention to the character issue is almost inevitable because it fits the media's own needs and preferences. Whether a nominee has ever engaged in sexual or criminal misconduct is a simple factual inquiry. Reporters do not need to learn or teach view-ers complex financial concepts or foreign policy positions. Rather, they investigate titillating and provocative allegations. President Clinton's statement during the Monica Lewinsky scandal is the ar-chetype of binary, yes–no coverage: "I did not have sexual relations with that woman, Miss Lewinsky." Similarly, when it was revealed in the closing moments of the 2000 campaign that Governor Bush had been arrested for drunk driving many years before, the media immediately fell into the "scandal frame" style of coverage. Who knew? When did they know? What efforts were taken to cover up the story? Not only are these stories easier than true issues stories, they are also much more likely to attract viewers.

Some journalists believe it is their duty to report nearly everything they can discover about a candidate and let the public decide which facts are relevant. Is it responsible for the media to decide what truths are relevant to voters? If potential candidates believe nothing is off limits and that every aspect of their lives will be exposed in the national press, many qualified and talented people will choose not to run for office.

Do scandalous stories about candidates hurt their chances for victory? One detailed study suggested that personal sins and past misconduct stories tended to affect those who already had a negative impression of a candidate rather than changing the minds of supporters. "Tabloid" information about the candidates was ultimately disregarded by voters in the study.[25] However, study participants may be reluctant to admit that their decisions were affected by trashy revelations, even when they are. Moreover, even if scandals move relatively few votes, scandal coverage, much like horse race coverage, sucks up airtime that might be spent on real issues.

The media's coverage of the general election, to the extent that it focuses on issues, tends to put issues into the frame of the horse race. Candidates strive to avoid specifics on issues that could offend important social groups and produce negative horse race assessments from the media. At the same time, the media focus on the personal attributes and record of the candidates to such an extent that sometimes the issues are almost an afterthought.

The Presidential Debates: An Unfiltered Media-less Moment?

One of the highlights of every presidential general election since 1976 has been the debates among the major party candidates. Debates give the candidates a chance to speak directly to millions of Americans without the filter of the media affecting how their images and words are interpreted. Yet the media play a role in nearly every aspect of presidential debates, including setting the expectations, choosing and delivering the questions, and deciding the victor or the crucial mistakes. To avoid mistakes and to promote the most positive spin, candidates are rigorously rehearsed by their campaigns in preparation for the debate. There are very few spontaneous moments in modern presidential debates, which may help explain

TABLE 10.1   Presidential Debates: Vanishing Viewers?

Year	Number of Debates	Viewers, Presidential Debate (average in millions)	Percent of Population	Viewers, Vice Presidential Debate (in millions)	Percent of Population
1960	4	63.1	35	Not held	*
1976	3	65.4	30	43.2	20
1980	1	80.6	35	Not held	*
1984	2	66.2	28	56.7	24
1988	2	66.2	27	46.9	19
1992	3	66.4	26	51.2	20
1996	2	41.2	15	26.6	10
2000	3	40.6	15	28.5	10
2004	3	53.4	19	43.5	15

Source: Commission on Presidential Debates (www.debates.org), Population Estimates Program, Population Division, U.S. Census Bureau, 2004. Percents calculated by the author.

why fewer and fewer Americans tune in. As shown in Table 10.1, the percentage of Americans who bother to watch a presidential debate has dropped nearly every year since the Kennedy–Nixon debates in 1960. Much like the party conventions do, debates today struggle to keep viewers. Even in close elections like the Bush–Gore race of 2000, the debates were seen by a mere 15 percent of the U.S. population.

Even so, debates remain the single most important media moment of the general election campaign. Prior to the debate, the campaigns work the media constantly to lower expectations for their candidate's debate abilities. If a candidate is perceived as the underdog going into the debate, a tie or unclear outcome can be quickly spun as a victory. When the debate actually takes place, the national press descends on a site as if it were covering a political Super Bowl. Prominent journalists are always the moderators and ask all the questions with the exception of the "town hall" format, in which questions come from the carefully screened audience. During the debate itself, networks maintain a studied silence and allow the candidates to joust without interpretation. However, as soon as the event is over, reporters crowd into "Spin Alley," a large room off the debate floor where campaign professionals immediately put the best face on any mistakes made by their candidate and cast the opposition candidate's performance in the worst possible light. Pundits and academics weigh in on debate performance in studio interviews, and groups of "average" voters who watched the debate on camera are interviewed for their reactions. Some networks also arrange for "dial-response" panels of typical citizens to watch the debate and react second by second with positive or negative spins on an electronic dial. Along with overnight polls of hundreds of viewers, these results help the media decide who won the debate and what the key moments were.

As we might expect, most media coverage focuses on how these contests affect the horse race and on minor factual errors made by the candidates rather than assessing the strength of the arguments put forth. The media also focus on how the debates reveal the personalities and characters of the candidates.

One of the key effects that television has had on debates is to shorten the amount of time candidates are permitted to make their arguments. As Neil Postman and other media analysts have observed, television is opposed to lengthy, complex arguments. In 1948 two candidates for the Republican nomination met for a televised debate at a time when very few homes had televisions and debates still followed nontelevision norms. The debate began with twenty-minute opening statements from each candidate, with eight and a half minutes allowed for rebuttals. By the 1960 Kennedy–Nixon debates, when television was far more influential, the opening statements were reduced to eight minutes, and much less time was allowed to answer questions or rebut points made by the opponent. Since 1988, no opening statement, question response, rebuttal, or closing statement has been permitted to run longer than two minutes. It is nearly impossible to say anything of depth in two minutes; thus candidates are reduced to reciting prearranged scripted responses to expected questions.[26] In 2000 a new low was reached when candidates had only one and a half minutes to respond to questions, sixty seconds to rebut, and a measly thirty seconds to respond to the rebuttal. The spectacle of watching politicians try to say something meaningful about national and international issues in thirty seconds was hardly edifying.

Who sets these rules? The campaigns negotiate every four years about the ground rules for the debates: how many, where, when, moderators, audience, response length, and even such minutiae as podium height and studio temperature. Although the media play no direct role in these negotiations, they are influential in two ways. First, since 1988 the debates have been sponsored by a bipartisan commission made up of politicians and party officials. This group determines who is invited to participate in the debates by consulting five national polls, including some of the major media polls. Candidates who do not average 15 percent of national support are not invited. The more important influence the media have on the debates is that without pressure from the media, debates would not have happened in some years. There is no legal requirement that candidates take part in debates, and a candidate well ahead in the polls or who is simply a poor debater might prefer to avoid debates entirely. Why risk a gaffe or misstatement that could make the election suddenly competitive? The media, however, portray any nonpartici-pating candidate as cowardly, thus forcing at least some debates every four years.

Do debates matter if fewer Americans watch them, responses are more and more scripted, and the time candidates are given to speak is spliced into smaller and smaller bits? Absolutely. In an image-driven, media-dominated election campaign, the debates are rare opportunities for candidates to contest their existing images. They may not be able to make content-laden issue arguments, but they can use a debate to come across as more caring, sympathetic, smart, or some other desired trait that challenges what Americans might have been taught to think of them.

NEW MEDIA: TALKING TO LETTERMAN ABOUT THE LAW

In 1992 Bill Clinton signaled to the country that he was a different kind of candidate by playing the saxophone as a guest on the late night *Arsenio Hall Show*.[27] Clinton was not the first presidential can-didate to appear on an entertainment show, but he was the first to make the "new" media an important part of his campaign. **New media outlets** are nontraditional media outlets such as late night comedy shows (Leno, Letterman, *The Daily Show*), daytime talk shows (*Oprah, Dr. Phil*), and talk radio ("Imus in the Morning," Howard Stern). Some take the view that such appearances on new media are more issue oriented in that the hosts tend to let the politi-cians talk longer about their policies and often allow audience par-ticipation. Typical viewers, unlike reporters, are less concerned with the horse race and more concerned with at least some of the issues. On the other hand, interviewers like Leno, or CNN's Larry King, are unlikely to ask tough or probing questions of politicians. They are easier to spin and often focus on trivialities about the candidate's family or favorite movies.[28]

Given that the number of Americans who read a daily newspaper or watch the local or national network news broadcast is declining, the increasing popularity of the new media among political campaigns is easily understandable. A campaign must speak to the voters if it is to succeed. If the voters are not listening to traditional media, candidates must go where the voters are. However, the danger is that politics will become increasingly viewed as just another form of entertainment rather than as a more serious civic matter.

PAID MEDIA AND MODERN POLITICAL JOURNALISM: LEVERAGING AND TARGETING

One response by politicians to the increasing power of the televised media in U.S. elections has been to devote more campaign resources to television advertising. Because the all-showing-eye of television news has become the greatest source of information about the campaign, politicians have been forced to wedge their messages in the advertising space between the media's coverage. Television advertising has become the single largest expenditure for all modern presidential campaigns. Many in the media attribute great swings in the polls to particularly effective ads. Every campaign media strategy includes both **free media,** which is getting the press to cover your candidate, and **paid media,** in which your candidate runs his or her own ads. Free media has the disadvantage of being unpredictable and uncontrollable; paid media has the disadvantage of tremendous expense. A thirty-second spot in a major media market can cost hundreds of thousands of dollars.

As with presidential debate comments, ads have gotten shorter and shorter. In the early days of television, candidates might purchase thirty minutes or more of airtime to deliver a speech to the nation. Five-minute ads were not uncommon. The 1964 and 1968 campaigns were turning points: ads became far shorter and more emotional in content. Today, a thirty-second ad is the norm, and with the exception of Ross Perot's surprisingly effective hour-long presentations in the 1992 campaigns, long paid speeches are a thing of the past.

Television advertising is blamed for a lot of negatives also associated with television journalism: weakened parties, depressed participation, and campaigns that focus on unsubstantiated allegations and negativity instead of debates over the issues.[29] However, some studies suggest that political ads are actually more informative than television news.[30] Why do ads convey more? Perhaps it is because even in the brief seconds of airtime any campaign story gets on the news, an effort is made to provide at least some semblance of balance. In an ad, however, the message is coherent and one-sided, without the clutter of hearing from two or more sides.[31] Another explanation is that television news conveys very little actual information, so doing better than that is no great accomplishment.

Can candidates, through the use of ads, "buy" elections? It is surely true that a candidate who has extremely deep pockets and can afford massive media buys can treat the media differently. In both 1996 and 2000, billionaire Steve Forbes was able to self-finance his campaign for president. By normal standards of electability, Forbes was not qualified: he had no experience in elected or appointed office, low name recognition, few important endorsements, and was not a powerful or charismatic speaker. Forbes's willingness to spend millions on advertising in the primaries pushed his ideas about lower and flatter taxes into the campaign. The media did not grant Forbes "electable" stature, but his paid media ads pushed up his popularity enough for him to briefly become one of the major candidates in the nomination race. Advertising may be most influential in primaries because there is often little existing knowledge of the candidates, the voters are without party loyalty to guide them, and free media coverage outside New Hampshire and Iowa can be quite scant.[32]

Sometimes campaigns succeed at getting the free media to cover their paid media extensively, thus **leveraging** their campaign dollars into more publicity for their point of view. The textbook examples are the Willie Horton and Daisy ads of 1988 and 1964, respectively. The Horton ad, produced by an independent Republican political action committee, linked the Democratic nominee, Michael Dukakis, to a horrific rape of a white woman perpetrated by a black murderer who escaped on a weekend furlough while Dukakis was governor. The ad, which luridly appealed to white fears of black crime, barely ran as paid advertising, but it was extensively covered in the free media.[33] A similar process occurred in 1964 when Democrats suggested Republican Barry Goldwater would make a reckless president who might start a nuclear war. The Daisy ad used the electrifying image of a mushroom cloud exploding in a cute little girl's eye to scare Americans into rejecting Goldwater. Although

MAKE YOUR OWN CAMPAIGN AD

You cannot truly understand how video politics has limited debate until you have tried to express a political message in a thirty-second ad. With the increased availability of low-cost digital cameras and video editing software, most college students can make surprisingly professional political ads, albeit with a great deal of effort. Many colleges also have substantial audiovisual staff and resources. Ask your professor if such an assignment would work in the class you are taking. Be warned: done correctly, making an ad takes many more hours of work than most research papers. It will also require teamwork.

There are seven main stages to the project: scenario creation, strategy, targeting, writing, staging, shooting, and editing/production. In scenario creation you create a campaign that will be the basis of your project. Choose a real political office, and recruit a candidate to "run" against the incumbent. Have the candidate choose a few issue positions, and then devise a strategy for the ad. Upon which issue(s) do you want to focus, if any? Is your ad negative to the incumbent, positive toward your candidate, or comparative? You may need to think about targeting as part of the strategy. Which demographic group(s) is supposed to be affected by your ad? What shows will you run it on? Why should this issue work with this group, and how will the ad text

"Daisy" ran only once on paid television, the mass media trumpeted it at no charge to the Democrats.[34]

Sometimes paid advertising is used to go under the radar of the free media, to **target** a message. In 2000 groups linked to the Democratic Party ran an ad during shows watched by African Americans linking George Bush to a monstrous lynching of a black man in Bush's home state of Texas. It featured a voice-over by the victim's daughter, emotionally accusing Bush of making her feel like her father "was killed all over again" when Bush opposed hate crimes legislation in Texas. Combined with a speaking campaign in black churches by the victim's family, the ad allowed Democrats to rally black support for Gore without alienating many whites who would have labeled the ad race-baiting if they'd seen it.[35] Similarly, and images work to do that? Very few ads are directed at the general voter anymore. More often ads are targeted at suburban white mothers or so-called NASCAR dads. Few are directed at college students because they do not vote in high numbers. Maybe you could create an ad that would show how to reach your generation?

Targeting and strategy lead into writing the actual ad script, which should include both the spoken words and descriptions of the action. Most amateur ads are far too heavy on spoken and written words. Study political ads online that you admire for tips on what works. Next, you have to set the stage. Make sure you have the location and the props you need. Pay attention to recruiting an experienced camera operator or spend time learning how it is done. Test your sound equipment in your locations. All of the preliminary steps will help make your ad shoot go better. Be sure to get multiple takes of every needed shot. Don't expect to get every shot right the first time, or even the first day. In editing remember the power of music and sound effects. Unless you have a background in video editing, you will probably spend more time editing the ad than on any other step.

If you are doing this for a class assignment, be sure to document every stage and prepare a strategic memo defending your choices with reference to ideas about campaigns in this book and in other sources.

in 1995–96 Democrats exploited the fact that most national reporters watch television only in a few major media markets to hide their strategy of massive early ad buys. This unprecedented strategy was largely ignored by the media because it was targeted at rural and suburban areas far from the homes of national reporters.[36]

Targeting advertising is made easier by the advertising data available to all buyers of commercials. Presidential campaigns target particular ages, races, income classes, and states with different ads, and expert buyers tell them which shows and which stations to reserve.

The success or failure of these two strategies of paid media, leveraging and targeting, relies on the campaign's ability to anticipate the media's decisions. Sometimes these strategies backfire. In 2000 a local Republican group ran an ad that tried to link Democrats to school integration in Kansas City, which was very unpopular with many area whites. The national media covered the local ad, thus preventing effective targeting.[37] And, of course, most national ads fail to get significant free media, thus denying campaigns the leverage they might desire.

POLLS AND EXIT POLLS: PREDICTING THE VOTE OR ALTERING IT?

One constant in modern media coverage of political campaigns is the centrality of polls to most election stories. Prior to the invention of random sample national polling in the 1930s and 1940s, journalists were much less certain in assessing political races. They relied on their sources to tell them how a candidate was doing in a particular state, and they analyzed the race based on their sources, gut instincts, and experience. Today many major news organizations sponsor national polls, and all of them report on them extensively. In a presidential campaign, the polling becomes so frequent in the weeks leading up to election day that independent Web sites track the daily average of major polls state by state.

Extensive focus on polls prior to an election may have a number of negative influences on campaigns. First, instead of merely predicting electoral outcomes, polls may harden a momentary lead for one candidate into a permanent advantage because those who support the trailing candidate may lose hope. Studies show that voter turnout in presidential elections is higher in states that are nearly tied between the two major candidates. The same may well be true of the nation as a whole: the presidential election of 1996 was widely seen to be over before it began and had an extremely low turnout, whereas the high turnout election of 2004 was expected to be quite close throughout the election year. The opposite may also be true: news about polls may create changes in the public mood by reporting minor changes as major shifts. Even if polls accurately depict the electorate at any given moment, they may enhance the volatility of the electorate as voters respond to daily shifts in the standings of the candidates.[38]

Polls are proliferating in news coverage because they give the appearance of scientific accuracy to the media's horse race coverage. Small shifts in poll numbers can be linked by media analysts to various actions or inactions by the candidates. Polls can also be used in issue coverage, such as assessing how many Americans support the president's Iraq policy. Unlike assessing the worth of the president's Iraq policy, which could expose the media to charges of bias, simply covering the results of a poll seems fairly neutral and fact-based.

Even as polls become more prominent in the horse race news coverage, they may be becoming less accurate. More and more voters are avoiding such polls entirely. Using call-screening technology, cell phones, or simply saying "No," many Americans are refusing to participate in polls. Cooperation rates are down to around 38 percent in many national polls, far lower than ever before.[39] As poll refusal rates go up, accuracy inevitably declines despite pollsters' creative efforts to adjust polls to account for refusers.

Exit polls are the source of yet another problem in media coverage: reports about election outcomes before all voters have had a chance to express their opinion.[40] In 1980, when President Carter concluded from exit polls that he had been defeated by Ronald Reagan, he conceded long before polls closed in Hawaii, Alaska, and parts of the West Coast. Some believed that Carter had hurt Democratic turnout in those areas because voters tend to care most about the presidential race. A similar phenomenon occurred in 2000 when some networks "called" the state of Florida while polls were still open in several Florida counties.

By sponsoring polls, the media actually manufacture news. Putting a poll into the field is almost certain to produce some kind of news during a political campaign. Even if there has been no significant event or shift in public opinion, the result is unlikely to be entirely unchanged from the previous poll, however recent, due to statistical chance. And there is an ironic way in which a badly done poll, or a poorly worded question, is actually more "newsworthy." A poll that confounds the accepted wisdom about a campaign or a candidate will make more headlines because it is unexpected. Few reporters will be savvy enough to discover that the numbers are different because of a shift in the quality or structure of the poll.[41]

CONCLUSION: REFORMS FOR BETTER CAMPAIGN JOURNALISM

After every recent presidential campaign, many members of the press have engaged in a series of self-criticisms about the low quality of the coverage given to the race. Among the most criticized races was the 1988 campaign between George Herbert Walker Bush and

Michael Dukakis. Twenty elites of the news industry met and discussed seven major defects in the press coverage of the campaign: too much horse race coverage, too much meaningless photo opportunity coverage, not enough issue analysis, failure to refute false claims in advertising, too much emphasis on polls and pundits instead of voters, too much emphasis on past personal scandals of the candidates, and candidates not given enough uninterrupted time in news coverage to make their points.[42] Unfortunately, these problems are still present, and many are substantially worse than they were in 1988.

Several proposals have been put forward to improve campaign journalism. First and foremost, **campaign finance reform** (CFR). Although CFR is not directly targeted at the media, its purpose is to reduce the role played by paid advertising. Several countries strictly limit the amount of airtime that campaigns can purchase, and some even ban it entirely.[43] However, many conservatives argue that all CFR will do is weaken campaigns and strengthen the media. If the media are currently deeply flawed, how will giving them more power improve the situation?

Another popular reform that would seek to lessen the power of both paid and unpaid media is free television time for all candidates. This would lessen the fund-raising burden on campaigns and theoretically make them less dependent on the media for coverage. Several countries including Japan already impose this rule on their broadcast media. However, many logistical problems loom in trying to make free television time part of American campaigns. First, the networks have always resisted this reform, and they are very politically influential. Second, in an era of cable television, it is quite likely that a half hour or hour from a candidate for the presidency would be largely unwatched, even if all three broadcast networks covered it. Third, would free television time be given to third party and independent candidates? Should all the dozens of minor party candidates for president be given equal amounts of free airtime? Fourth, how would it work for campaigns for Congress, which frequently cover from two to five different media markets? Alternatively, one media market may have as many as twenty-five congressional campaigns. Viewers living in the greater New York City media market would quickly tire of seeing free television from incumbents and challengers. One point to remember is that the major parties already have some access to "free" television because tax money finances the general election presidential campaign, and much of that is used to buy ads. Still, it isn't quite free. Any money spent on television cannot be spent on another campaign task.

Political scientist Larry Sabato asks whether libel laws in the United States should be strengthened so that political figures who are abused by the press have the option to sue the media, as they do in Britain and several other democracies.[44] This solution might do something to rein in the intense scandal coverage so prominent in modern campaign journalism. However, tougher libel laws might well fail to pass constitutional scrutiny given how strongly protected First Amendment freedoms are in this country.

Political scientist Tom Patterson argues that the media's influence on presidential primary campaigns could best be reduced by shortening the primary process and holding four regional primaries or one national primary on the same day rather than allowing the media to set the expectations game in New Hampshire and Iowa every four years. A shorter campaign would also address what Patterson sees as an overall "negativity" bias in the media. His research shows that the longer the campaign, the more the media's coverage becomes cynical and negative.[45]

One media reform widely adopted after 1988 was to offer more sustained analysis of claims made in paid advertising. These **ad watches** appeared in both print and broadcast journalism. Initially, these programs were somewhat ineffective. The analyses would typically begin by rerunning the controversial and allegedly deceptive ad, yet again giving false claims an uninterrupted and, to the casual viewer, unchallenged airing. More recent ad watches try not to broadcast the entire ad, showing it only in a portion of the screen so that it is clear that a critique is taking place. Comparing negative ads in presidential campaigns from 1988 to 2004, it is clear that documentation of claims as part of the visuals and voice-overs of ads has become far more prevalent today, perhaps because of enhanced media oversight.

Other reforms for campaign journalism call for greater fairness to third party and independent candidates. In 2000 and in 2004 it was very hard to get news about Ralph Nader or other non-major-party candidates. But it is difficult to say whether third party candidates don't get coverage from the media because they are unknown and fringe candidates, or whether they are unknown and fringe candidates because they get little media coverage.

Many of the media's deficiencies in covering campaigns are probably here to stay. Consider horse race coverage, perhaps the broadest and most common criticism about campaign journalism. One reason not to cover the issues is that they remain largely fixed from the convention to the election. Even if newspapers and television news covered each candidate's issue positions once, why do it again? Journalism always has a preference for the new over the old, and an update on the standings of the candidates, in certain states and across the nation, will always be new, even if the headline is only "Bush maintains narrow lead." Would a headline in October that read "Kerry, Bush policies on Social Security remain different" be read by many people? If the media did attempt to offer detailed and comprehensive analyses of the issue positions of the candidates, there would be two problems. First, campaigns often choose to be vague and incomplete in their proposals to maintain their appeal to the largest number of voters. The shallowness of some of the media's treatment of the issues is not the media's fault but the campaigns'. Second, would the public watch fifteen-minute news segments on the complexities of Social Security policy, or read seven-page *Newsweek* articles about it? Perhaps the people are getting the campaign journalism they desire, even if it is not the coverage that the country deserves.

The change that has most affected campaign journalism recently seems to have been the intrusion of the newest form of media, the Internet, into campaign journalism. Rather than a targeted reform chosen by academics and media elites, the Internet arrived without warning onto political campaigns, making them move to an even faster rhythm than before. But that is just one change among many that the Internet has brought about in political journalism, and it is to that seminal development that we now turn our attention.

KEY TERMS

ad watches
campaign finance reform
exit polls
expectations game
free media
frontloading
great mentioner
horse race coverage

Iowa caucus
leveraging
New Hampshire primary
new media outlets
paid media
pre-primary poll
targeting

DISCUSSION QUESTIONS

1. Do you believe the media have too much power in deciding who the "qualified" nominees to be president are? Is there any way for the parties to fight back?
2. Do you think the media spend too much time on horse race coverage? Or is that just what the public wants covered in campaigns?
3. Think of all the ways a voter could find out about the issues in a presidential campaign: television, radio, print, Internet journalism, paid advertising, debates, or talking with friends. What ways are best, in your opinion, in terms of the most meaningful information for casting an intelligent vote?
4. Looking over the proposed reforms discussed in this chapter, which one do you think is most important, if any?

ADDITIONAL RESOURCES

Out of Order, by Tom Patterson, is the best book on the media in presidential campaigns.

The Making of the President 1960, by Theodore White, created a whole new style of campaign coverage and remains a classic. Many of the sequels are also strong, but White's first account of the presidential campaign trail remains his best.

Road to the White House, by Stephen Wayne, is a broad account of presidential campaign politics and is useful if you want to put the media's role in the campaign into a broader context.

ONLINE RESOURCES

www.livingroomcandidate.org is an amazing library of presidential campaign ads covering some of the most famous spots from 1952 to 2004.

www.c-span.org/vote2004/campads.asp provides a smaller collection of 2004 campaign ads.

NOTES

1. Thomas E. Patterson, *The Mass Media Election* (Westport, CT: Praeger, 1980), 3.
2. Quoted in John William Cavanaugh, *Media Effects on Voters* (New York: University Press of America, 1995), 13.

3. Ibid., 156.
4. Susan Page, "Poll Majority Say They'd Be Likely to Vote for Clinton," *USA Today,* May 27, 2005: A1.
5. Sandy Maisel, *The Parties Respond: Changes in American Parties and Campaigns* (Boulder, CO: Westview Press, 1998).
6. William Mayer, *In Pursuit of the White House: How We Choose Our Presidential Nominees* (Boulder, CO: Westview Press, 1995).
7. Doris A. Graber, *Mass Media and American Politics,* 6th ed. (Washington, DC: Congressional Quarterly, 2002), 239.
8. Ibid., 240.
9. Tom Patterson, *Out of Order* (New York: Knopf, 1993), 185.
10. Jeremy D. Mayer, *Running on Race: Racial Politics in Presidential Campaigns 1960–2000* (New York: Random House, 2002).
11. Patterson, *Out of Order,* 188.
12. Graber, *Mass Media,* 239.
13. Charles A. Thomson, *Television and Presidential Politics* (Washington, DC: Brookings, 1956), 32.
14. Stephen Wayne, *Road to the White House* (New York: St. Martin's Press, 2000), 178.
15. Thomson, *Television,* 120.
16. John Zaller, *The Nature and Origin of Mass Opinion* (New York: Cambridge University Press, 1992).
17. Philip E. Converse, "The Nature of Belief Systems in Mass Publics." In *Ideology and Discontent,* David Apter, ed. (New York: Free Press, 1964); but see Robert Lane, *Political Ideology: Why the American Common Man Believes What He Does* (New York: Free Press, 1962).
18. Wayne, *Road to the White House,* 231.
19. Patterson, *Out of Order,* 197–98.
20. S. Robert Lichter, "A Plague on Both Parties: Substance and Fairness in TV Election News." *Press/Politics* 6, no. 3 (2001): 8–30.
21. Wayne, *Road to the White House,* 227.
22. Thomson, *Television,* 148.
23. Wayne, *Road to the White House,* 228.
24. Richard W. Waterman, Robert Wright, and Gilbert St. Clair, *The Image-Is-Everything Presidency* (Boulder, CO: Westview Press, 1999), 53.
25. Cavanaugh, *Media Effects,* 158–61.
26. Commission on Presidential Debates, www.debates.org
27. Graber, *Mass Media,* 243.
28. Patterson, *Out of Order,* 169–71.

29. Edwin Diamon and Stephen Bates, *The Spot* (Boston: MIT Press, 1992), 365.
30. Kathleen H. Jamieson and David S. Birdsell, *Presidential Debates* (New York: Oxford, 1988), 125.
31. Graber, *Mass Media*, 249.
32. Ibid.
33. Mayer, *Running on Race*.
34. Wayne, *Road to the White House*, 242.
35. Mayer, *Running on Race*.
36. Wayne, *Road to the White House*, 244.
37. Mayer, *Running on Race*.
38. Jeremy D. Mayer and Lynn Kirby, "The Promise and Peril of Presidential Polling: Between Gallup's Dream and the Morris Nightmare." In *Is This Any Way to Run a Democratic Government?* Stephen J. Wayne, ed. (Washington, DC: Georgetown University Press, 2004).
39. Richard Morin, "Don't Ask Me: As Fewer Cooperate on Polls, Criticism and Questions Mount," *Washington Post*, October 28, 2004: C1.
40. Graber, *Mass Media*, 235–36.
41. Joel Best, *Damned Lies and Statistics* (Los Angeles: University of California Press, 2001).
42. Cavanaugh, *Media Effects*, 156.
43. Jody C. Baumgartner, *Modern Presidential Electioneering* (Westport, CT: Praeger, 2000), 46.
44. Larry J. Sabato, *Feeding Frenzy* (New York: Free Press, 1991), 218–19.
45. Patterson, *Out of Order*, 208–11.

CHAPTER 11

The Internet and the Future of Media Politics

Political communication in the United States is in a period of rapid and unpredictable change as the video era inevitably gives way to the Internet era. This chapter examines the advantages and possible dangers of Internet politics for American democracy and predicts what aspects of American politics will be most changed by the coming dominance of the Internet.

Television remains the most influential medium in American politics today in terms of number of consumers and campaign dollars spent, but it is clear that television has a challenger on the scene: the Internet. By June of 2006 more than two hundred million Americans were regularly using the Internet, and the number grows each day. The United States is also the most wired large country in the world, with nearly 69 percent of all Americans logging on, behind only New Zealand and Iceland in popularity of the Web.[1] A study by the Pew Research Center for the People and the Press found a precipitous fall in the number of Americans who followed politics through broadcast news and a rapid rise in the use of the Internet for that purpose.[2] A 2004 study found that local television news was still the most popular source of information among young people ages eighteen to thirty-four but that the Internet was second, and rising rapidly.[3] Among more educated and wealthier young Americans, the Internet was clearly the dominant source. As a political medium, the Internet has risen faster than any previous method of communication—from introduction to the public to mass utilization in a decade.

The arrival of the Internet challenges us to reimagine media politics. What can be done through e-mail, the Web, wireless messaging, and other emerging computer-based technologies to improve the ways in which we get news, form opinions, campaign for causes and candidates, cast votes, and comprehend our public rights and responsibilities? Just as occurred with video, the Internet may alter the very nature of American democracy, republican government, political culture, campaigns, and political journalism.

Before discussing the effects of the Internet, it is useful to define what constitutes the "Internet." As with interstate highways, nineteenth century railroads and canals, and modern airports, government played a key role in the creation of the modern "information superhighway." In the late 1960s scientists working for the Defense Department's Advanced Research Projects Agency (ARPA, later DARPA) created the very first connection between computers that could exchange packets of information.[4] As more and more defense and university computers joined the network, it became a national, decentralized method of exchanging data. In the 1980s the increasingly widespread availability of personal computers forever changed the Internet as more and more individuals began to access and use the burgeoning network. The *Internet* refers both to the World Wide Web of graphic sites, some with downloadable content, and to e-mail and file exchange programs such as Napster.*

The Internet is extraordinarily dynamic and is evolving even as these words are written. The latest method of political communication mixes talk radio's passion, the Ipod's portability, and the Internet's accessibility: **podcasting.** Individuals can record political commentary using inexpensive home microphones, post their thoughts to the Internet, where others can download them to their MP3 players, and listen to them at their convenience. Some even subscribe to specific podcast shows and get automatic downloads to their computer each week. The medium is experiencing explosive growth: one New York station posted its first podcast in January 2005 and by June casts were being downloaded 125,000 times a week. When Itunes.com began offering podcasts in June 2005, it received a million subscribers in its first two days.[5] Although most

---

*The definition of the Internet remained so troubling that in 1995 the Federal Networking Council passed a resolution attempting to settle the question. They concluded: "'Internet' refers to the global information system that—-(i) is logically linked together by a globally unique address space based on the Internet Protocol (IP) or its subsequent extensions/follow-ons; (ii) is able to support communications using the Transmission Control Protocol/Internet Protocol (TCP/IP) suite or its subsequent extensions/follow-ons, and/or other IP-compatible protocols; and (iii) provides, uses or makes accessible, either publicly or privately, high level services layered on the communications and related infrastructure. . . ."

podcasts focus on music and entertainment, many are political in nature. In 2008 podcasting will certainly be a part of the presidential campaign. Some congressional candidates already post podcasts of speeches on their campaign Web sites.

Not only are citizens finding new uses for the Internet, but the Internet is absorbing other media, or at least merging with significant aspects of them. Although the telecommunications industry has suffered spectacular setbacks, the percentage of American homes with broadband connections to the Internet quadrupled between 2000 and 2002.[6] One-fifth of U.S. home Internet users (twenty-four million Americans) switched to the higher priced connection so that they could move at higher speeds, see more multimedia messages, and remain online without having to tie up their telephone lines. The top five political blogs in the United States attract more than half a million visitors each day.[7] The advent of online radio, downloadable videos, podcasts, and audio file exchanges only hints at what may be coming next. The Internet is a moving target for analysts and political activists alike.

THE PROMISE OF THE INTERNET

The rise of the Internet as a major force in the American media offers four promising changes in politics: interactivity, independence, global reach, and depth.

Interactivity

When television broadcast news is the main source of political information, and when Americans learn about politicians and their stances through televised presidential debates and campaign ads, there is little opportunity for individual citizens to feel involved in the process. By contrast, while reading a story on the Internet or watching a streaming video of an interview with a journalist or a politician, a citizen can shoot an e-mail off to a federal agency or make a monetary contribution to the politician. Newspapers and broadcast stations conduct online political polls at their Web sites and report the unscientific results. Media companies like online polls even though they are of dubious accuracy because they are amazingly cheap. Interactivity between journalists and consumers becomes far easier. Consider the ease and immediacy of sending an e-mail to Bill O'Reilly at Fox News versus writing a letter to Walter Cronkite in 1974. Media companies even monitor from day to day which pages of their Web sites are looked at and by how many people. Consumers of online journalism vote with every mouse click and download about the issues they want the media to cover. Newspapers and television stations conducted market research and polling before the Internet, but these did not approach the amount of information provided by online monitoring of media consumption.

The Internet may also bring about higher levels of **interactivity** between citizens and the government itself. Arizona and other states are exploring voting online. Enthusiasm for computer voting went even higher after the debacle in Florida during the election of 2000 in which nineteenth-century voting technology was exposed as deeply flawed and widely utilized. Many of these same problems appeared again in 2004, further spurring the investigation of online solutions.[8] All fifty state governments and many localities distribute information on the Web, and every month more government services are available online, from paying parking tickets to applying for government contracts. Elected officials may not read every e-mail they receive, but they would be foolish to ignore an outpouring of e-mails from individual voters.

The interactivity of the Internet has also been utilized by presidential campaigns, most notably that of Howard Dean in 2004. Dean was a little-known governor of Vermont when the election season began. Using the Internet, he advertised his strong opposition to the war in Iraq and began to attract more crowds than any other candidate for the Democratic nomination during the second half of 2003. Dean began raising shockingly large amounts of money through the Internet, often in response to rapid e-mail requests targeted at specific goals. Dean's tactics were so successful they were emulated by the campaigns of both Bush and Kerry, as well as by many independent political groups.

Interest groups, new and old, have rushed to exploit the possibilities of the Internet. The Internet allows far-flung individuals with little political experience to coalesce around a cause with remarkably little financial outlay. In 1998 a husband and wife team formed Moveon.org, a political action committee that capitalized on citizen outrage about Clinton's impeachment. Years after impeachment ended, Moveon.org remains one of the most powerful groups on the left. Moveon.org exists almost entirely online, yet it attracts hundreds of thousands of members who donate money, sponsor (and even create) television ads, and disseminate and respond to news stories.[9] On the right, FreeRepublic.com has thousands of Republican and right-wing activists who use it each day to discuss politics and plan demonstrations against Democrats and liberals. The interactivity offered by the Internet will, in the view of some, ameliorate one of the chronic problems in American politics during this century: low levels of citizen participation, particularly in voting. By making information more readily available, by lowering barriers to citizen input and interaction, and by making voting and donating easier, cyberpolitics may enhance citizen interest, influence, and participation.

Independence

The Internet may also weaken the media's control over what citizens learn about politics. Citizens can become more independent of the power of media gatekeepers in the age of the Internet than at any time in human history. Compare a daily newspaper to a thirty-minute evening news broadcast to a CNN Web site. The forty thousand words of text available in the newspaper represent the editors' view of what an educated citizen should know about current events that day. There is some degree of independence; a committed Republican could choose not to read any reports of the torture and murder of prisoners in secret CIA detention centers overseas,[10] and a committed Democrat might choose not to read any positive stories about President Bush. By contrast, in watching an anchor deliver the few thousand words of a typical news program, the viewer is passive; he cannot dart ahead or jump back in the newscast to follow his interest.* The Internet consumer of news is in control. She may click only on the stories that interest her and can request that a news Web site only show her stories on topics of concern.

Independence also applies to the number of media outlets available today. Throughout this century, concern among political scientists and media analysts has grown about the concentration of media power in fewer and fewer hands.[11] By some estimates, fewer than ten multinational corporations control the most influential media outlets in the country. The Internet may well change that. Although

---

*At least he cannot without using a VCR or a TIVO machine. And, of course, with the ubiquitous remote control, he can now surf to another news channel quite easily. Cable has changed television as well, since a conservative can watch Fox News while a liberal can choose a more liberal outlet.

the most popular sites on the Web are often affiliated with major news corporations (CNN, MSNBC, Yahoo, AOL, and so forth), some of the most influential Web sites, such as The Drudge Report, are run by individuals. Anyone with a computer and Internet access can set up a Web site with his or her own political views. **Blogs** or "weblogs" are sites set up by individuals to publicize their experiences and their opinions. They are often vulgar, unsourced, and by definition nonauthoritative. Even though the number of blogs is growing exponentially, it would be a serious error to assume that most blogs are political in nature. A 2003 study found that "the typical blog is written by a teenage girl who uses it twice a month to update her friends and classmates on happenings in her life."[12] However, one of the leading opinion journalists of the day, Andrew Sullivan, has set up his own Web site where his thoughts and essays are available to readers without the filter of editors or the delay of publishing.* As newspaper editor Dan Gilmour put it, "I think we've moved profoundly from the older period in which news was a lecture. Now the job is that we tell you what we have learned, you tell us if you think we are correct, then we all discuss it."[13]

The Internet may also contribute to nonconformist thought in politics. During the height of television's media dominance, some feared that the media were contributing to a "spiral of silence." Those with minority views would see no support for their opinions in the media, which emphasized conformist and majoritarian views, and they would keep silent for fear of social ostracism.[14] Today, thanks to the Internet, almost no opinion is so isolated that it cannot find at least one kindred spirit somewhere on the Web. The Internet, because it lacks gatekeepers and filters, is simply a profoundly different medium than any that has come before.

The Internet fosters independence by providing more points of access to political information, to both consumers and producers. The network is practically limitless in its capacity to send, store, and grant access to information. Online search engines such as Google can rapidly search billions of Web pages for information. And Google

---

*www.andrewsullivan.com. Sullivan is a particularly interesting case of a "blogger" because, unlike the vast majority of online writers, Sullivan has had an illustrious and influential career in the traditional media, both print and more recently television. Sullivan is also quite an iconoclastic figure, a gay Catholic conservative Brit writing on American politics. Sullivan's blog got him in trouble with a traditional publication: when he criticized the *New York Times Magazine* one time too many online, they decided not to carry his pieces anymore.

MOST POPULAR BLOGS

The blogsite Truth Laid Bear has created a ranking system for blogsites that tracks daily traffic and then ranks them. In early March of 2006, these were the top-ranked political blogs:

1. Michelle Malkin
2. Instapundit.com
3. Power Line
4. Daily Kos
5. Boing Boing: A Directory of Wonderful Things
6. Little Green Footballs
7. Captain's Quarters
8. Hugh Hewitt
9. The Volokh Conspiracy
10. Talking Points Memo: by Joshua Micah Marshall

One indication of how new the political blogosphere is, is that the rankings change rapidly. The top national newspapers and the top cable networks are comparatively stable, but blogs rise and fall, appear and disappear, from any ranking system. A single post can move a blog up in the rankings like a rocket going into orbit and bring it crashing down almost as fast. It should be noted that this list leaves out some of the most prominent political blogs, such as Free Republic, because its content is entirely made up of posts by its readers. Nor does it include Slate or CNN or some of the pure media outlets where none of the content is created by the readers.

underestimates the breadth of the Internet because it does not index e-mail, a medium that has been widely used for political purposes.

The Internet allows more people to engage in journalism, campaigning, and less public modes of politics (such as leaking, lobbying, and administrating). In the mass media era, publicly available messages about, say, the United States Senate essentially came from the Senate offices, registered lobbyists, and journalists with permission to enter the Senate Press Gallery. Today, if you, the online citizen, have something to tell the world about the U.S. Senate, you can express yourself in any number of Net forums. Your declaration will not be amplified by the *New York Times* in all likelihood, but it could well be indexed by Google, especially if you are wise to the ways of online publicity.

The Internet has also given citizens an independent means to challenge the media's monopoly on facts. In 2004 CBS News ran a major story on documents that allegedly showed that President Bush had refused a direct order to appear for duty during his service in the Texas Air National Guard during the Vietnam era. Although the public had long known that Bush used family connections to get into the Guard during a time when it was a popular way for wealthy men to avoid the draft, the documents revitalized the issue of Bush's wartime conduct and his later failure to fulfill the terms of his enlistment. Very quickly, thanks to conservative bloggers, questions emerged about the documents' authenticity. Experts and amateurs pointed out numerous factual and stylistic problems with the documents. In a massive humiliation for CBS News and the main reporter on the story, Dan Rather, the network was forced to admit that the documents were probably forgeries. Rather, who had long been accused by conservatives of having a liberal bias, faced difficult questions about how he had so quickly accepted as legitimate anti-Bush documents that had been rejected by other mainstream media outlets as highly questionable. Without the Internet's amazing ability to link people rapidly, citizens would have lacked the ability to quickly challenge the CBS story.

Citizens may be most empowered at the state and local level. One of the underreported stories of 2004 was the influence of local bloggers on some local, state, and congressional races.[15] Recall that some research suggests there is a greater concentration of media power in state and local politics, in part because of low information levels among voters about local issues and elections. In localities with one major radio station, television station, and newspaper, owned by corporations with similar views, a single blogger could make a difference.

Clearly the Internet has expanded the boundaries of political journalism. That is not the same as guaranteeing equality: wealthy and official voices still hold advantages. Internet advertising is one of the main ways to increase online traffic to Web sites, and the cost and sophistication of Web ads is growing. Few private citizens can afford to run a banner ad on Yahoo seeking hits for their political blog. Even with these inequalities, the Internet confers an opportunity for influence previously unimaginable for average citizens.

Global Reach

The video era made international politics more vivid and immediate than ever before, and the Internet has only accelerated this process. The conflict in Iraq is not just brought home vividly by embedded reporters broadcasting on the networks. Many Americans log into Web pages written by American troops participating in the occupation and Iraqis blogging live from Baghdad. These insights, highly individualistic and subjective compared to the traditional media, not only are unfiltered but also convey an immediacy and candor often absent from the mainstream media.

As more and more foreign newspapers go online, the ability of an individual citizen to follow foreign affairs in real time grows. Due to the pace of mail deliveries, surveying the print media in a foreign country from the United States had previously been delayed by a week or more, but today it can take place instantaneously. The Internet has also made it easier to fact check and hold accountable global publications. The Middle East Media Research Institute (MEMRI) provides daily translations of important articles from Arab and Islamic media outlets that would have previously been ignored by all but the most careful Middle East watchers. The ability of Middle East leaders to say one thing in English and another thing through the Arab language press has been curtailed by the constant surveillance of MEMRI and other online monitors.[16] The Internet has also begun to shake the tightly controlled media in places like China, Iran, and even North Korea.[17] Totalitarian governments can attempt to control access to the Internet, but the Internet produces so many economic benefits that many countries have been forced to allow it. Once an authoritarian or totalitarian government allows some access, regime opponents located in other countries have the opportunity to speak to their countrymen outside the control of the government. Were Thomas Paine alive today and still interested in sparking revolutions, there is no doubt he'd been using the Internet to fight tyranny.

Depth

Consider a typical cable news networks Web page. It will have streaming videos available that reproduce the fragmented and personalized broadcast coverage, but it will also give viewers access to much deeper knowledge. Links to online encyclopedias, long articles, or even books at Amazon.com are frequent. The same is true for campaign Web sites. The candidate's flashy thirty-second video ads can be viewed, but they are almost always accompanied by detailed issue statements. Combined with such nonpartisan civic Web sites as www.vote-smart.org (Project Vote Smart) and www.dnet.org (Democracy Net), voters now have access to position papers, transcripts of debates, and links to legislation.

Consumers of politics on the Web may initially be presented with a fragmented and incomplete picture of an event or a candidate, but they are given the tools to put the issue into a deeper context. Of course, one might note the same about an article in *Time* magazine or a story on CBS News. It was never impossible for consumers of the news, intrigued by a particular issue, to educate themselves on it through a trip to the library if nothing else. What the Internet changes is the ease with which depth is available. Context is just a click away.

THE DEFECTS OF THE INTERNET FOR MEDIA POLITICS

Each of the positive changes wrought by the introduction of the Internet can be subjected to cross-examination. Not only may the Internet fail to rectify existing problems in American media politics, it may have created new ones.

Unequal Access

The **digital divide** describes the inequality in access to the Internet. From its birth until this moment, the Internet has been a medium far more often used by the wealthy, the educated, the male, and the white citizens of this country than by others. The skew in usage on each of those factors has lessened since 1996, but it has not vanished. Similarly, the first schools to get wired were wealthier ones, and this remains true today.

One could complacently observe that similar patterns were evident at the dawn of radio and television and that those "electronic divides" rapidly disappeared. The digital divide is certainly getting smaller. According to a Pew Center poll, home computer ownership went from 36 percent to 59 percent and venturing online went from 21 percent to 54 percent in just the four years, from 1996 to 2000.[18]

Unequal access may not be as large a problem, or at least as new a problem, as some see it. Even newspapers in the colonial era were not equally distributed, with many in the lower classes lacking either the literacy to appreciate papers or the money to buy them.

However, there is reason to think that this divide will be more resilient than previous ones. First, many of the educated and wealthy who frequently use the Web do so from their workplaces. It is unlikely that autoworkers, waitresses, busdrivers, and plumbers will soon be granted worksite access to the Internet. People accessing the Internet from the workplace must consider the possibility that their movements, words, and activities will be monitored by their employers. Such surveillance is more common in working-class jobsites, thus adding another class divide to Internet politics. Second, the cost of access is continually changing. Although basic access (cost of the computer plus cost of an Internet service provider) may have declined in price, the costs for faster access are much greater. Many features on the Internet are increasingly geared toward those who can download large quantities of data quickly. The divide in access to that quality of service is very great. Third, even with more Americans learning how to use computers with each passing moment, there remains a generational gap in Internet usage. A sixty-five-year-old in 1960 had little difficulty plugging in a television set and watching the Kennedy–Nixon debates. But many senior citizens today still find computers daunting and confusing. For these reasons, if the Internet becomes the most important form of political discourse, it will be a conversation that leaves millions of Americans out of earshot for years to come.

Overload

When there were only three television news networks, and only a few nationally influential newspapers, the major media outlets had tremendous power to set the nation's agenda. With so many diverse outlets today, there is far less sense of a unified national agenda to which politicians have to react and the public has to pay attention. Presented with the chaotic, shifting, and massive amount of political information available on the Web, the citizen today may simply retreat from the **overload** of data.

The overload of data comes at Americans at an increasingly dizzying pace, making politics rapid and dynamic. Because the Internet conveys information almost without discernible delay, in hotly competitive political, media, and media/political situations, there are more cycles of action–reaction communication. This affects political elites as well as ordinary citizens. For example, on September 17, 2000, the Bush and Gore campaigns for president strafed reporters on their press e-mail lists (consisting of 2,000 and 1,200 names, respectively) with fifty-six e-mails. Most of these concerned a sixteen-page "Blueprint for the Middle Class" issued by the Republican nominee. The Democrat's "pre-buttal" was twenty-four pages long. The fifty-six e-mails spun and re-spun around the topic of which candidate had the better economic plan for America.[19]

The Internet creates a **real-time news cycle** in which political communication can occur literally at any time. Real-time politics has more players, more messages, and less preparation time for any single person to digest all that is being said, and shown, and perhaps substantiated.

Government's response to the news cycle's expansion has been to accelerate, but the response of the citizen to this rapid overload of competing claims may well be exhaustion and even alienation. The overload may also expose interactivity with government officials as a sham and a false hope. See what ensues when you send an e-mail to a public official you've watched at C-SPAN.org, for instance. (Hint: not much.) In 1992 when Ross Perot advocated an "electronic townhall" in which all of America would debate and then vote on the issues of the day, perhaps Americans imagined that technology could take us back to New England townhall democracy. But the overload problem with regard to interactivity is even greater than it is with regard to information: there are too many of us for government to process our inputs on issues beyond the shallowest up or down opinions. The dream of restoring direct democracy is not new in American public life. Pollster George Gallup imagined in 1939 that public opinion polling would lead to a responsive and participatory democracy, and that certainly has not occurred.[20] Cyberpolitics has not magically erased the classic problems of the "one and the many"; the overloaded circuits of the Internet may have actually exacerbated it.

Filterlessness

If the Internet grants us independence from the centralized power of the mass media, this independence is inextricably tied to the problem of **filterlessness.** Political, civic, and media institutions use filters to improve the quality of the information they depend on and release to the public. They check facts, revise sentences, select photos and video footage, and so forth. The Internet's virtue of no authoritative control permits dissidents and eccentrics to promulgate their views to the world, but this is also a significant weakness. A book that was released by a reputable academic press went through a lengthy peer review by knowledgeable experts. A story printed in the *New Yorker* underwent careful and redundant fact checking. As the anecdote had it, a reporter should not print a story about how much his mother loves him unless he can verify it with two independent sources. CBS's "Rathergate," involving the fake Bush documents, as well as other recent scandals involving the *New York Times* and other major media outlets, are cited as evidence that the mainstream media are no better than bloggers, but no one engages in systematic fact checking of Web sites. Moreover, it is in part the rapid pace of the media in the era of cyberpolitics that has removed much of the filtering process. Because of the pressure created by the Internet, rumor, falsehood, and innuendo quickly move into public discourse. Matters about the private sex lives of public officials that would never have been printed in previous eras are now fodder for Web gossips like Matt Drudge, which creates pressure on newspapers and television networks to cover these stories. The mainstream media are responsible and largely accurate, if only by comparison with the online alternatives.

One can point to examples of the media abusing their gatekeeping authority in the past, such as their refusal to inform the nation of philandering presidents whose preoccupation with illicit sex arguably raised questions about national security and judgment.[21] However, the loss of gatekeeping power by the mass media has made politics a less appetizing field of endeavor, for both citizens and politicians. The first story about the Monica Lewinsky affair appeared on the Drudge Report because an "old-media" editor at *Newsweek* refused to run it. Similarly, during the ensuing impeachment, the Drudge Report ran a controversial account of an alleged rape committed by Clinton decades ago, an account that no mainstream media outlet would cover because they did not believe it had been fully sourced. Pressured by the coverage on Web sites and in chat rooms, the mainstream media eventually ran both stories.

The permeability and universality of the Internet raises questions about the nature of truth itself. Who is an authority, and how do we know? Students conducting research for term papers often mistake cranks and kooks for reputable scholars based on the slick presentation of their thoughts on a Web site. Of course, fringe groups who deny the Holocaust or assert anti-Semitic canards as fact have been publishing books and magazines for years. However, librarians had acted as a filter to most of these materials, separating legitimate challengers to conventional wisdom from irrational ideologues. The Internet puts the laughable claims of racist or anti-science groups only a click away from any college student, a student who may lack the intellectual training and critical tools to assess and reject these groups' counterfactual assertions. Postmodernist followers of the philosophies of Nietzsche and Foucault may welcome this assault on established truth, but it poses real challenges to rational discourse.

Parasitism

The major blogs that cover politics are free, giving their content away to any reader. However, when they are covering a breaking news story or a complex political issue, most of them include links to mainstream media outlets. The national newspapers have beat reporters on topics such as health care and national security who often have decades of expertise on these topics, and they have international news bureaus around the world. It is rare for a political blogger to do the kind of research that the national news outlets do every day. This type of reporting is costly and must be paid for in advertising and subscription dollars. Although some newspapers are beginning to realize significant profits from online advertisements, most newspaper Web sites are still losing money for their parent companies.

Blogs may represent "independence" from corporate control, but they also present news outlets with a conundrum. If news outlets do in-depth quality reporting that becomes widely circulated on the Internet without any fee or sometimes credit, how long can they continue to subsidize this content? Blogs can be thought of as parasites who benefit from the hard work of the mainstream media without contributing to the creation of its content. Television news has been a parasite on print journalism for decades, with many broadcast reporters using the newspapers to tell them where the good stories are. The difference is that television was not providing exactly the same content as the newspapers, which blogs often do.

Blurring

The Internet has begun to alter political journalism in fundamental ways, most importantly by altering the definition of who is a journalist. In the past, a journalist was someone who worked for the established print or electronic media. Credentials to cover the White House or other major political institutions were granted on the basis of employment by a respected media outlet. Is someone who sets up a Web site that talks about politics a "journalist"? What if the Web site is basically a subsidiary of one of the political parties and only covers news that favors that party?

During President Bush's first term, an obscure news service, Talon News, which shared a Web site with a Republican group, hired a "journalist" by the name of Jeff Gannon, whose qualifications for journalism were, to be charitable, remarkably scant. Denied permanent press credentials by the White House press corps because he lacked any credible experience, he was mysteriously issued day passes to the White House press briefings for months, asking questions that almost always reflected a pro-administration position. When one of his questions to the president was found to be factually incorrect, as well as taken directly from the Rush Limbaugh broadcast, reporters began to investigate Gannon and found that not only were his credentials thin, but his past employment included work as a prostitute. When politics and sex meet, a media firestorm predictably ensues, and such was the case here. Reporters wanted to know how an unqualified partisan with an extremely shady past had managed to get daily passes into one of the most secure sites on earth. But amid scandal a deeper question remains: Who exactly is a journalist?

This question goes deeper than the simple matter of credentials. The definition of journalist affects campaign finance regulation most directly. If a citizen is hired by a congressional campaign to write and distribute political leaflets, every dime spent must be reported to the Federal Election Commission (FEC). The author of the leaflets isn't a journalist, and no one reading them would think so. If a campaign hired a newspaper columnist to write for it, on the other hand, both the campaign and the journalist would be seen as violating the sanctity of elections and the free press. But when a campaign paid two political bloggers to secretly advocate on its behalf, as a Republican campaign did in a 2004 Senate campaign, most of the media ignored it.

In 2005 the FEC held hearings on whether bloggers should be given the same general exemption to campaign finance regulation that journalists receive. Either option poses risks for our democracy. If anyone can become a journalist just by paying a few dollars a month to have a Web site, the privileges of the press such as immunity to campaign finance laws and the confidential source shield laws will become cheapened by their universality. On the other hand, prominent political bloggers fear that government regulation of the Internet will kill its vitality and vibrant freedom. Ultimately, the FEC decided not to regulate the Internet's role in campaigns except in requiring that all expenditures by the campaign upon the Internet be reported, as with any other expense. For now, the broader question of who is a journalist under the law and under custom remains blurred by the new force of the Internet.

Impermanence

As outlined in Chapter 1, one of the drawbacks of oral political culture was the impermanence of political communications. Centuries later, does the Internet reintroduce that defect into politics? In the print or video era, the White House had a tough time denying that a particular statement was made, even after questions had emerged about the accuracy of the statement. The printed version was released and dated. If we consider George W. Bush the first president of the emerging Internet age, his administration has already demonstrated how the Internet can help change inconvenient truths. When the White House Web site first covered President Bush's speech about the defeat of Saddam Hussein, the headline read "President Bush Announces Combat Operations in Iraq Have Ended." As the occupation of Iraq began to result in the deaths of more and more American troops, the Web site was quietly edited to add the word "major" before "combat operations." Of course, Bush had said "major" in his speech, so the editing was arguably not inaccurate, but it did show how revisionist editing of past statements was newly possible thanks to the Internet. Of a more serious nature was the shift that occurred when the government removed a transcript in which an administration official on the eve of war promised the public that no more than $1.7 billion would be required from American taxpayers for the reconstruction of Iraq. This wildly optimistic estimate proved highly embarrassing for the administration when the reconstruction costs rose into the dozens of billions of dollars with no end in sight. Rather than admitting error or discussing why the estimate was so inaccurate, the administration simply removed the transcript and made all links to it inoperative.[22]

The problem of online impermanence goes far beyond incidents in which the government removes embarrassing facts from public circulation. The average Web page is estimated to last only seventy-five days before removal. Any Web site that connects to hundreds of other sites must be constantly monitored and updated to prevent the accumulation of dead links. The ability to constantly edit and improve a Web page is often a marvelous benefit to accuracy, but at the same time it can become a loss to history. As more and more think tanks, government agencies, academics, corporations, and individuals move away from print and create documents that exist only online, deleting or editing a page can result in the loss of the original document forever. As a partial correction of this, several archives of the entire Internet have been created. The most famous, the Internet Archive, attempts to take a snapshot of the entire Internet on a regular basis, preserving billions of Web pages so they can be examined by future researchers.[23]

One organization, thememoryhole.org, sets out to more directly challenge those who would alter the online historical record. In 2004 the liberal group Moveon.org held a contest in which members were invited to make their own thirty-second anti-Bush ads. Out of fifteen hundred ads, two made crude analogies between Bush and Hitler. After an outcry from conservatives complaining about the use of fascist rhetoric (including some who had frequently used the term "femiNazis" to describe liberal women), Moveon.org removed the ads, but they are still available today at thememoryhole.org.

Even with projects like thememoryhole and the Internet Archive, the Web remains a medium highly susceptible to deletions, alterations, and edits. Its size and complexity make any attempts to preserve it inevitably incomplete. Billions of new Web pages are created each year, and storing even a fraction of them involves millions of gigabytes of disk space. Fortunately, bloggers on the left and the right have independently been monitoring Web pages to look for changes in important documents and pages.

Cocooning

> We live in self-imposed exile from communal conversation and action. The public square is naked. American politics has lost its

> soul. The republic has become procedural, and we have become
> unencumbered selves. Individualism has become cancerous. We
> live in an age of narcissism and pursue loneliness.[24]

Although philosopher Albert Borgman wrote these words while the
Internet was in its infancy, they capture many of the far-reaching
problems some see inherent in this new medium. The growth of
technology's role in American life may contribute to a sense of
hyperindividualism as we **cocoon** ourselves away not only from
politics but also from real-world human connections. Champions of
the Internet's possibilities rave about the potential for spacially separated individuals to form interest groups through the Web, but perhaps such groups fail to provide community, solidarity, and other
group benefits that are necessary to civil society. Consider the difference between a union hall gathering of workers in 1950 and an
Internet chat room on politics today. The union hall meeting requires
physical presence and interactions beyond the level of typing and
reading. Those present see each other as complete beings who have
left their private domains to enter into public discourse. The patterns of listening and speaking, of debate and discussion, would not
be unfamiliar to a colonial Virginian or an ancient Greek. By contrast, the denizens of a chat room or the readers of a bulletin board
may hide behind pseudonyms and misrepresent their true selves or
opinions with careless abandon. Most important, they may not feel
the same sense of connection to each other as do people who meet
in person.

Thinkers as diverse as De Toqueville[25] in the nineteenth century
and political scientist Robert Putnam in the late twentieth century
have emphasized that America's civil society rests on the health of
voluntary associations among citizens. Civic activities that build up
"social capital" have been declining in the last forty years, and this
troubles many scholars, politicians, and citizens. One of the more
intriguing findings in Putnam's influential 2001 book, *Bowling Alone,*
was that for every hour of newspaper reading, civic engagement
increased, whereas for every hour of television watching, it de-
creased.[26] Comparable data are not yet available for Internet usage,
but it seems plausible that local activities decline as Internet usage
expands. Thus it becomes important to find out whether the com-
munal activities on the Web can produce the same connectedness
that characterize traditional groups. As one recent article asked,
"When it comes to . . . building community, is the Internet more like

a Girl Scout troop or a television set?" Unfortunately, given current patterns of usage, it seems that the Internet is far more similar to the dreaded idiot box, television, than to a meeting with other citizens.[27]

Cocooning may represent the most subtle and insidious danger in cyberpolitics. Even before the Internet, many worried that Americans were increasingly unconnected to each other. More and more of the upper class live in gated communities, send their children to private schools, and fail to interact in any meaningful way with less wealthy Americans. Demonstrations and marches and rallies have declined in effectiveness as Americans no longer congregate in public spaces but in privately owned malls. With the dawn of Internet shopping, telecommuting, and Web-based entertainment, leaving home becomes almost superfluous. Perhaps the new media possibilities of the Web will provide Americans with access to new and unfiltered information about politics. But if we do not have a sense of community, of shared obligation and values, will we care about political news from home or abroad? Instead of "Thinking globally and acting locally," will we now "Entertain individually and disappear locally"?

In this sense, the Internet may be the apotheosis of what America's first great media critic, Walter Lippmann, described as "pseudoreality."[28] In Lippmann's original conception, the media provided the citizen with a useful simplification of the complex real world. The citizen's reaction to that pseudoreality would eventually have real-world implications. However, the Internet may create a "virtual reality" all its own, in which behaviors and interactions that never leave cyberspace become an end in themselves.

Cocooning is not just a physical phenomenon of people leaving their homes less; it can also be seen as citizens isolating themselves from information and topics they disagree with. The Internet allows for more independence from the media's agenda, but in allowing each news consumer to pick his or her own news topics, the Internet may prevent full discussions. News Web sites allow regular visitors to pick the type of news they want to read: someone could read only about sports and movie news if he or she wished. Others may choose to read only liberal or radical or Christian news sites. Cass Sunstein, a law professor at the University of Chicago, in his book *Republic.com*, worries that the Internet causes extremism and polarization as more and more citizens isolate themselves from any viewpoints other than their own.[29] True believers can cocoon themselves away from troubling facts by surrounding themselves with Web sites that deny the truth. The mainstream media print corrections; many political blogs simply repeat their errors until they and their readers believe them.

Cocooning will surely be more of a threat tomorrow than it is today. The trend in the Internet is toward more and more integration, both of content and of methods of transmission. Broadband technology offers the potential for a grand unification of all media into a single giant data stream. The future American home may have one connection to the outside world, and through that broadband cable will stream news, movies, telephone, e-mail, Web sites, votes, political donations, shopping orders, bills, banking, and everything necessary for life save water, food, and air (and our orders for all those things may be encoded in the pipeline as well). The effects this will have on America's political culture are incalculable at present. Perhaps the unified media will be more subject to centralized control. Perhaps the Web will retain the virtue of independence, and Americans will take advantage of greater choices in sources of political information. Whatever happens in this brave new world of unified media, the incentives to leave home will be lessened, and the tendency to cocoon in one's own space more common.* Those who confidently predict a revolution caused by blogging and the Internet have to contend with the wry observation of Wonkette (Ana Marie Cox), one of the most prominent political bloggers: "A revolution requires that people leave their houses."[30]

Surveillance

The ability of government to monitor our activities and invade our privacy has been greatly enhanced by the Internet. Even before the Internet was invented, the French political philosopher Michel Foucault worried that modern governments had become far too intrusive, putting citizens into a "Panopticon," or visual prison, in which we are all constantly under surveillance by government and

---

*Cocooning can be exaggerated as a threat. The Internet can be a medium for civic connection, in which two or more people come to see the world from each other's perspective, and so mature as classic liberal Enlightenment theory would have it. Online communities can promote dialogue between citizens of differing views, and they can knit families and other necessary social groupings closer together. A Harris poll found that 48 percent of U.S. Net users said they communicate more often with family and friends than before. (Michael J. Weiss, "Online America," *American Demographics,* March 2001.)

our fellow citizens. The Internet has fundamentally altered our conceptions of privacy in ways that are only partially understood. As Senator Patrick Leahy put it in a speech in 2004:

> The marriage of information-gathering technology with information storing technology, manipulated in increasingly sophisticated databases, is beginning to produce the defining privacy challenge of the information age. Modern databases, networks and the Internet allow us to easily collect, store, distribute and combine video, audio and other digital trails of our daily transactions. We are on the verge of a revolution in micro-monitoring—the capability for the highly detailed, largely automatic, widespread surveillance of our daily lives.[31]

As with all new media technologies, the Internet challenges regulators of the media to strike new balances between privacy, freedom, safety, and efficiency.

CONCLUSION: THE INEVITABLE INTERNET

There is no way to unring the bell of technological change. The Internet has expanded by leaps and bounds during the last ten years because it filled needs that Americans had, even if they did not know they had them: interactivity, faster news, easier contacts, greater media independence. It has changed the way Americans learn about politics, and it has begun to change the way they participate in politics. The ordinary citizen can now readily correct for media biases of many varieties and see politics more fully than before the Internet arrived.

Ironically, this new technological innovation has produced changes in journalism that are revitalizing older forms of media behavior. Partisan Web sites such as Freerepublic.com or Moveon.org are at least as deeply biased as the newspapers of the 1790s when each party controlled a number of newspapers. Even more recently, participatory news Web sites have emerged in which "citizen journalists" write about issues that affect them, typically at the local level. These are usually unpaid part-timers who post with little editing or oversight to a local "newspaper" Web site. Just as with some of the very first newspapers, much of the content is informal and produced by an unprofessional staff.[32] The millions of bloggers who write daily on subjects as diverse as Middle Eastern politics to auto maintenance are reminiscent of a free speech corner, a town center where the public can communicate without restriction or fil-tering. The death of actual public space may be partially healed by the new public cyberspace.

But the improved capacity for political learning is not the same as an improved capacity for political action. Protesters, dissenters, and opponents can get their messages out, and the sympathetic can find them. But there's quite a psychological road to travel between perception and action: the viewers must believe they have a chance at victory before they will organize to act. By encouraging cocooning, the Internet may act as a barrier to political action. Furthermore, the Internet also has sinister implications for government and corporate surveillance of our actions and thoughts. Allied with video cameras, the Internet can be used to monitor citizens in public spaces. "Cookies" can track where viewers have browsed. Post-9/11 legis-lation gave the government new powers to read e-mails at home and abroad.

Will the Internet become a source for positive political change, or will it exacerbate existing ills in American media politics as well as adding new ones? It is difficult to say because the Internet era has not yet even officially begun. We have not yet had the Internet equivalent of the Kennedy–Nixon debates of 1960 in which one could definitively say that the medium changed the outcome. The Howard Dean campaign of 2004 was tantalizingly close, but the Internet has yet to win a decisive victory over video in a presidential campaign. When campaigns begin spending as much money on their Web sites as their television ads, perhaps we will be able to say that the Internet has become dominant.

There remains much for media critics to study, and much data are yet to be examined before we will understand how the Internet has affected the fundamental nature of American media politics. It is too early to say where the Internet is taking political communication because the nature of the medium is rapidly evolving. Ten years ago there were no "bloggers" in America; today there are more than ten million.[33] Once we know for sure that the Internet has produced broad systemic changes, we will be closer to judging the long-term implications of those changes.

What we can say is that these changes will have mammoth implications for the nature of American political journalism and American politics generally. In the twentieth century, Walter Benjamin and Neil Postman, along with many other media analysts, pondered how the new medium of video would shape politics and culture. Both those who saw video as a looming menace and those who saw it as a possible solution to many governmental problems agreed that the manner in which a political message is conveyed is sometimes as important as its content. The Internet poses even more profound challenges to popular government and media power. Whether the Internet becomes a force for furthering democracy and civil liberties or a means for centralizing power and elite dominance remains uncertain. It will take vigilance and activism by many American citizens to make certain that this new medium does not damage fundamental aspects of the American political system but rather expands and revitalizes the media's role in our republican democracy.

KEY TERMS

blogs	interactivity
cocooning	overload
digital divide	podcasting
filterlessness	real-time news cycle

DISCUSSION QUESTIONS

1. Do you use the Internet to learn about or participate in politics? Do you think learning about politics on the Internet is different from learning through video or print? How?
2. Do you read any political blogs, such as Andrewsullivan.com or Freerepublic.com? Do you think they are "better" in some ways than the mainstream media?
3. Do you think there is a danger of "cocooning" produced by the Internet?
4. Would you feel comfortable voting online, or do you think it is important to vote in person?
5. What form of political communication might one day replace the Internet?

ADDITIONAL RESOURCES

Republic.com by Cass Sunstein is a dense but powerful argument that the Internet is harming political discourse in the United States in sometimes subtle ways.

Smart Mobs: The Next Social Revolution by Howard Rheingold is a remarkably positive view of how new technologies such as cell phones and palm pilots are altering culture and even helping to bring down oppressive governments.

The Revolution Will Not Be Televised: Democracy, the Internet, and the Overthrow of Everything by Joe Trippi is a somewhat rambling personalized account of how the Internet is changing politics, business, and culture, largely in positive ways, from the perspective of Howard Dean's campaign manager.

ONLINE RESOURCES

www.archives.org is the Web site that tries to keep a record of all Web sites.

www.thememoryhole.org tries to keep track of how government, corporations, and media outlets use the Internet for deceptive purposes.

www.freerepublic.com is the most influential conservative Web site.

www.moveon.org is one of the most influential liberal Web sites.

www.memri.org tracks the Middle East media.

www.andrewsullivan.com is one of the most influential blogger Web sites.

www.robinsloan.com/epic is a link to a short, powerful movie that outlines a dark media future of corporate dominance and information control. Called "Googlezon," it highlights many of the negative possibilities outlined in this chapter.

NOTES

1. Internet world stats, internetworldstats.com
2. Pew Research Center, "Internet Sapping Broadcast News Audience," June 11, 2000. www.People-press.org/media00rpt.htm
3. Merrill Brown, "Abandoning the News," *Carnegie Reporter,* Spring 2005.
4. "A Brief History of the Internet," The Internet Society, 2000. http://www.isoc.org/Internet/history
5. Anjali Athavaley, "Mainstream Media Is Tuning in to Podcasting," *Washington Post,* July 18, 2005: A1.

6. Pew Internet & American Life Project, "The Broadband Difference," June 23, 2002. www.pewinternet.org

7. Daniel W. Drezner and Henry Farrell, "Web of Influence," *Foreign Policy*, November–December, 2004.

8. Jeremy D. Mayer, "The 2004 Presidential Election: Bush Wins Another Broken Election," *Relações Internacionais*, the journal of the Instituto Português de Relações Internacionais, 2005.

9. Ibid.

10. Dana Priest, "CIA Holds Terror Suspects in Secret Prisons," *Washington Post*, November 2, 2005: A01.

11. Ben Bagdikian, *The Media Monopoly*, 6th ed. (Boston: Beacon Press, 2000).

12. Drezner and Farrell, "Web of Influence."

13. Ben Hammersley, "Time to Blog On," *The Guardian* (UK), May 20, 2002.

14. E. Noelle-Neumann, *The Spiral of Silence: Public Opinion—Our Social Skin* (Chicago: University of Chicago Press, 1984).

15. John McArdle, "Blogging Locally: Web Sites on State and Local Politics Gaining Prominence." Roll Call, May 12, 2005.

16. www.memri.org

17. Drezner and Farrell, "Web of Influence."

18. Pew Research Center, "Internet Sapping Broadcast News Audience."

19. Bob Davis and Jeanne Cummings, "Hot Buttons: A Barrage of E-Mail Helps Candidates Hit Media Fast and Often," *Wall Street Journal*, September 21, 2000.

20. George Gallup, "Polling the Public." In *Public Opinion in a Democracy*, Charles William Smith, ed. (New York: Prentice-Hall, 1939).

21. Thomas C. Reeves, *A Question of Character: A Life of John F. Kennedy* (Rocklin, CA: Prima, 1992).

22. Dana Milbank, "White House Web Scrubbing: Offending Comments on Iraq Disappear From Site," *Washington Post*, December 18, 2003: A5.

23. Paul Boutin, "The Archivist: Brewster Kahle Made a Copy of the Internet. Now, He Wants Your Files," *Slate*, April 7, 2005.

24. Albert Borgman, *Crossing the Postmodern Divide* (Chicago: University of Chicago Press, 1992), 3.

25. Alexis de Tocqueville, *Democracy in America* (New York: Signet, 2001). (Orig. pub. 1840.)

26. Robert Putnam, *Bowling Alone: The Collapse and Revival of American Community* (New York: Touchstone, 2001).

27. Margie K. Shields, Susan E. Linn, and Stephen Doheny-Farina, "Connected Kids." *The American Prospect On-Line,* December 26, 2000.
28. Walter Lippmann, *Public Opinion* (New York: Free Press, 1997). (Orig. pub. 1922.)
29. Cass Sunstein, Republic.com (Princeton: Princeton University Press, 2002), 3–8.
30. Drezner and Farrell, "Web of Influence."
31. Patrick Leahy, "The Dawn of Micro Monitoring: Its Promise, and Its Challenges to Privacy and Security." Speech given at the Conference on "Video Surveillance: Legal and Technological Challenges." Georgetown University Law Center, March 23, 2004.
32. Ariana Eunjung Cha, "Do-It-Yourself Journalism Spreads: Web Sites Let People Take News Into Their Own Hands," *Washington Post,* July 17, 2005: A01.
33. David Von Drehle, "Fighting Words," *Washington Post Magazine,* July 17, 2005.

Index